MYTHS, BELIEFS AND ASTROLOGICAL TRADITIONS IN MUGHAL INDIA (A.D. 1526 TO 1748)

MYTHS, BELIEFS AND ASTROLOGICAL TRADITIONS IN MUGHAL INDIA (A.D. 1526 TO 1748)

KANTA SINGHANIA

AUTHORSPRESS

Worldwide Circulation through Authorspress Global Network
First Published in 2023
by
Authorspress
Q-2A Hauz Khas Enclave, New Delhi-110 016 (India)
Phone: (0) 9818049852
E-mail: authorspressgroup@gmail.com
Website: www.authorspressbooks.com

Myths, Beliefs and Astrological Traditions in Mughal India (A.D. 1526 To 1748)

ISBN 978-93-5529-548-4

Printed in India at Kensington Press

Dedication

In the Memory of
My Revered Father
Late Dr. Swarup Chand Singhania
who is the Main Source of
Inspiration

Preface

Myth is the result of a purely psychological operation and is the oldest effort of human mind because the psychological ideas behind these myths and beliefs were, somehow, originated from a logic or facts, such as the idea of astrology, which is nowadays, supposed to some extent, as a myth and belief, moreover, a superstition also. Though it is purely based on astronomy which has a scientific ground and basis

Astronomy is the oldest scientific discipline which humanmind has ever known. Being an ancient culture, India has a long tradition of astronomical and related activities. Several names of astronomers and astrologers are found from the *Vedic* period to medieval period of India, such as Gargya, Parasara, Saktya, Gautam, Vamdeva, Aryabhata, Srisena, Varahmihira, Brahmagupta, Bhaskara I etc. in ancient times. Al-Beruni, Pheru Thakkar, Mahendra Suri, Bhaskara II, Nilkantha Somayaji etc. acquired the deep knowledge of astrology. In mughal period, we find a long list of astrologers, who were patronised by the imperial courts. The important names were Maulana Chand, Jotik Rai, Fath-ulah-Sirazi, Maulana Alyas, Mulla Farid Munajjam, Raja Sawai Jai Singh, Raghunandan Nilkantha, Vedangraya etc. Moreover, Abul Fazl has illustrated a long list of astronomers and astrologers, who were reputed in Central Asia, before advent of Mughals in India.

Emphasis has been made on Mughal history regarding the political, economic, social, and cultural aspects but nothing has been found in this area except a little bit in some contemporary sources i.e., Humayun-nama, Akbar-nama and Ain-i-Akbari of Abul Fazl, Tabaquat-i-Akbari of Nizammuddin Ahmad, Tuzuq-i-Jahangir, Shahjahan-nama, etc.

Nowadays, the impact of the subject on society and polity can be seen increasing rapidly. Thus, such a popular subject creates a curiosity to know about its history and utility. I am also fascinated and motivated to know the psychological impact of the subject thoroughly in historical perspective.

In Mughal period of India, the astronomical calculations were made through observations, astrolabes, astronomical canons, tables, and astral charts, which had a scientific basis, as I found Abul Fazl's description about scientific basis behind the comet appearance in Akbar's reign. He has described the position of Zodiac sign, planetary position, and its effects on universe, when the comet appearance occurs. He further describes the predictions of various astrologers at the movement. Such pertinent questions were raised through astrology during mughal rule. Emperors deliberately chose the favourable time to enter the capital, to go for a battle, to lay the foundation of a city or fortress and many more.

Hence, this attempt covers the cultural aspect and also scientific astronomical calculations. The review of literature covers primary, modern, and secondary sources and articles. The foreign travellers' accounts are also referred to. The practice of astrology was not only prevalent in medieval India, but it was a world phenomenon. It was subjected to science in most of the countries in 16th and 17th centuries. There were several world reputed astronomers like Riccioli, Danzig Johannes Hevelius, Jean Picard, Giovanni Donenico Cassini etc.

Today, various programmes on astrological calculation, position of stars and their effects on different aspects of life can be read and seen as regular feature in many newspapers, magazines, and television. Nowadays, most of the politicians and highly placed officials also take important decisions according to the calculation of their stars' position.

Hence, this research work is an attempt to study the development and impact of astrology on polity and society pertaining to a specific period of mughal India i.e., from Babur to Aurangzeb including the contribution of Sawai Jai Singh II of Jaipur (1526 A.D. to 1748 A.D.). It is hoped that present study would provide a new outlook in viewing and understanding India's cultural heritage and assimilation of two cultures. The objectives of the study are to find out the history of astrology and astronomy and its development during mughal India, to analyse its impact on mughal emperors in particular and on society in general. Its influence on architecture, painting and literature has also been described in historical perspective,

The study of my research work is mainly based on primary source material, particularly various contemporary writings like, Baburnama, Humayun Nama, Quanun-i-Humayuni, Ain-i-Akbari,

Akbarnama, Tabquat-i-Akbari, Tuzuk-i-Jahangiri, Shahjahanama, astral charts like, Zich-i-Shahjahani and Zil-i-Jadid-i-Muhammad-Shahi. In mughal India, the astronomical calculations, the basis of astrology, were made through observations astrolabes, astronomical canons, table, and astral charts. Hence, these sources have also been analysed by understanding the working of devices used in these observations and astrolabes.

The secondary sources and travels' accounts of Manucci, Barnier, Pelseart etc., as given in bibliography, which contains the cultural impact in every respect have been studied and evaluated, keeping in mind the research methodology of our discipline. For the proper treatment of the subject, the thesis has been divided into seven chapters excluding bibliography, in a very systematic and scientific way.

The first Chapter contains the origin of myth, belief and superstition regarding astrology and its development and impact in ancient India in historical perspective. In Chapter II, the meaning of astrology and astronomy, their relation and impacts have been described. The Chapter III deals with early mughal period, i.e., from Babur to Akbar (1526 A.D. to 1605 A.D.) in the context to the development of astrology and its impact. The Chapter IV contains the development of astrology and astronomy and its impact during the period of Jahangir, Shahjahan and Aurangzeb including the contribution of Sawai Jai Singh in astronomical sciences. The Chapter V deals with the impact of astrology on contemporary society, learning and literature, art and architecture and painting. While the Chapter VI describes about Abul Fazl who was a courtier as well as a contemporary historian, was an astronomer and astrologer also. Lastly the Chapter VII concludes the study.

It is indeed my proud privilege to express gratefulness to Professor R C Sobti (Padamshree Awardee) former Vice Chancellor Panjab University Chandigarh and Baba Saheb Bheem Rao Ambedkar Central University Lucknow Uttar Pradesh, who has so generously blessed this work with his scholarly 'Forword'.

I am also grateful to Dr Vipin Sobti, former Principal, Govt College Mohali Punjab, who has motivated and helped me in many ways.

I take the opportunity to acknowledge my gratitude to my research guide Prof. R.S. Sangwan, the Chairperson, History

Department, Kurukshetra University, Kurukshetra, who accepted to supervise me for this rare topic. I am also thankful to Prof. R.S. Tanwar, the Registrar, Kurukshetra University, and Kurukshetra, who helped me in different ways. I would like to specially thank Dr. Y.S. Khyalia, the former Registrar, Kurukshetra University, Kurukshetra, for his continuous inspiration and assistance in my enrolment for Ph.D. I am very much thankful to my friends especially Dr Anita Sharma, Dr. Neelam Prabha Sharma, Dr. Priti Nath and Dr. Anuradha Bhattacharya who helped me in different ways. I would like to thank my colleagues Dr. Bannuelhar Patra, Mr. W. Shaiza and Dr. Karan Singh, who have edited the manuscript and inspired me. I am also thankful to Mrs. Renu Oberoi and Mrs. Jaspal Kaur, the library staff of Postgaduate Govt. College, Sector 11, Chandigarh. I am greatly indebted to my parents, Late Dr. S.C. Singhania, who was the main source of inspiration, and Smt. Neelam Singhania and all brothers and sisters who always encouraged me for writing work. My husband, Mr. Mahendra Kumar, and my sons, Devrishi and Tanmay deserve my heartfelt thanks for their stringent cooperation in different ways and for bearing with me. Tanmay has gone through the manuscript and made necessary suggestions also. I am thankful to my daughter in law Shivani who motivated and cooprated me continuously.

I am thankful to the Librarians and the staff of the Pt. Jawahar Lal Nehru Library, Kurukshetra University, Kurukshetra and Library of the Panjab University, Chandigarh, and the Haryana State Archives, Panchkula for providing me the facilities of consultation and photocopying of the material.

I am also thankful to Mr. Sohan Lal Sharma, who has typed the manuscript and the publisher Authorpress, New Delhi, who has given consent to publish it in the book form.

Above all, I thank the Almighty to bestow me with his constant grace and strength.

Kanta Singhania

Professor R.C. Sobti
(Padmashree Awardee)
M.Sc. (Hons. Sch.), Ph.D., D.Sc., F.T.W.A.S.,
F.N.A., F.N.A.Sc., F.Z.S., F.N.A.A.S.,
F.A.M.S., F.P.A.S., F.A.M.I., F.S.C.G.
INSA Sr. Scientist
&
Professor Emeritus
Former Vice-Chancellor,
Panjab University Chandigarh
& Babasaheb Bhimrao Ambedkar
(Central) University Lucknow

PANJAB UNIVERSITY,
Chandigarh, *India* 160 014

31.3.23

FOREWORD

Fascination with the heavenly bodies has been one common trait among mankind since early civilization. Such fascination has resulted in multiple streams of study. In ancient era, these studies were known as astronomy and astrology while in contemporary times, we use terminologies like – cosmology, astrophysics, space science, etc. Despite multiple names and forms, such studies have influenced and continue to influence human thought and its understanding of the world. However, among them, the study of Astrology has managed to penetrate much more into the social, cultural, economic and political fabric of human lives.

History should be seen in its multiple facets and with the lens of Astrological traditions, one can notice its influence and prevalence across multiple eras and cultures. In the present work, entitled "Myths, beliefs and astrological traditions in Mughal India", the author Dr. Kanta Singhania provides the reader with a clear lens to understand the extent of influence of Astrology and its traditions on the lives of the Mughal Kings and the overall society. The author illustrates the activities performed with astrological guidance, contribution of the then rulers towards the literature and its patronization. This research also includes multiple evidence to advocate its credibility. It is expected that this work will inspire numerous historical studies with the lens as provided here by the author.

I highly appreciate the hard work put in by the author in compiling this excellent book.

(R.C. Sobti)

Corresponding Address : Deptt. of Biotechnology, Panjab University, Chandigarh
Res. : 2917, Sector 42-C, Chandigarh | E-mail : rcsobti@pu.ac.in

Contents

Preface 5

Foreword 11

1. Historical Background Ancient and Delhi Sultanate Period of India 15

2. Astrology and Astronomy – Meaning, Their Relation, Scientific Basis and Effects 49

3. Development and Impact of Astrology and Astronomy during Mughal Period (A.D. 1526 – A.D. 1605) 69

4. Astrology and Astronomy under the Mughals: A.D. 1605 to A.D. 1750 107

5. Impact of Astrology and Astronomy on Society, Literature, Education, Architecture and Painting in Mughal Period 134

6. Abul Fazl's Vision of Astronomy and Astrology 159

Conclusion 178

Bibliography 186

Illustrations 193

Index 203

CHAPTER 1

Historical Background Ancient and Delhi Sultanate Period of India

Through the ages, Indian culture has a vast area of Mythology. The mythology offers a window opening towards the world of ideas as also inferentially towards the material life of the people, who create the myths, beliefs etc. But these myths and beliefs are born in the collective unconsciousness of men and there is a vast area common in this level; hence myths and beliefs from different lands bear some resemblance to each other which ultimately stem from the primordial myth-making activities in very ancient times.[1]

"Mythology as a whole, says M. Renan in his *Studies in Religious History*, is a vast play upon words. The myth is formed by the inevitable misuse of a language in which each substantive was an animated being, in which every verb signified a physical action. Myths are multiplied by the misuse of synonymous and by means of popular etymology, a fruitful source of fables even in our days".[2.]

By referring to the great primitive work of the Aryan religions, the *Vedas*, M. Breal discovers the first essentially naturalistic germ of the myth. Knowing nothing whatever of physical forces, the men of that time interpreted the action of nature only by the analogy of their own actions. The only force they knew was the force of will, of which they were directly conscious. Accordingly, they imagined all the outward world to be endowed with volition and to be directed by it. Thus, they personified everything – sky, clouds, sun, moon, planets, ocean, earthquake, etc. In this way Myth[3] is the result of a purely psychological operation and is, together with the language, the oldest effort of human mind, because the psychological ideas behind these myths and beliefs, somehow are originated from some logic and facts, such as an idea of Astrology which is nowadays, supposed to some extent, as a myth, and belief, moreover a superstition also. Though it is purely based on Astronomy and has a scientific ground and basis also.

Astronomy is the oldest scientific discipline, as humanmind has known. Being an ancient culture, India has a long tradition of astronomical and related activities. Though at present, we have no definite clues to the astronomical knowledge of the Harappan people,[4] but a recent attempt by Finnish philologists to read the Indus Valley script using a computer method seems to indicate that the '*Nakshatras*' are of Harappan origin, as also are the later Dravidian names of the five planets related to their colours (such as: Mars, the red star).[5.]

Recurring order of the morning, noon, and night, of one season after the other and repetition of the same season after a large number of days and nights, must have been observed even by the most primitive of men in very early times. These bare observations provided man with a rough estimate of time of the day, the number of days in the increasing and the decreasing phase of the moon i.e., in a month. Man could now keep a record of the passage of time and thereby knew also when he ought to sow or harvest his crop, or for that matter, how many sets of seasons or years had passed since he was born.

Besides his observations, the starry heavens attracted the attention of man. Initially, he looked at the sky with a sense of awe, admiration, and curiosity. Then he observed that the heavenly sphere carrying the stars rotated from the east towards the west (although now it is proved that it is the earth that rotates). Gradually, he noticed that the moon at night and the sun during the daytime moved along a certain fixed heavenly path (i.e., now known as Zodiac – a belt or zone of the sky, sixteen degrees wide in which the sun, moon, and planets travel). It was also noticed that there were certain groups of moving stars in this path and the sun had reached near such a group of stars on a particular day or a season. Passing of the sun through all these stars and its restart provided man with an alternative and relatively more accurate method of determining the number of days in a year. This was man's first important landmark in his knowledge of astronomy.[6]

Astronomy and Astrology in Vedic Period

India, as can be expected from an ancient culture, has a long astronomical tradition. The oldest astronomical text in India is the *Vedanga Jyotisha* (astronomy as a part of the *Vedas*), one part of which is attributed to Lagadha. It is dated about 1400 B.C. The earliest interest in astronomy was in observing equinoxes and solstices for ritualistic purposes, in making rather inexact luni-solar calenders and in observing conspicuous stars (*Nakshatras*) as a guide to the motion of the moon and the sun.[7]

Calculation of time was part of the sacred ritual with the Vedic Aryans. Religious sacrifices that they performed were of different types. While some of them were performed at a particular time of the day, the others were performed at full or new moon or when the days and nights were of equal length and occasionally a sacrificial ritual lasted even for a year or more. Not only that, the sacrificial altar had to face a particular direction also, as for example, the east. So, we see that the Aryans had to have a fairly broad-based idea of the time and the direction from very early times.

Even during the early Vedic period in India, there was a class of men well versed in the art of recognizing and noting the position of the various stars and calculating therefrom the time of the performance of different religious sacrifices. *Yazurveda*[8] mentions *nakshatra-darsha* (star gazer) and *ganaka* (calculator or astrologer) as important functionaries in connection with the performance of these sacrifices. Chhandogya Upnishad[9] mentions *nakshatra* Vidya (astronomy) as one of the subjects known to Narada. In the *Grhya-sutras*, a section of *Kalpa-sutras*, it is recorded that on arrival in their new home, the bridegroom pointed out to the bride the pole star (*Dhruva*) indicating thereby the constancy of their wedded life. During the *Sutra* period, astronomy, and astrology (*Jyotisha*) formed one of the six *Vedangas*, the parts of the *Vedas*. Jainas considered astronomy as one of the principal requisites in their priests.

There is no regular text of astronomy available to us for the early stages of the Vedic period, which could tell us the amount of astronomical knowledge possessed by the Vedic Indians. Hence, we have to depend upon the indirect references as given in different *Samhitas* and other texts of Vedic literature. These references reveal a lot of astronomical information. But this knowledge was, however, immersed and amalgamated with religious and mythological traditions. The growth of astronomy was the outcome of the worship of planets and their movements. Since the Vedic period the auspicious time for the performance of *Yajnas* and sacred rites have been determined by the respective position of planets in the solar system. In every Veda, there is a reference to astronomical treatise in which is explained the calender for the fixation of the time for the performance of religious duties. This science was the favourite pursuit of the Brahmins. In the ancient '*Brahmans*', it is stated that there is no rising and setting of the sun and days and nights are the result of the revolving movement of the solar system. Many planets were known to the ancient people of India according to the *Taiteriya Aranyaka.*[10] About the discovery of planets, Weber writes, "whether Hindus discovered the planets independently or whether the knowledge came to them, cannot yet be determined, but the systematic peculiarity of the nomenclature points in the meantime to the former view.[11]

The Rigvedic hymns are generally devoted to praising and describing the attributes of the celestial gods – the personified heavenly bodies, although the descriptions are full of imagination of the poets.

Rigveda[12] mentions a year to have twelve months, 360 days and divided into four quarters of 90 days each. Rigvedic Aryans noted the heliacal rising of Sirius at the vernal equinox.[13] Two stanzas have been interpreted to mean that the year commenced from the time of summer solstice, with the sun in the *nakshatra Phalguni.*[14]

Sun is described as the source of light. It outstrips all other heavenly bodies in its speed of travel. It measures the day and the night and drives away the stars and the night, as one drives away the thieves. There is one sun in the world and that the rising and setting of the sun makes the days and the nights.[15]

The moon is said to be born again and again. The sun and the moon ascend alternately and move in close succession.[16] Of course, the moon plays a subordinate role only.

Some hymns imply the knowledge of planets. In some places seven and in other, five planets are mentioned.[17] Planet Jupiter (*Brihaspati*) finds mention in a hymn. Jupiter is said to have been identified in Rigveda times, by Vamadeva, son of Gotama.[18] Another planet Venus is also mentioned in one of the hymns.[19]

Eclipses are mentioned without their real cause. The hymn, that says that 'The sun, whom Asura's son Svrabhanu had hidden, was found out only by the Atri people, as no one else had power to find it', perhaps, indicates that Atri people had some idea of predicting the solar eclipse.[20]

In Rigveda, a hymn mentions the 7 planets and 27 nakshatras.[21] In Yajurveda also, a list of 27 *nakshatras*, commencing with Kritika is clearly mentioned. It also mentions that the full moon in *Phalguni nakshatra* is the beginning of the year and moon shines because of the sun's light.

In *Atharvaveda*, the description of frequent eclipses is mentioned. Demon of *Rahu*[22] is stated to be the cause of the eclipses and the gods *Soma* and *Rudra*, the remover of the eclipses. It also mentions Sirius and Orion group of stars.

Satapath Brahmana mentions planet Sukra. *Taittiriya Brahmana* says about planet *Brihaspati* (Jupiter) that when it was first born it was near *Tishya nakshatra.*[23] First born here, perhaps, means when it was first noted.

In *Mahabharat*, the cause of eclipses was said to be devouring of the sun or the moon by the demon of *Rahu*, Planets are mentioned as five or seven in different places. And sun was considered as the central point around which the planets rotate.[24] *Mahabhararta* refers to disappearance of one of the *nakshatra* namely *Abhijit.*[25] *Vishnu Purana* mentions the distances, in *yojanas* of the orbits of different heavenly bodies from the earth.

Vedanga Jyotisha

Vedanga Jyotisha was a regular astronomical text of the Vedic period. This is the first systematized text of *Jyotisha* that is available to us now. It is said to have been composed by Lagadha, who lived sometimes between 1200 – 900 B. C. But now, the available text of *Vedanga Jyotisha* seems, however, to belong to a period around the beginning of the Christian era. Calculation based on astronomical data provided in this text indicates that it was probably composed in Kashmir Valley.[26]

In this text, 27 *nakshatras* mark 27 division of the *ecliptic*, each being equal to 13.20". Chief characteristic of the text is that it gives the calculation of the position of the sun and the moon relative to the *nakshatras*, division of *Yugas*, *Savana* time, measurement of the time and *Tithis* (Lunar days).[27]

The main purpose of the astronomy of this period was to fix time for the performance of the religious sacrifices. Calculation of the time based on the principle mentioned in *Vedanga* were used even in the third century B.C. by Emperor Ashoka to calculate the precise duration of his intended Buddhist pilgrimage. This fact shows clearly that Vedic astronomy was then in common use.[28]

Astrologers and Astronomers in Ancient India

Gargya is known to be the first person, according to *Vedas*, to have enumerated all these *Nakshatras*. In the Nineteenth Book of the *Atharvaveda* the hymn nos. 7 & 8 are associated with the name of Sage *Gargya*.[29] When did *Gargya* live? is not known with certainty. He is said to have determined the position of various stars at the time of the birth of Lord Krishna. At the time of *Mahabharat*, he was an astrologer of Arjuna.[30] He was thoroughly acquainted with calculations of time by the observation of the stars. In *Vishnu Puran*, according to a mythological story, *Gargya* propitiated Sesha, the cosmic serpent and from it, acquired the knowledge of the science of stars.

Gargya Samhita, which was possibly composed about the beginning of Christian era, is said to have embodied the teachings of *Gargya*. There are references about it in later works but the treatise itself seems to have been lost long ago. In this treatise a mention has been made of the Greek invasion of India and a conquest of Greeks by a Saka king. And these episodes occurred about the third century B.C. This treatise also mentions that "The Greeks (Yavanas) are *mlechchhas*, but amongst them this science of astronomy is well established and therefore they are honoured as sages; how much more than an astrologer (should be honoured) who is a Brahmana."[31.]

In later times, Varahmihira's *Brihat Samhita* appears to have been based on *Gargya Samhita*.

Sunahsepa, the son of "Ajigarta, was one of the great observers of stars. His seven hymns of the Rigveda are very significant. In *Vishnu Puran*, Sunahsepa is known to be the son of Visvamitra and is also known as *Devarata* or God-given. Visvamitra is associated in mythology with the creation of seven stars, *Saptarsi*, and the Seven *Nakshatras*. Perhaps, Sunahsepa, also known as Devarata, is regarded as the adopted son of Visvamitra and was a real son of Ajigarta.[32] He worked in the Astronomical Academy of Visvamitra, both of them collaborated in a large number of astronomical observations especially of stars.

Parasara Saktya and Gautama were also reputed for their astronomical observations. The constellations, they observed were known as 'str', a word that has come down to us as star in English.[33]

Vamadeva, son of Gautama, is to be credited with the first identification of *Brhaspati* or the planet Jupiter, a reference to which is found in the *Rigveda* and in the Atharvaveda also.[34]

Just as the credit of identifying *Brhaspati* or Jupiter goes to Vamadeva, similarly Vena, the son of Bhrgu, for the first time identified the planet, Venus. There are two hymns of 20 verses associated with the name of Vena Bhargava in the Rigveda: IX.85 and X.123.

Though, these references of Vedic literature points towards very old traditions of astronomy in India, yet it cannot be said in unequivocal terms that the knowledge of these *nakshatras* is Indian in origin.[35]

After *Vedanga Jyotisha*, we do not have any astronomical text extent with us for the next about a thousand years. *Kautilya sastra*, around 300 B.C., mentions some astronomical observations. *Surya prajnapati* of the Jainas, around 200 B.C., mentions almost similar astronomical concepts as are in the *Vedanga Jyotisha*, except for its different cosmology with two suns etc. Next, we hear about Aryabhata's astronomy in the fifth century A.D. Although we do not find any written work in between aforesaid period, but it is very much clear by the available evidence that there was a confluence between Indian astronomy and Greek astronomy.

It is difficult to say when India had first contact with the Greeks. An indirect trade between India and the Levant seems to have existed from very ancient times. Perhaps, for the first time India to the east of Indus was first made familiar in Europe by the historians and men of science, who accompanied Alexander the Great in 327 B.C. Their narratives, although now lost, are condensed in the writings of Strabo, Pliny and Arrian.[36] Alexander built two memorial cities on the scene of his victory – Bucephalia, and Nicaea. He also built a town known as Alexandria. A Greek garrison and *satrap*, left there by Alexander, laid the foundation of a lasting influence. After his death in 323 B.C., Bactria and India eventually fell to Seleucus Nicator, the founder of Syrian monarchy. This period coincided with the rise of Chandragupta, who founded an empire in 316 B.C. with Pataliputra as a Capital. He made an alliance with Seleucus, after defeating him in war. Seleucus gave his daughter to Chandragupta in marriage and stationed an ambassador Megasthenes at the Court of Chandragupta. This was the period when Indian astronomy besides architecture and sculpture came under the influence of the Greeks.[37]

It was during this period that the Indian astronomers came into contact with Greeks and other neighbours. Indian astronomy now came under the influence of Greek astronomy. This was the period when the five astronomical systems, called *Siddhantas*, developed in this country, partly indigenous and partly in collaboration with Greek astronomy. These *Siddhantas* were named as *Surya*, *Paitamaha*, *Paulisa, Vasistha* and *Romaka*. The *Romaka* and *Paulisa Siddhantas* were foreign in origin as their names implies. *Romaka* was after the Roman Empire and Paulisa, according to AlBiruni was written by *Paulus al Yunani*.[38]

The *Surya Siddhanta* was a composition in *Slokas* in four parts, which underwent many changes in course of time. *Paitamaha* belonged to a period when science had not yet well established itself in India.

There was an apparent difference between the Indian and Greek ideas about Astronomy. *Surya Siddhanta*, though in general agreed with Ptolemy's observation, yet it had difference in many respects. It has been argued by scholars that the amount of Greek influence in Indian astronomical thought cannot be estimated correctly.[39]

Professor Whitney (who translated the *Surya Siddhanta*) has expressed the opinion that the absence from the Hindu system of any of the improvements introduced into Greek astronomy by Ptolemy seems to favour the conclusion that the original transmission of astronomical knowledge into India took place before Ptolemy.[40] Macdonell says that "The uncertainty is all the greater since we have no more of the date of the five *Siddhantas* than that they were regarded by Varahmihira as authoritative works.[41]

Thus, considering the influence of Greeks on Indian astronomy, the fact remains that astronomy in both the countries grew in collaboration with each other. Whereas India has been indebted to the Greek thought, Greek astronomy also must have been equally influenced by the *Siddhantas* propounded in this country.[42]

Thus, it can be said that Indian astronomers came into contact with the best literature of the Greek astronomy also and vice versa. They were not satisfied with preparing workable almanacs only. Both the countries collaborated in many sciences, and the Greek and Indian astronomy developed as a joint effort. Whereas India gave to the west astronomers like Ptolemy; the Greeks gave to the east such personalities as *Bhaskara* I and *Brahmagupta*.[43]

Paitamaha Siddhantas was similar to *Vedang Jyotisha* and was prevalent in the beginning of the 4th century A.D. Its year consisted of 366 days and included two intercalary months in a *Yuga* of five years and operated with *Nakshatra* and not with *Rashis* (signs). *Vashishtta Siddhanta* (400 A.D.) shows further progress in astronomy, Sign (*Rashis*) displaced the *Nakshatras* and the idea of *Lagna* (i.e., the point of ecliptic that is on the eastern horizon at any time) is also adumbrated. Its year consisted of 365 days and hence it was more accurate than that of *Paitamaha Siddhanta. Paulisa Siddhanta* (380 A.D.) shows advancement in the lunar and solar astronomy. It lays down a rough rule for calculating eclipses. *Romaka Siddhanta* (500 A.D.) shows further advancement in science. It is completely based upon astronomical theories. Its theories are mainly reference of the works of Hipparchus and Ptolemy.[44]

Thus, it can be said that before Aryabhatta, like astronomy, *Jyotisha* (astrology) was very popular and firmly rooted in India. It was a part of the *Vedanga* and no rites whether secular or religious could be undertaken with/out reference to good or bad omens. The Yajna, marriage, penance, or any other undertakings by an individual or by the society as a whole, could not be performed without the favourable and auspicious coincidence of the stars and *Nakshatras.* Whatever might have been the development of Astrological sciences, it was an indispensable factor in human life and society. The advice of the astrologers was always sought both by the kings and the common men both. Thus, astrologers were always maintained by the kings at their courts, and they got high patronage from all sections of the people. The Brahmins were principally in this profession and but with the raising supremacy of Buddhism their hold was considerably lessened. Buddhism had no belief in its efficacy.[45]

Astronomy in Jain Literature

The Jains displayed extensive literary activity from early times and their canonical literature contains information about scientific subjects. Their basic texts are classified as *Angas*, *Upangas, Prakirnakas, Chedasutras and Mulasutras.*

The *Angas* are twelve in number. Two of them, the *Sthananga* and *Bhagavasti sutra* contains information of mathematics and astronomy.

Out of twelve *Upangas, Suryaprajapati Chandraprajnapati* and *Jambudip prajnapati* also have a detailed information of astronomy. *The Mulasutras* are four in number. The first Mulasutra, viz. *Uttaradhyayana* contains astronomy. The individual texts i.e., *Nandisutra, Anuyogadvarasutra* and *Prakirnakas* deal with numerous topics on astronomy.[46]

Jain Canons relating to astronomy, mathematics, geography have been collected in the *Ganitanuyoga.* The Jain Canons speak of astronomy as an important branch of study and as an essential equipment for a Jain priest for computing the correct time for religious performances.[47] The *Trilokaprajnapati* by *Yati Versabha* (between A. D. 473 and 609) is an encyclopaedic work in 7000 verses, and its chapter seven, has a long discourse on astronomy. *Jyotisakarndaka*, possibly, written by an early author named *Padaliptacharya*, is based on the *Suryaprajnapati* and contains the entire gamut of Jain astronomy.

Aryabhata

Aryabhata was the earliest astronomer, who had written the earliest preserved Hindu astronomical and mathematical text known as *Aryabhatiyam.* This text and its later commentaries and quotations are the only material available which tell us about Aryabhata and his work.

Nothing is known about his family, parentage, and the person himself. He is said to have belonged to Kusumpura (Patna in Bihar). According to his work, he was born around 476 A.D. He wrote this famous book at the age 23 or 24. This was the period, which, in the social and cultural history of India, is called "The Golden Age of India", when under the Gupta emperors there was an outburst of intellectual activity in science, literature and other spheres.[48]

His *Aryabhatiyam* consists of two parts – (1) *Dasagitika-Sutra* and (2) *Aryashtasta.* Although some scholars suggest that these are two different books,[49] but according to Dr. O. P. Jaggi both are the different parts of the book Aryabhatiyam only.[50] He advocated that the rotation of earth was responsible for causing day and night. And the planets like moon were not luminous bodies but it was sun which made them shine. He obtained correct equation for the orbit of a planet. He introduced correct angular diameter of the earth shadow at the moon orbit, and he knew how to find half the duration of an eclipse and total obscuration. He also framed a rule to ascertain what part of the moon will be observed in an eclipse.[51] He also declared that it was not caused by Rahu but by the shadow of the earth and moon.

There are indications that he had written one more book which is not available. It is being thought that the book might have contained description of astronomical instruments used in his time.[52]

He seems to be a contemporary of Paulus.[53] And he expounded Paulisa and *Romaka Siddhantas.* His disciples were *Nissanka*, *Pandurangasvamin* and *Latadev*, who was *sarvsiddhanta* Guru.[54]

On the occasion of the anniversary of the renowned astronomer Aryabhata, the French astronomer Dr. Roger Billard said, in New *sarvsiddhanta* Delhi, "I think the history of Indian astronomy to be as a whole the most extraordinary monument of history of sciences, a very epistemology by its very self and perhaps the most enlightening knowledge of man's search for knowledge. In particular, the new history of Indian astronomy leads us to discover how and why Aryabhata was the leading astronomer of the scientific astronomy in India and furthermore how and why he will soon be great figure in the history of astronomy in general. Aryabhata's work was more accurate and advanced than that of Claudins Ptolemy."[55]

Srisena

Srisena is generally recognised as the original author or probably a recastor of the astronomical treatise called *Romaka Siddhanta*, which was composed sometime before 500 A.D. It is one of the earliest Indian astronomical treatises which clearly indicates the influence of the early Greek astronomy. According to *Romaka Siddhanta*, a year has 365 days, 5 hours, 55 minutes, and 12 seconds. The beginning of the day in *Romaka Siddhanta* is not reckoned in the original Indian fashion from midnight or sunrise but from sunset and also not from the meridian of Ujjayani but from that of Alexendria (*Yavanapura*).[56] This clearly shows the influence of Greek astronomy. It also gives methods for the calculation of the mean places of the sun and moon, length of the revolution of the moon's node, the greatest and the true latitude of the moon. Besides it gives 150 tables of the equations of anomaly.

Varahmihira's *Panch-Siddhanta* (550 AD) includes *Romaka Siddhanta* as one of the five *Siddhantas* and our current knowledge of *Romaka* is based on that description. Brahmagupta, a later distinguished astronomer-mathematician did not have a high opinion of Srisena of *Romaka Siddhanta.* He wrote in his *Brahma-Sphutra-Siddhanta* that "Srisena took from Latadev the rules concerning the mean motions of the sun, moon, mars, mercury, Jupiter, venus and saturn and from

Aryabhata the rules concerning the epicycles and true motions of the planets and thus *Romaka Siddhanta* which was a heap of jewels had by Srisena been converted into a sort of patched cloth".[57] AlBiruni (1031 A.D.) in later times remarked that the calculations made according to *Romaka* and *Paulisa Siddhanta* were not very correct.

Romaka Siddhanta of Srisena seems to have been lost long ago. There, however, is known to exist a spurious *Romaka Siddhanta* in the India office library in London which seems to have been fabricated around 1600 A.D.[58]

Varahmihira

After the Vedic period, widening horizon of knowledge in various spheres such as different schools of philosophy, coupled with the prosperity of the Gupta period created an interest in the study of various astronomical phenomenon, for the better understanding of the universe in which the man lived. Contacts with the people from other lands such as Greece, brought about exchange of ideas and views in astronomy, like in other fields of human endeavour.

In such environments Varahmihira, son of Aditya Dasa, a Brahman lived in Ujjayani in Magadha kingdom (central India) at the end of fifth century (499 A.D.) and died in 587 A.D. Ujjayani was an important city for astronomical activities during those days.

Varahmihira was a prolific writer in astronomy and astrology. Much of his work is still extent and about the rest we know from his commentator, Bhattotpala (968 A. D). His entire work is divided into three parts. The first part is on astronomy and the second and third on astrology. The first part of his work is called "*Pancha Siddhanta*". This is essentially based on the five astronomical *Siddhantas* in vogue i. e. *Paulisa, Romaka, Vashishtta, Surya* and *Paitramaha Siddhantas.*[59]

AlBiruni, later on (1030 A.D.), did not have high opinion of the work of Varahmihira as he wrote, "Varahmihir has composed a small compass called *Panch-Siddhanta* which ought to mean that it contains the pith and marrow of the preceding five *siddhantas*. But this is not the case, nor is it so much better than they, as to be called the most correct of the five".[60.]

Varahmihira mentioned various aspects of astronomy which an astronomer of his time was supposed to know. He perfectly knew the divisions of heaven and of time, in ages, years, half years, months, half months, days *muhurtas, ghatis, palas, vipalas, prativipalas* etc., as described in five *siddhantas*.

The second part of Varahmihira's work relates to astrology. The work entitled "*Vrihat Jataka*" is still available. It consists of 25 chapters and deals purely with horoscopic astrology. The other two portions of part second, called *Vrihad-Yatra* and *Vrihad-Patale* dealing with journeys and weddings, have probably not yet been recovered.

The third part of his work generally known as *Vrihat-Samhita* is still available in complete form. It contains about 4000 couplets, distributed over more than a hundred chapters. It contains useful information such as the movement of heavenly bodies and their effects upon men, geography, architecture, construction of images, excavation of tanks, laying out of garden, special characteristics of different classes of women and animals, jewellery, augury, marriage etc. In his writings, we find quite a lot of influence of Greek astronomy. He uses in his astrological works certain terms which are said to be Greek or derived from Greek. He frequently quotes them in his treatise *Vrihat Samhita.*[61]

His other works were *Yoga Yatra, Jyotish-Shastra, Hora-Shastra,* and *Laghu-Jataka* in which he explained the technique of foretelling about the future of living beings. Varahmihir was a compiler rather than a researcher, and an expert on omens.[62]

Brahma Gupta

After Aryabhatta and Varahmihira, the two great mathematician-astronomers, Brahmagupta came. He was later assessed by AlBiruni as the most distinguished mathematician of India. Brahmagupta, son of Jishnu, was born in 598 A.D. in the town of Bhillawala near Multan in Punjab. After the downfall of the glorious Gupta empire, though cultural and literary prosperity was still continuing yet astronomy was certainly on the decline.

On the basis of his knowledge of mathematics and astronomy and his own original contributions to the subject, in 628 A.D., at the age of 30, Brahmagupta composed a treatise called "*Brahma-Sphuta Siddhanta*" (sphuta means corrected). This *Siddhanta* appears to have been based on a much earlier compilation called *Brahma* or *Paitamaha Siddhanta*, which had become out of date because its observation and calculation did not match with the latest prevailing knowledge. Another work was *Karana Khanda Khadyaka*, composed in his later life in 665 A.D. He had a very deep knowledge of algebra, and also used it in solving various astronomical problems. He is, perhaps, the first in the world to have used algebra effectively for astronomical calculations. Consequently, he along with later Indian workers brought astronomy to a high degree of perfection.[63]

Brahmagupta's knowledge and contribution in the field of astronomy, though significant, is marred by his prejudices. In his *siddhanta* he described the principles of his astronomical system and gave methods for the calculation of the motion and places of various planets, their rising and setting, conjunctions, calculations of moon and sun eclipses and many other problems. He also mentioned Puranic and religious matters.

Brahmagupta criticized and differed from Aryabhata and upheld wrong orthodox notions particularly about the non-rotation of the earth and the cause of the eclipses. Here, it is worth remembering that during Brahmagupta's time, astronomy, was very much admixed with Brahmanical religion and still believed in the orthodox astronomical explanations. A denial of those views was tantamount to sacrilege of the religion. It is possible that Brahmagupta was under pressure of the priests and also the king under whom he composed his *siddhanta* and uphold orthodox views. His work *Brahma-sphuta Siddhanta* was introduced to the Arabians in 771 A.D. through an Indian, who travelled to Baghdad. Arabs called it as "Sind-Hind", and from this book the elements and methods for calculation of astronomical tables were adopted in the Islamic lunar year.[64]

Bhaskara I

Bhaskara I, the celebrated author of the '*Mahabhaskariya*' the '*Laghu Bhaskariya*' and a commentary on the *Aryabhatiya*, lived in the seventh century. He was the contemporary of Brahmagupta (628 A.D.) and a follower of Aryabhatta (born 476 A.D.). He describes the certain places lying on the Hindu prime meridian.[65] Such list of the places is also given by other astronomers as *Lalla, Vatesvara, Sripati* and *Bhaskara II* (12th century A.D.).[66]

Kalyanavarman

Kalyanavarman enjoyed a high reputation as an astrological writer and the importance attached to his only known work, the *Saravali*. However, considerable uncertainty prevails about the date of the astrologer Kalyanavarman and his work Saravali. Scholars have suggested various dates for him between the flourishing periods of *Varahmihira* whom he mentions and *Bhattotpala* who quotes his works. But Kalyanvarman also refers to the astronomer Brahmagupta who completed his *Brahmasphuta Siddhanta* in 628 A.D. Thus, the author Kalyanavarman must have flourished sometime between 628 and 730 A.D.[67]

Bhattotpala

Bhattotpala was an erudite astrologer of the early medieval period. But there is uncertainty regarding his flourishing period, and on the basis of the concluding stanzas of his commentaries on Varahmihira's *Vrihda Jattak* and *Vrihta Samhita* mentioning the Saka year 888, it is generally believed that he lived about the middle of the tenth century A.D. He is also cited by the Arabic writer Abu Mashar, who died in 886 A.D.[68] He wrote "*Horasastra*" and commented on Varahmihira's work in the tenth century. After a deep and thorough study of existing works he gave new interpretation to the subject. He also revised a text of Kalyanavarman i.e., *Saravali*, written in the seventh century A.D., perhaps he might have completed it also.[69]

Bhaskara II

Bhaskara, son of Maheshwara, was born in the year 1114 A.D. at Vijjadavida in modern Maharashtra state. He composed his great treatise "*Siddhanta Siromani*" in the year 1150 A.D., when he was only 36 years old. Another of his works is named *Karana-Katuhale* which he composed in the year 1183-84 A.D. The period when Bhaskara lived generally speaking, was of decline and decadence in all spheres of cultural and literary activities in India due to the Mohemmedan invasions and the increasing influence of Islam.

"*Siddhanta* Siromani" is a voluminous treatise divided into four parts namely *Patiganita* or *Lilavati* which deals generally with arithmatic, *Bijaganita* which deals generally with algebra, *Grahaganitadhyaya* and *Goladhyaya* which together deal with motions of the planets and calculations of the sphere. In *Grahagaintadhaya* of *Siddhanta Siromani* describes Bhaskara's astronomy which is based on *Surya Siddhanta.* In confirmity with it he attributes the motions of the planets to winds, distinguishing clearly between them and atmospheric currents. He explains the revolution of the planets by developing a theory of epicycles and analyses the motion of the sun by considering changes in longitude not only from day to day, as his predecessors had done, but over the shorter periods, so that its motion be uniform during small intervals. In his Goladhyaya, Bhaskara gives two values for the ratio of the circumference to the diameter.[70]

Bhaskara II was the last great mathematician astronomer of ancient and medieval India. Later on, scholars have generally confined themselves to writing commentaries on the works of their predecessor.

Lalla (C.638 or C.768), *Munjala* or *Manjula* (932), *Shripati* (1039), *Prithudaa* (864) were also known as astronomers and commentators.[71]

According to Kashyapa, we have eighteen names in the galaxy of astronomers in ancient India as follows as:[72.]

(1) *Surya* (2) *Pitamaha* (3) *Vyasa* (4) *Vashistha* (5) *Atri* (6) *Parasara* (7) *Kashyapa* (8) *Narada* (9) *Garga* (10) *Marichi* (11) *Manu* (12) *Angiras* (13) *Lomasa* (14) *Paulisa* (15) *Chyavana* (16) *Yavana* (17) *Bhrgu* (18) *Saunaka.* This list indicates the assimilation of Greek astronomers with Indian astronomers. According to *Parashar*, the leading astronomers were nineteen. He adds only one astronomer known as '*Visvasrd*' in above list.[73]

Astrology in Everyday life during Ancient India

The history of astrological beliefs in India goes back to early ancient period, as we see that Vedic civilisation exhibits beliefs in the *sakunas*, prognostications and omens.[74] In the *Chandogya Upnishad* (VII.1.2.4), *Daiva* and *Nakshatra Vidya*, i.e., the knowledge of the *Utpatas* or natural disturbances and *Jyotisa* respectively, are included in the list of the sciences studied by Narada. Panini refers to the belief in divination from bodily signs and to fortune-telling by soothsayers. But it was also mentioned in the *Rgayanadigana* that *utpata, samvatsara, muhurta and nimitta* were the subjects of study of astronomy and omens in those days.[75]

There was a great importance of an astrologer in daily life of common people as well as for the king of the state in ancient India. Here, we can mention Varahimihira's strongest advocacy for the astrologer's cause and he devotes one full chapter i.e., *Samvatsara-Sutradhyaya (Chap. II)* for the description of the qualifications and importance of the *Samvatsara* (astrologer) for the state and society. He advises the king to respect and secure the services of a learned

Samvatsara. If he does not honour a learned astrologer, he is destined to destruction.[76]

We find the king's dependency on the astrologers as he describes in his other works also viz. the *Gautama Dharmasutra* (XI. 15-16), the *Visnudharmasutra* (III.75), the *Yajnavalkya-Smriti* (I. 307, 333, III.171-2), the *Visnudharmottara* (II.4.5.-16) and the *Kamandakiya Nitisara.*[77] Even *Kautilya,* who was against the reliance on astrology, mentions, '*Kartantika', 'naimittika'* and *'mouhurtika',* in the list of royal officers drawing an allowance of 1000 *panas.*[78]

However, the practice of astrology was unequivocally condemned as an unorthodox science, by early Buddhist, Jaina and Brahmanical writers. Manu also condemned this practice. But these strong condemnations show that the astrologers enjoyed great popularity with the common folk.

According to Varahmihira, a *Samvatsara* (astrologer) should be highly ideal, master of three branches of *Jyotisha* viz. mathematics, horoscopy and natural astrology and possess necessary intellectual attainments. He should also have a sagacious bent of mind. But he condemned such astrologers, who made predictions only for the sake of material gain. He brands such people as '*naksatra-dusakas*' (II.16 B.S.)

Varahmihira mentions a very wide range of astrological beliefs of ancient time. He records superstitions relating to the sun, the moon, planets, constellations, and zodiacal signs. He also interprets of the movements of the limbs, bodily marks, the signs of the great men and the sakunas. Angavidya or the science of prognostication through the movements of bodily limbs is a very ancient science. It is mentioned in early Buddhist, Bramanical and Jain works. A detailed work of this science is to be found in *Puvvayariya's* prakrit work '*Angavijjapainnayam*' in about fourth century A.D. The popularity of this science in Varahmihra's time is evident from his statement that one well-versed in it was always respected by the king and the people.[79] In prognosticating good or bad results, the prognosticators took note of the direction, and the place of the query, the utterance of the questioner, any article brought at the time of the query and the movements of the limbs of the questioner. Proper care was taken to select an auspicious direction, spot, and time for the query. In a query concerning pregnancy, the sex, the number of children, the time and the *nakshatra* of the birth and abortion, were determined from the behaviour of a pregnant woman. Various effects –good and bad– were also believed to occur from the position of the pimples (*pitaka*), ulcers (vrana), *tilakas*, *moles*, auspicuous mark and heary circles (*aVarta*) on the different parts of the body.[80] A special class of the interpreters of bodily signs called *Samudravid* and *Laksanajna*, had come into existence. According to Varahmihira they were highly respected in society.

As many as eleven chapters of the *Brihat Samhita* of Varahmihira (LXXXV-XCV) are devoted to the *Sakunas* or indications of future events in the life of a human being derived from the movements of birds and animals, especially during journey. The philosophy behind the belief in the efficacy of omens is that an omen indicates the fruition of one's good and bad deeds in a previous life.[81] Thus the events revealed by birds and animals were regarded as the outcome of a man's deeds in a previous life and omens had only an indicatory value.

A noteworthy feature of Indian life through the ages is the persistency of beliefs, superstitions, and omens are not an exception. The idea, for example, that a dog entering a house with a dry bone into its mouth or barking facing the sun[82] or during the night[83] bodes evil, still persists. The belief that crows assembling in a town or village without any apparent reason foreshadow evil[84] is still perserved. Similarly, sneezing before starting a journey or any kind of work was, like today, regarded as inauspicious[85] some objects, the sight of which was regarded as auspicious at the commencement of a journey, as mentioned by Varahmihira. In fire-worship, the priest was invariably associated with the *samvatsara*, while the priest offered oblations into fire, the *samvatsara* interpreted omens. It is said that if at the conclusion of fire worship, the fire blazes forth of its own accord, is glossy and its flames turn to the right, it indicates victory to the king.[86]

Jyotish (Astrology) as a subject of Learning and Education

Manu accepts three sciences –*trayi, Varta* and *Dandaniti.* But Brihaspati refers to only two main *Vidyas*[87] – *Varta* and *Dandaniti.* But in *Varta* he gives a long list of education for livelihood, the art of acting, painting, soothe saying, the knowledge of cocks, horses and elephants, astronomy, grammer, mathematics and the knowledge of supreme soul etc.

Kalidas refers to 14 Vidyas (knowledge) – 4 Vedas (Rigveda, Yajurveda, Samveda, Atharveda); 6 Angas (Shiksha, Kalpa, Sutra,

Nirukta, Chhanda; Jyotish (Astronomy and Astrology); Dharamshastra, Puranas, Mimansa, and logic.

Varahmihir states that the science of *Jyotisha* can be divided into three departments (*skandhas*), the first branch called *Tantra* deals with the determination by mathematical calculation of the heavenly bodies, the second known as Hora treats of horoscopy or the casting of the horoscope; and the last is natural astrology which is also called *Angavinischaya* or *Sakha (Phalgranth)* and the whole course of *Jyotisha* is named as *Samhita*. *Utpata* considers the word *Samhita* in a wider sense. According to him, only one who knows *Jyotisha* in its three sections viz. *Ganita, Jataka* and *Sakha* are considered to be well-versed in *Samhita*. Varahmihira tells us that a real astrology is one who knows both text and meaning of the works on mathematical astronomy, natural astrologer and horoscopy and explains *Samhita* as *Phalagrantha*. A person fully accomplished in natural astrology can be an efficient diviner.[88]

Further, Varahmihir has laid down the contents of works belonging to different branches of the science. According to him, Indian astronomical works are usually classified under three heads. (1) *Siddhantas* (2) *Tantras* and (3) *Karanas*. A clear-cut distinction between them cannot be drawn. According to the popular definition, however, such works as start their calculations from the beginning of the Kalpa are known as *Siddhanta*. He again tells that such books as do not reach the standard of a *Siddhanta* are mostly called *Tantra* or *Karana*.[89]

The next branch of the science, according to Varahmihira, is horoscopy. It includes the following topics: – the strength or weakness of zodiac signs (rasi), half signs (*hora*) third parts (*dreskana*) ninth parts (*navansh*), twelfth parts and degrees, determination of various kinds of power of the seven planets due to the direction, belonging to the department of each planet, conception, time of birth, instant death of a child, span of life, destiny and intervening changes, the most favourable combinations of planetary positions such as *Raja-yoga, Chandra-yoga*, etc., the constellations formed by only two planets, the celestial constellations and effects of all these *yogas*, character, the planetary aspects, calculation of lucky period according to *mahadasas* and *antardasas*. Auspicious and inauspicious moment, travelling, marriage and like matters, are the function of *Hora*. All are the subjects of this branch.[90]

Lastly, the natural astrology, which is known as *Samhita, Sakha, Anga* or *Phalagranth*, covers the effects of planetary position on individual and on whole universe, and its good and bad influence and its remedies etc. Some unscientific topics like omens are also included in this branch.

Thus, the astronomy and the astrology were the fullfledged subjects for learning and education. So, it can be said in other words that these two had a great impact on ancient society of India.

Astronomy and Astrology during the period of Delhi Sultanate

During the medieval period, people in general, were very superstitious like ancient period. Belief in supernatural and the influence of the stars on the life of an individual were universal. Although rulers showed more rational attitude in many cases, yet they were very particular about the auspicious and inauspicious moments and wanted to know them from their astrologers. Both the Hindus and the Muslims shared this common faith in the supernatural.[91]

Astronomy, as practised and understood in this period, had its origin in the Arabs world, also in Persia and Central Asia. Thus, we must know about the origin and development of the subject in its birthplace and land.

Origin and Development of Astronomy and Astrology during Arab Empire

In the Sultanate of Ghazani, at the time of *Mahmud* and his son *Masud*, Abu Rayhan Muhammad ibn Ahmad-al-Biruni (A.D. 973-1048) made a treatise on astronomy which was known as *Quanun-al-Masudi. Ibn Yunus* and *Ibn-al-Haytham* were famous researcher and obse,rver of astronomical phenomenon at the court of *Fatimid-al-Hakim* (AD 909-1171).[92]

A fresh impetus was given to the pursuit of astronomical studies, when *Abu-al-Fath Omar Ibn Ibrahim al-Khayyam* reformed the calendar (C. 1075) and made it probably superior to the Gregorian. A fresh cultural and scientific activities were encouraged after the destruction of the flourishing cities of *Samarqand, Bokhara, Bulkh* and the *Khwarizm shahi Sultanate* by the *Mongol, Chingiz Khan* and *Hulaqu*. Thus, a centre of astronomical studies grew up at *Maragah.*[93] Here an observatory was built under the supervision of *Nasir-al-din Tusi.* He made very useful observation with his successor. Under Ilkhan of Persia (AD 1256 – 65) Tusi was instructed to compile a new set of astronomical tables. These *Ilkhanian* Tables dealing with Greek, Chinese, Persian and Arabic chronology, planetary motions, ephermerides and astrology, occupied the observatory staff for around twelve years (A.D. 1260 – 72) and comprised both new observations and the earlier results of Hipparchos, Ptolemy and muslim astronomers such as Ibu Yunus etc. The most important of the astronomical treatises of *Al-Tusi* was the *Tadlikira* which gave rise to a series of commentaries.[94] Here an illustration from *Tabaqat-I-Nasiri*, may be pointed out, that Chinghiz Khan also selected an auspicious moment for marching his army into the territory of Iltutmish of Hindustan.[95]

The last and best equipped of the observatory due directly to Islamic influence was established about A.D. 1420 at Samarqand, Turkestan, by Ulugh Beg (A.D. 1393-1440), grandson of Tamerlane. His greatest work was an independent star catalogue, based entirely upon new observations. His instruments, though entirely lost, are considered the best made upto that time.[96]

In fact, the family of the *Barmika*[97] was responsible for opening the floodgate of Indian science and wisdom literature to the Arabs. Their ancestors were from the Nava Vihara (Nav Bahar) of *Balkh* in modern Afghanistan and they had a natural interest in India. Sachau observes that they encouraged Hindu scholars to come to Baghdad and ordered them to translate from Sanskrit into Arabic, books on medicine, philosophy, astrology, and other subjects.[98] *Al-Jahiz*, the famous writer of several books of Belle letters, wrote in his article about the superiority of the Indians to others that Indians are advanced in astrology-astronomy, mathematics, medicine, painting and sculpture.[99]

Abu-Rihan Al-Biruni

Al-Biruni's real name was *Abu Raihan Muhammad bin Ahmad Al-Biruni.* The surname Al-Biruni indicates that his birth placed was situated somewhere in the suburb of the city of *Khwarazm*, metropolis of the territory. The residents of this suburb were known as Biruni, i.e. people who resided outside the metropolis. The ruling dynasty of Khwarazm at that time was known as the Al-i-Iraq dynasty and its last ruler, the patron of Al-Biruni was *Abu-Abdullah Muhammad Khwarazm Shah.* At this time, Al Biruni was twenty- three years old and he had benefited from his association with scholars and scientists of eminence attached to the royal court. Here, the name of *Abu*

Nasrbin' Ali, may be mentioned. He was the cousin of the reigning Khwarazm Shah. And he is said to have stimulated Al-Biruni's interest in mathematics and astronomy. Al Biruni calls him his patron and teacher. Soon after the fall of his patron he was invited by *Shamsul Ma'ali*, the ruler of *Jurjan* and *Tabristan*, to join his court. In Jurjan, Al-Biruni had completed his famous work '*Asar-ul-Baqid*', which was dedicated to *Shamsul-Ma'ali*. This work shows his interest in astronomy as well as mathematics, geography, history, and medicine. He describes the achievements of ancient people in different sciences and also makes comments on past discoveries.[100] Al Biruni also appears to have been interested in improving astrolabes. For example, he explains a flattened astrolabe.[101] In Jurjan Al-Biruni also successfully worked out the circumference of the earth by determining the distance between two altitudes.[102] He completed his treatise *Tajrid ul-Shu'at* also in *Jurjan*. Al Biruni, after returning from Jurjan, stayed in Khwarazam till its conquest by Sultan Mahmud of Ghazna in A.D. 1017. He established an observatory where he observed the movements of planets. He mentions his observations and research there from the year A.D. 999 to 1016 in his *Qanun-i-Masudi*. In 1017, however, Al-Biruni was arrested by *Sultan Mahmud* along with the dignitaries of Khwarazm. But, as he was a distinguished intellectual, particularly famous for his knowledge of astronomy, he was set free and allowed to proceed to India, where he probably stayed for thirteen years.[103]

In India, Al-Biruni travelled in Punjab, Sindh, and other places, and made friendship with Hindu scholars. He also acquired knowledge about Indian sciences and culture through a study of Sanskrit and interacted with the people of India. Thus, Al-Biruni was able to have access to important Indian works dealing with astronomy and astrology. He translated several Sanskrit treatises on astronomy. One of the treatises, entitled *Gharat-ul-Zijat* a translation into Arabic of *Karan Tilak* on astronomy and astrology, is available in the Pir Muhammad Shah Library in Ahmadabad.[104] It records observation of solar and lunar eclipses. It was completed before Al-Biruni started his famous *Kitab-ul-hind-fi Tahqiq Milal Hind* (India).

Al-Biruni also acquainted the Indian scholars with Ptolemy's work and the invention of astrolabe (*San'at-al-usturlab*) as well as techniques of using it. Al-Biruni seems to have returned to Ghazna during the last years of Sultan Mahmud's reign. And here, he sat to write the *Qanun-i-Masudi* which is a work of high standard on astronomy. But, except the *Kilab-ul-Hind*, *Asarul-Baqia* and *Qanun-i-Masudi*, his work remains unpublished.[105]

Al Biruni probably enjoyed the reputation of a great *munajjim*, i.e., astrologer-astronomer, and he was a master of astrology, both according to the Greek and the Hindu system and indeed Eastern writers of later centuries seem to consider him as having been the court astrologer of King Mahmud.[106]

Al-Biruni wrote many works and is said to have executed several translations from the Greek, and to have summarised the *Almagest* of Ptolemy. Those most spoken of are astronomical tables, a treatise on precious stones, one on *Materia Medica*, an introduction to astrology, a treatise on chronology and the famous *Kanun-ul-Masudi*, an astronomical and geographical work frequently cited by Abu-l-Fida, especially in his tables of Latitude and Longitude. For this last work he received an elephant load of silver (from the emperor Masud), which however, he returned to the "Royal Treasury".[107]

Influence of Astrology during the Period of Delhi Sultanate

Many references about the influence of astrology and other beliefs can be seen in early sultanate period. One instance can be mentioned from *Chach-Nama* such as, when Dahir Rai was informed about the attack of Arabs, i.e. (Muhammad Kasim), he took certain precautions for the safety of his dependants. And he himself went out to a distant place from Arabs. Dahir then said to an astrologer, "I must fight today, tell me in what part of the heavens the planet Venus is, and calculate which of the two armies shall be successful and what will be the result". After the computation, the astrologer replied, "According to the calculation, the victory shall be to the Arab army, because Venus is behind him and in front of you". Rai Dahir was angry on hearing this. The astrologer then said, "Be not angered, but order an image of Venus to be prepared of gold". It was made and fastened on his saddle traps, in order that Venus might be behind him, and he be victorious".[108.]

Another instance is found in *Tarikh-i-Tahiri*, i.e., the foundation of *Tatta*, a town. It is mentioned that brahmans and astrologers having settled a lucky day and having sought a spot in the neighbourhood of Samui, they selected an eligible place, where now stands the city of *Tatta* and there the foundation was laid.[109]

One of the instances is mentioned by a contemporary *Minahaju-s-siraj* in his work '*Tabaqat-i-Nasiri* that in A.H. 636 Sultan Iltutmish led the armies of Hindustan towards Banyan. In this journey, he fell sick and was obliged by his severe illness to return home. Wednesday morning, the 1st of Shaban was fixed by the astrologers for his entrance into Delhi the (the capital) and he entered the city.[110]

As the progress in astronomy and astrology in central Asia and Khurasan, before the foundation of the Sultanate of Delhi, has been discussed earlier. So, Indian Muslims were also influenced by this. One common feature found in historical literature produced in India by the emigrant writers was that all seem to have believed in the effect of stars and planets on the fate of man and the universe. But Minhaj-i-Siraj Juzjani was an exception of it. In fact, astrology had become a part of astronomy in Central Asia under Buddhist influence, Fakhr-i-Mudabbir opens the introduction of his *Shajra-i-Ansalb* (Book of Genealogy) with a description of the dome of the heavens with their seven skies, each with its presiding planet – all testifying to the glory of the creator.[111] However, Minhaj-i-Siraj-Juzjani was free from such influence, but he considered the study of astronomy a cultural pursuit. Hasan Nizami mentions the Zodiac and the seven planets influencing man's destiny. And Sadiduddin Muhammad Awfi calls Nizam-ul-Mulk Juwaidi a Sahib-i-Qiran, or one born during the conjunction of two auspicious stars.[112]

Some evidence are found in contemporary sources, which shows the passion of scholars for the knowledge about intellectual heritage of Hindus, especially astronomy, medicine, mathematics and yoga.[113] Amir Khusrau speaks highly in his *mathanavi Nuh Siphr* of the contribution of Brahmins to logic, prognostication, scholasticism and physics.[114] In this mathanavi, he has divided the work into nine chapters (*Siphirs*), his first chapter corresponding to the top-most and the ninth sky, second to the eighth sky and so on, in a descending order. Each chapter is dedicated to a planet which is presiding star of the respective sky.[115] In fact, this shows how deeply astronomy went into literary composition of the early 14th century and played a vital role in the life of the medieval people. In his *Qiran us-Sa'dain Amir Khusrau* says, "The movement of the earth has been linked with time, hence day and night, the season of spring and autumn. These changes constitute the source of life and comfort for living beings".[116]

Zia-ud-din Barani has given a good instance about the influence of astronomy and astrology during Ala-uddin Khalzi's period. That shows that astronomers and astrologers also received royal patronage. He narrates those women in the *haram* of Alauddin Khalzi lavishly rewarded Hindu and Muslim astrologers for drawing horoscopes on the birth of princes. They were held in favour for their expertise and experience. He again mentions that the elite of Delhi could not start any work or undertake any project without consulting the astrologers. In fact, the astronomers also practised astrology to earn their livelihood.[117] Although the condemnation of astrology is justified according to the teachings of Islam, yet it was not justified to condemn astronomy. In defence of astronomy, *Shams Siraj Afif*, the late fourteen century's historian writes in his work '*Tarikh-a-Firojshahi*, that "Astronomy is one of the fourteen sciences known to scholars. But the study of astrology has been forbidden by the Prophet. It is, however, permissible to know the rules concerning the shadow of the sun and that in a particular month in what degree of what sign of the zodiac the sun would be, the hours of the short night and the long night and when the night turned into the day".[118.]

In the period of Alauddin Khalzi, the contribution of Thakkura Pheru (1291 to 1323 A.D), in the field of astrology, can not be ignored. He has written several books on different subjects i.e., *Vastu Shastra*, *Ratna Pariksha* (Gemology) etc., but his work *Jyotisar*, written in Prakrit language in 1272 A.D. is a remarkable contribution to know the planetary position, their astronomical calculation, different astrological combinations of planets and their effects on daily life. It contains 474 shlokas.[119]

The simultaneous use of two eras (i.e. Indian and Hijri) in India from the eleventh century onwards, probably brought the problem of converting the dates of one era into another, Thakkura Pheru had made the first attempt probably to formulate a rule for the conversion of era.[120] He was employed at the treasury and the mint of several Sulans of Delhi viz., Allauddin Khalzi, Shihabuddin Umar, Qutbuddin Mubarak, possibly also Nasiruddin Khusrau and Ghiyasuddin Tughlaq. Thus S. R. Sarma has called him a 'pioneer in popularising the science'.[121.]

Zij Astronomy

Zij astronomy appears in India, for the first time, under the patronage of Sultan Firozshah Tughlaq (A.D.1351–1388). Arabic and

Persian Zijes were copied and commented upon. Several books on astronomy were written during his reign and astrolabes constructed. On his orders, an astrolabe was placed on the highest tower in his capital Fiorzabad (in Delhi). Afif associates two astrolabes with the name of Firoz.[122] In addition, Firozshah also took steps to Sanskritize instrumentation astronomy.[123] It was the period of beginnings of the Indian response to Islamic astronomy. Under this enlightened monarch, *Mahendra Suri* composed in 1370 a Sanskrit work on the astrolabe called *Yantraraja*, on the basis of an Arabic text not yet identified,[124] and several Sanskrit works on astronomy and astrology were translated into Persian, notably *Varahmihira's Brhatsamhita* with Utpala's commentary.[125] About three hundred books were captured by Firoz Tughlaq from Jwalamukhi temple. Later on, some of these on astronomy were translated into Persian. The famous writer of the age, Izzaj-ud-din Khalid Khani translated into Persian version, one of the books on rising and setting of the 7 planets, their good and evil impacts, important auguries, and omens. This book was named after the Sultan as *Dalail-i-Firoz Shahi.*[126]

A number of magical events are mentioned by some historians. Such references are noticeable in the Tarikh-Dαudi, a history of the Lodi and Sayyad Sultans of Delhi. In the reign of Sikander Lodi (1489-1517) a magician was known to be capable of creating a fruit garden in Jodhpur in the twinkling of an eye".[127]

There was a great impact of such motivating factors on the social life of common masses in medieval period of India. Sultan Firoz Shah Tughlaq believed in the augury, and he was in the habit of consulting the Quran, deriving omen from certain passages. The Medieval people took augur from sneezing. People believed in lucky and unlucky days and had very strong belief in omens. The Muslim community like the Hindu, believed in superstitions and astrology had a great hold on them. They used to consult the astrologers before entering on an enterprise. Very often, they consulted the book of *Hafiz of Shiraz for omen.* According to Barani the age of Alauddin Khalzi produced great astrologers and astronomers. Every quarter of the city had astrologers, and they prepared the horoscopes of the notable persons like maliks, vazirs and amirs.[128]

As we have noted above a number of works were produced on astronomy and astrology in India during the ancient and medieval periods. These works can be described briefly under three categories viz. *Siddhantas, Karanas* and instrumentation texts.

1. *Siddhanta* literally means the established end or result. This *siddhant* astronomy, which was mathematical, came about as a result of interaction with Greece in post-Alexandrian period. The *Siddhantas* are the text books.
2. *Karanas* are easy form of books. It gives practical rules for carrying out computations. A noteworthy feature is that *Karanas* choose a contemporaneous epoch rather than follow the *Siddhantas*.
3. The instrumentation texts in Sanskrit were composed during the reign of Firozshah Tughlaq for the first time. These texts are written about astronomical instruments.

Above three categories of works are shown in the following three tables: [129.]

Table 1 Important *Siddhantas* in Ancient and early Medieval Period

	Year	Author	Place	Work
1.	b. 476	Aryabhata I	Patna	Aryabhata-*Siddhantas* Aryabhatiya (499)
2.	c. 505	Latadeva	–	Redactions of Saura – *Romaka*, Pautisha-*Siddhantas*
3.	c. 620-700	Brahmagupta	Bhillamala Rajasthan	Brahma-Sphuta-*Siddhanta* (628)
4.	Fl. 629	Bhaskara I	Valabhi Gujrat	Maha-Bhaskariya (629) Lughu-Bhaskara
5.	8th Cent.	Lalla	Dasapura Malwa	Shishya-dhi-vriddheda (748)
6.	c. 800	Anonymous	–	*Surya Siddhanta*
7.	b. 880	Vateshvara	Vatanagara N. Gujarat	Vateshvara-*Siddhanta* (904)
8.	c. 953	Aryabhata II	–	Maha-*Siddhanta*
9.	c. 1000-1050	Shripati	Rohinikhand South of Ujjain	*Siddhanta*-Shekhara
10.	b. 1114	Bhaskara-II	Vijjalavida Bijapur	*Siddhanta*-Shiromani (1150)
11.	b. 1444	Nilkantha Somayaji	Kundapura Kerala	Tantra-Sangraha
12.	c. 1475-1525	Juanaraja	Parthapura Godavari	*Siddhanta*-Sundara (1503)

Table 2 Important Karanas

	Year	Author	Place	Work
1.	505	Varahmihira	Ujjain	*Pancha-Siddhanta*
2.	c. 620-700	Brahmagupta	Bhillamala Rajasthan	Khanda-Khadyaka (665)
3.	c. 650-700	Haridatta	Kerala	Graha-Chara-niban-dhana (683)
4.	c. 650-700	Devacharya	Kerala	Karana-Ratna (689)
5.	c. 900-950	Manjula or Munjala	Prakashpattan	Lughu-Mavasa (932)
6.	c.1000-1050	Shripati	–	Dhi-Kotida-Karana (1039)
7.	c.1050-1100	Brahmadeva	Mathura	Karan-Prakasha (1092)
8.	C.1060-1110	Shatananda	Puri, Orissa	Bhasvati-Karana (1099)
9.	b. 1114	Bhaskara II	Vijjalavida, Bijapur	Karana-Kutuhala (1183)
10.	c.1280-1350	Chakresh-vara Mahadeva	Rasina, Godavari	Mahadevi (1316)
11.	13–14th Century	Vararuchi	Kerala	Vakya-Karana (1282/13.6)
12.	1367	Mahadeva	Trymbak, Godavari	Kamadhenu-Karana
13.	c. 1360-1455	Parameshvar a	Alattoor, Kerala	Drig-ganita (1430)
14.	1375	Ishvara	–	Karna-Kautirava
15.	1417	Damodara	–	Bhata-tulya
16.	c.1450-1510	Keshava	Nandgaon Maharashtra	Graha-Kautuka (1496)
17.	c. 1475-1550	Chitrabhanu	–	Karanamrita (1530)
18.	c. 1500-1560	Shankara-Variyar	Kerala	Karana-Sara
19.	b. 1507	Ganesh Daivajna	Nandgoan, Maharashtra	Graha-Laghava (1520)

Table 3 Instrumentation Texts in Sanskrit

Year	Author (Place)	Work	Instrument
1370	Mahendra Suri (Delhi)	Yantraraja	Astrolabe
c. 1400	Padmanabha	Yantra-Kiranavali	Astrolabe-Dhruva-Bhramana-Yantra
1428	Ramachandra (Sitapur, U.P.)	Yantra-prakasha	Misc.
15th Cent.	Hema (Gujrat)	Kasha-yantra	Cylindrical sundial
b.1507	Ganesh Daivajna	Pratoda-Yantra Sudhiranjana-yantra	Gruateded strip

End Notes

1. Sukumari Bhattacharji, *Myths, Vedic Buddhist and Brahmanical*, Progressive Publishers. Kolkata (July 2002) Preface.
2. As quoted by Sukumari Bhattacharji, *Ibid.*
3. G. N. Banerjee, *Hellenism in Ancient India*, Chapter XIII, Munshiram Manoharlal, New Delhi (1998), pp. 268-269,
4. Rajesh Kochhar and Jayant Narlikar, *Astronomy in India: A Perspective*, Indian National Science Academy, New Delhi (1994), pp.1-3.
5. A. L. Bhasham (ed.), *A Cultural History of India*, Clarendon Press, Oxford (1975), p. 161.
6. O.P. Jaggi, *History of Science and Technology in India*, Vol. II, Chapter 9, Atma Ram and Sons: Delhi (1984), p. 99.
7. Rajesh Kochhar and Jayant Narlikar, *Op.cit.*, pp. 2-3.
8. *Yazurveda*, XXX, 10 as quoted by O. P. Jaggi, *op. cit.*, p.112.
9. *Chhandogya Upanishada* VII, 1, 2, 4; 2.1; 7.1 as quoted by O.P. Jaggi, *op. cit.*
10. M.L. Bhagi, *Ancient India: Culture and Thought*, The Indian Publication, Ambala Cantt (2001), p. 187.
11. *Ibid.*; Also see, B. Basu, "Vedic Astronomy: Its Relevance Today", *Journal of Asiatic Society*, Kolkata (2005), Vol. XLVII, pp. 41, 43-45.
12. *Rigveda*, I, 164.11, 48 as quoted by O.P. Jaggi, *op. cit.*, p.128; also see, G.T. Garral (ed.), *The Legacy of India*, Black and White Sandip Prakashan, New Delhi (2005), pp. 846-47.
13. *Rigveda* I, 105. 11; *Ibid.*
14. *R. V.*, VII, 103.9 & X 15.13; *Ibid.*
15. *R. V.*, I 50, 95.3; *R. V.*, VIII, 58.2; *R. V.*, IV 53.3; *Ibid.*
16. *R. V.*, X, 85.18; *Ibid.*
17. *R. V.* III, 7.7; *R. V.*, I 105.10; *R.V.*, IX, 114.3; *Ibid.*
18. *R. V.* IV, 50.4; *R. V.*, IV, 50.4, *A.V.*, XX 88.4; *Ibid.*
19. *R. V.*, X, 123, 1.2.5; *Ibid.*; also see, Basu, Vedic Astronomy, *Journal of Asiatic Society*, *op. cit.*, pp. 47-48.
20. *R. V.*, V, 40.9; *Ibid.*
21. *R. V.*, X, 55.3 *Ibid;* also see, B. Bose, Vedic Astronomy, *op. cit.*, p. 47.
22. A.V., V 6.4, XII, 3.8, *Ibid.*
23. T. B. III, 1.1, *Ibid.*
24. *M. B. Bhishma parva* 100; *Ibid.*
25. M. B., III, 42.24; *Ibid.*
26. O.P. Jaggi, *op. cit.* p. 109.
27. *Ibid.*, p. 110.

28. *Ibid.*, p. 111.
29. Swami Satya Prakash Sarasvati, *Founders of Sciences in Ancient India*, Part I, (Pb. Vijay Kumar, Govindram Hasanand, Nai Sarak, Delhi (1990), p. 128 (footnotes)

    (1) चित्राणि साकं दिवि रोचनानि सरीसृपाणि भुवने जवानि। तुर्मिशं सुमतिमिच्छमात्रे अहानि गीभि: सर्पयामि नाकम्।

    (2) सुहवमग्ने कृत्तिका रोहिणी चास्तु भद्रं मृगशिर: शमार्द्रा। पुनर्वसू सूनृता चारू पुष्यो भानुराश्लेषा अयनं मघा में।।

    (3) पुण्यं पूर्वाफल्गुन्यौ चात्र हस्तश्चित्रा शिवा स्वाति सुखो में अस्तु।

    राधे विशाखे सुहवानुराधा ज्येष्ठा सुनक्षत्रमरिष्ठ मूलम्।।
30. O.P. Jaggi, *op. cit.*, p. 113.
31. *Ibid.*, p. 114.
32. Swami Satya Prakash Sarasvati, *op. cit.*, p. 135.
33. *Ibid.*, p. 136.
34.

Ibid., p. 137, बृहस्पति: प्रथमं जायमानो महो ज्योतिष: परमे व्योमन्।
सप्तास्यस्तु वि जातो रवेण वि सप्तरश्मिरधमत् तमाँसि।।
- *R.V.*, IV, 50.4; *A.V.*,.XX.4, 88.4

35. O. P. Jaggi, *Ibid.*, p. 115.
36. Svami Satya Prakash Sarasvati, *op. cit.*, p. 575.
37. *Ibid.*, p. 516.z
38. M.L. Bhagi, *op. cit.*, p. 188, also see G.T. Garrat (ed.), *The Legacy of India*, Black & White Publication, New Delhi (2005), p. 347.
39. *Ibid.*, p. 188.
40. sSwami Satya Prakash Saraswati, *op. cit.*, p. 517.
41. M. L. Bhagi, *op. cit.*, p. 188.
42. Svami Satya Prakash Saraswati, *op. cit.*, Vol. II, p. 518.
43. *Ibid.*, p. 519.
44. Haldhar Pathak, *Cultural History of the Gupta period*, Bhartiya Publishing House Delhi, Varanasi (1978), p. 225; also see, G.T. Garrat (ed.), *op.cit., pp. 348-49.*
45. M. L. Bhagi, *op. cit.*, p. 189.
46. K. V. Sarma, *History of Science and Technology in India*, edited by G. Kuppuram K. Kumudamami, Sandeep Prakashan, Delhi (1990), Vol. II, pp. 336-37.
47. *Ibid.*, p. 338.
48. O. P. Jaggi, *Scientists of Ancient India and Their Achievement*, Atma Ram & Sons, Delhi (1966), p. 152.
49. Hardhar Pathak, *op. cit.*, p. 226.
50. O. P. Jaggi, *op. cit.*, p. 153.

51. Hardhar Pathak, *op. cit.*, p. 227.

52. Nem Kumar Jain, *Science and Scientists in India*, Indian Book Gallery, 2691, Gali Baradari Ballimaraw, Delhi (1982), p. 35; also see, A. K. Bag, "Aryabhatata-I's Achievement in Ancient Indian Mathematic and Astronomy", *Journal of the Asiatic Society*, Kolkata (2005), Vol. XLVII, pp. 14-17.

53. M. L. Bhagi, *Ibid.*, p. 189.

54. Hardhar Pathak, *Ibid.*, p. 227.

55. Nemkumar Jain, *op. cit.*, p. 34.

56. O.P. Jaggi, *op. cit.*, p.159.

57. *Ibid.*, p. 160; also see, Amalendu Bandyopadhyay, "Astronomy During the period from 5th to 12th Century A.D.", *Journal of Asiatic Society*, Kolkata, Vol. XLVII (2005), pp. 27-36.

58. *Ibid.*

59. G.T. Garrat, *op. cit.*, pp. 342-49; also see, S. N. Sen, and K. S. Shukla, *History of Astronomy in India*, Indian National Science Academy, New Delhi (1985), pp. 61-69.

60. Edward Sachau, *Albruni's India*, (Rupa Co., 7/8 Ansari Road, Daryaganj), New Delhi (2002), p. 139.

61. O.P. Jaggi, *op. cit.*, pp. 166-167.

62. Kochchar and Narlikar, *op. cit*, p. 1.

63. O.P. Jaggi, *op. cit.*, p.174; also see, *Brahmasphuta Siddhanta*, ed. Ramswarup Sarma, *Indian Institute of Astronomical and Scientific Research*, New Delhi (1966), Vol. IV, pp. 1385-89.

64. *Ibid.*, pp.177-78.

65. Swami Satya Prakash Sarasvati, *op. cit.*, p. 599 F.N.

    लंकातः खरनगरं सितारूगहें पाषाटो मिसितपुरी तथा तपर्णी।

    उतुंगस्सितवरनामघेयशैलो लक्ष्मीवत्पुरमपि वात्स्यगुल्मसंज्ञम्।।

    विख्यातवननगरी तथा ह्यवन्ती स्थानेशो मुदितजनस्तथा च मेरूः।

    अध्वाख्यः करणविधिस्तुमध्यमानामेतेषु प्रतिवसतां न विद्यते सः।।

    Mahabhas-Kariya II. 1-2 (1960) p. 47.

66. *Ibid.*, p. 600.

67. Ajay Mitra Shastri, *Varahmihira and his Times*, Kusumanjali Prakashan, Jodhpur (1990), p. 195.

68. *Ibid.* p. 201.

69. M. L. Bhagi, *op. cit.*, p. 189.

70. O.P. Jaggi, *op. cit.*, pp.185-86; also see *Sidhanta Shiromani of Bhaskaracharya*, (trans.) by A.A. Somayaji, Kondriya Sanskrit Vidyapeeth, Tirupati (1980), pp. 345-47.

71. Rajesh Kochchar and Jayant Narlikar, *op. cit.*, p. 1; also see, Ramkrishan Bhattacharya, "Science and Superstition in Indian Astronomy", *Journal of Asiatic Society*, Kolkata (2005), Vol. XLVII, pp. 50-54.
72. Swami Satya Prakash Sarasvati, *op. cit.*, p 595.
73. *Ibid.*, p. 596.
74. V. R. Pandit, "Omens and Portents in Vedic Literature", *Proceedings of the All India Oriental Conference*, Nagpur Session (1946), p. 76.
75. Ajay Mittra Shastri, *Ancient Indian Heritage Varahimbir India*, Vol. II, Aryan Book International, New Delhi (1996), p. 356.
76. As quoted by Ajay Mitra Shastri, *op. cit.*, Vol. II, p. 357.
77. *Ibid.*
78. *Ibid.*, Arthashastra, IX-4; V.3 as written by Ajay Mitra Shastri, *Ibid.*, p. 357.
79. *Ibid.*, p. 366.
80. *Ibid*
81.

    अन्यजन्मान्तरकृतं कर्म पुंसां शुभाशुभम्।

    यत्तस्य शकुनः पाकं निवेदयति गच्छताम्।। LXXXV.5(B.S.)

82. Varahimihira, *B. S.* (LXXX-VIII.2)
83. *Ibid.*(LXXX-VIII.5)
84. *Ibid.* (XCIV.8)
85. *Ibid.* (XC IV.60)
86. *Ibid.* (XLII.32)
    Haldhar Pathak, *op. cit.*, p. 167.
87. Vide Arthshastri :- वार्ता दण्डनीतिश्चेति बार्हस्पत्याः।
88. Ajay Mitra Shastri, *op. cit.*, Vol. II, p. 430.
89. *Ibid.*, p. 431.
90. *Ibid.*, p. 433.
91. O. P. Jaggi, *op. cit.*, p. 26.
92. *Ibid.*, p. 41.
93. *Ibid.*
94. *Ibid.*, p. 42.
95. *Ibid.*, p. 26, Tabaqat-I-Nasiri, pp. 1045-46, as quoted by O.P. Jaggi, *op. cit.*
96. *Ibid.*
97. M.A. Saleem Khan, *op. cit.*, pp. 179-179, Baramika was the family of the famous wazirs of Harun. They were the most powerful and wealthiest families only after the family of the Caliphs, and at the same time had a tradition of borning and patronised scholars, poets, scientist, and philosophers.
98. *Ibid.*, p. 179.

99. *Ibid.*, p. 180.

100. Siddiqui, *op. cit.*, p. 18.

101. *Islamic Culture*, Hyderabad, Vol. XIX, January 1945, reprint, New York (1971), pp. 49-50. Also quoted by Siddiqui, ibid.

102. Hasan Barani, *Albiruni: His Life and Works* (Urdu), Muslim University Press, Aligarh (1927), p. 53; also quoted by Siddiqui, *op. cit.*

103. Siddiqui, *op. cit.*, p. 19.

104. *Ibid.*, p. 20.

105. *Ibid.*, pp. 20, 24.

106. Edward Sachau, *Alberuni's India*, Rupa Co., New Delhi (2002), Preface I, p. XIII.

107. H.M. Elliot and John Dowson, *History of India by its own Historians*, Vol. II, Kitab Mahal, Allahabad, p. 3.

108. *Ibid.*, p. 169.

109. *Ibid.*, p. 273.

110. *Ibid.*, Vol. II, p. 328.

111. Siddiqui, *op. cit.*, p. 86.

112. *Ibid.*

113. *Ibid.*, p. 88.

114. *Ibid.*

115. R. Nath and Faiyaz Gwaliari, *India, as seen by Amir Khusrau*, Historical Research Documentation Programme, Jaipur (1981), p. 29 (Notes).

116. Amir Khusrau, *Qiran ul-Sa'dain*, ed. Ismail Meeruti, Aligarh (1918), p. 5, also in Ijaz-i-Khurravi, Vol. 2, p. 158.

117. Siddiqui, *op. cit.*, p. 88, and Barani Ziyaulddin, *Tarikh-i-Firoz Shahi*, Calcutta (1862), pp. 363-64.

118. *Ibid.*, p. 88.

119. Thakkur Pheru, *Ratna Parikshadi Sapt Grauthsangrah*, ed. by Agarchand and Bhanwar Lal Nahta, Rajasthan Prachya Vidya Prishthan, Jodhpur (1961), p. 45/1.

120. G. Kuppuram and K. Kumudamani (eds.), *op.cit.*, Vol. II, S.R. Sarma, *Islamic Calendar and Indians Eras*, p. 434.

121. *Ibid.*, p. 434.

122. R. C. Jauhri, Firoz Tughlaq, ABS Publication, Jalandhar (1990), p. 179, Afif TFSA, pp. 255, 369-70.

123. *Ibid.*

124. S.R. Sarma, *op. cit.*, p. 433.

125. *Ibid.*

126. R. C. Jauhri, *op. cit.*, p. 76.

127. Peter Mundi, *Travels of Peter Mundi in* Asia, ed. R.C. Temple, London, 1914, p. 65. I. H. Siddiqui (ed.), *op. cit.*
128. M.P. Srivastava, *Social and Cultural Trends in Islamic India*, Vohra Publishers and Distributors, Allahabad (1972), p. 45.
129. Rajesh Kochhar and Jayant Narlikar, *op. cit.*, pp. 3, 4 and 7.

CHAPTER 2

Astrology and Astronomy – Meaning, Their Relation, Scientific Basis, and Effects

Astrology, in the Vedic period, was known as one of the six *Vedangas*. It was called the eye of the *Vedas*, for it threw light on matters relating to timing events. The conduct of Vedic ritual had to be performed at a particular time of specific period. Hence Astrology was used to this purpose. In modern context, however, it is used to interpret the birth charts of an individual to have an overview of personal and professional future.

This Chapter deals with the meaning of astrology and astronomy and their relations, the basic concepts of Astrology, its scientific basis, its impacts on human being and on universe as a whole as conceived or understood by the medieval Indian society.

What is astrology? The question is taken up by scholars with their different views and opinions. Some define astrology as the science of stars, while others have opinion that it is the art by which the future of man can be known. It may also be defined in other words that it is the philosophy of discovery and analysing past impulses and future actions of both individuals and nations, in the light of planetary configuration.[1] According to Sandipan Chaudhuri, the word 'Astrology is derived from the two Greek words 'astron' meaning Star and 'logos' meaning cosmic reason or logic. Hence, Astrology is consequently, investigation of the cosmic reason in the structure and happenings of the starry universe from the practical point of view or a knowledge of the stars and knowledge by the help of the stars.[2]

According to Collins dictionary, 'Astronomy is the scientific study of the individual celestial bodies (excluding the earth) and of the universe as a whole. It means that it covers the study of planets, stars and other heavenly bodies.

Astronomy is derived from the Greek root 'Astron' meaning star and 'Nemo' meaning arrange i.e., astronomy is a science which states the geometrical position of the stars in the sky at a particular moment.[3] Thus practical astronomy implies study of stars and their influences upon human and mundane affairs. Astrology can be defined as a system of knowledge sharing correlation of astronomical facts with terrestrial events. Statistically, several astrological combinations are corroborated. However, it is in practice that thinkers and intellectuals of all ages have endorsed the truth of astrology and have consulted their horoscopes. Generally, astronomers are all lovers of astrology, such as discussed in Ist Chapter, like; *Arya Bhatt, Bhaskar, Varahmihir*, etc.

Indian astrology consists of its five parts i.e., *Hora, Siddhanta, Samhita, Prashan* and *Shakuna.*[4] '*Hora*'' means a study of impact of planetary position on human beings. '*Siddhant*' means the computing or calculating the position of planets or celestial bodies. *Samhita* means the study of effects of celestial bodies or planets on Universe as a whole, such as Earthquake, Solar or Lunar eclipses etc.

Prashna Shastra states/or claims that good or bad events occur due to particular auspicious or inauspicious moments. So, accordingly, the future may be predicted.

It is important to note that all parts of Indian astrology depend on astronomical phenomenon. Astrology cannot be studied without knowledge of astronomy. So, it is very necessary to know about the meaning and basic facts of astronomy, which deals with the solar system.

Zodiac

To understand the Solar system, firstly we must know about the *Zodiac.* It is a broad belt in the sky extending about 9 degrees on each side of the ecliptic. A path of the Sun, which passes exactly through the centre of the *Zodiac*, is known as *Ecliptic.* The *Zodiac* is an imaginary circle of 360 degrees, and it is further divided into twelve equal parts of 30 degrees each. Each equal part of 30 degrees is known as a Sign or a *Rasi.* The Zodiac is also known as *Bhachakra* in Sanskrit. It revolves on its axis in a day from east to west.[5]

Signs or Rasis

There are twelve signs in the *Zodiac*, namely Aries (*Mesha*), Taurus (*Vrishbh*), Gemini (*Mithuna*), Cancer (*Karka* or *Kataka*), Leo (*Sinha*),

Virgo (*Kauya*), Libra (*Tula*), Scorpio (*Vrischik*), Sagittarius (*Dhanus* or *Dhanu*) and Pisces (*Meena*). Each of these signs has a stretch of 30 degrees in the *Zodiac*. Each sign has its own Lord, shape, direction, and characteristics as follows:

Characteristics of Signs (Rasis)[6]

	Signs	Direction	Characteristics	Shape, Name & Lord
1.	Aries	East	Movable Sign, relates to kings having blood-red complexion, Preclominates in Rajoguna, Denotes great activity, Fairy sign	The Ram Lord – Mars
2.	Taurus	South	Fixed Sign, Represents finances, businessmen. An early sign having fair complexion.	The Bull Lord Venus
3.	Gemini	West	Airy Sign, Denotes intellectual/commercial activity common sign	The Twins Lord– Mercury
4.	Cancer	North	Movable Sign, Represents Brahmins and is Sattvic Watery Sign, Colour is Pale red	The Crale Lord – Moon
5.	Leo	East	Fixed Sign, Royal Sign with fair complexion. Sattvic in Nature and denotes good activity	The Lion Lord – Sun
6.	Virgo	South	Common Sign, Relates to Business Community and Tasmic in Nature. Earthly Sign	The Virgin Lord – Mercury
7.	Libra	West	Airy Sign, Predominant with Rajogunaa representing Sudra. It is dark in complexion and is movable	The Balance Lord – Venus
8.	Scorpio	North	Fixed Sign, Denotes Brahmins having reddish Brown colour. A Secretive Sign of the Zodiac and is watery in nature	The Scorpion Lord – Mars
9.	Sagittarius	East	Common Sign, Sattvic in nature and a royal sign giving a fighting tendency, Fairy Sign	The man with arrow and the horse as his lower part. Lord – Jupiter
10.	Capricorn	South	Movable sign, Tamsic in	The Crocodile

			nature, Earthly sign	Lord Saturn
11.	Aquarius	West	Airy Sign, Denotes mystic and research orientation. Fixed Sign, Tasmic in nature	The Water Carrier Lord – Saturn
12.	Pisces	North	Common Sign, Denotes Brahmins and religion, Watery Sign with Satvik guna	The fish Lord – Jupiter

Sattva, Rajas, and *Tamas* are the basic characteristics of any human being. *Tamas* denotes a constant desire for base things and satisfaction with basic instincts. *Rajoguna* denotes great worldly activity for desires at a higher plane than *tamoguna. Satvic guna* denotes a stage when man is able to control worldly desires for spiritual and moral advancement.[7]

Planets

There are nine planets, namely, Sun (*Ravi, Surya*), Moon (*Chandra*), Mars (*Mangal* or *Kuja*), Mercury (*Buddha*), Jupiter (*Guru* or *Brihspati*), Venus (*Shukra*), Saturn (*Shani*), *Rahu* and *Ketu.* The last two planets are called shadowy planets *Chhaya Grahas* as they do not have physical or celestial bodies like the other seven planets. The two places where the Moon crosses the ecliptic path i.e., the path of the Sun, the north shadowy point is known as *Rahu* and the corresponding south shadowy point, which is exactly 180° away from the former is called *Ketu.* In spite of the fact that they are not celestial bodies like other planets, they are very important and effective points. Hence, due to their powerful influence on the earth, they have been ranked as planets in Hindu astrology. There are three other newly discovered planets namely *Uranus* (also called *Herschel*), *Neptune* and *Pluto.* In Western astrology, these newly discovered planets have more importance than *Rahu-Ketu.*[8] However, in Indian astrology they are less important planets due to far away from the earth. Hence, their influence is more on the Universe as a whole rather than on individuals.

All planets have their own characteristics like *zodiac* signs. They represent different qualities or masters of capabilities as follows:[9]

	Planets	**Characteristics**
1.	Sun	Represents the soul of the native, also represents government/ father/king/sons. It is capable to make powerful.

2.	Moon	Represents mother, children, artistic features, watery places, quick movements, and the most important the mind of the native.
3.	Mars	Represents ego, anger, fire, weapons, police arrogance, younger brothers and earth or soil.
4.	Mercury	Represents intellectual capacity speech, education, friends, maternal uncle, sister and sister-in-law, accounts and law.
5.	Jupiter	Represents judge, teacher, logic, wisdom, learning, dignity, status, religion, husband, good conduct, piousness.
6.	Saturn	Profession, Karma, Labour, hard-work, slowness, refineries.
7.	Venus	Wife, treasure, money, wealth, immovable property, voice, sisters, artistic nature.
8.	Rahu	Grandfather, Muslim, deviant behaviour, Masking ability, tactfulness, tricky, arrogancy.
9.	Ketu	Law, lawyers, religion, renunciation, Christianity, obstructions.

According to *Varahmihir*[10], all planets are supposed to be a friendly enemity or neutral relation with other planets that can be shown by following chart:

	Planets	Friend	Enemity	Neutral
1.	Sun	Moon, Mars & Jupiter	Saturn, Venus	Mercury
2.	Moon	Sun, Mercury	–	Saturn, Mars, Jupiter and Venus
3.	Mars	Moon, Sun & Jupiter	Mercury	Venus, Saturn
4.	Mercury	Sun, Venus	Moon	Mars, Jupiter & Saturn
5.	Jupiter	Sun, Moon & Mars	Venus & Mercury	Saturn
6.	Venus	Mercury, Saturn	Moon & Sun	Mars & Jupiter
7.	Saturn	Mercury, Venus	Moon, Sun, Mars	Jupiter

Movements and Motions of Planets

- Each planet except *Rahu* and *Ketu* performs the dual function of revolving on their own axis from west to east and secondly rotate the Sun.

- Saturn is the most distant planet from the earth,
- Jupiter, Mars, the Sun, Venus, Mercury, and the Moon situate respectively in order to their distance from the earth.
- Hence, moon is the nearest to the Earth.
- The Earth moves around the Sun. Hence, it appears that the Sun moves around at the rate of roughly one degree of the zodiac in one day consisting of 24 hours and takes 365 days and 6 hours to complete a circle in the *zodiac*.
- The Moon moves at the rate of one hour and 48 minutes to pass a degree of this space.
- Mars moves at the average rate of 45 days for 30 degrees, means it takes one and half days per degree.
- Mercury moves at the rate of one and half degrees a day like Mars. But there is quite difference between the movement of Mars and Mercury. The reason is the Mercury is very close to the Sun. So due to solar influence, its movement becomes very much unstable and unsteady. When it comes in front of the Sun, it moves more rapidly. After that, it begins to move slowly and goes backward of the Sun. So, in this process, Mercury remains approximately on 28 degrees in either direction of the Sun. And it completes the run in 27 days in average.
- Jupiter takes almost 13 months in each sign of 30 degrees. But it is found generally that it remains in a sign for a little less than a year.
- Venus takes almost one day to cross one degree.
- Saturn moves within a sign of 30 degrees in almost two and a half years or 30 months. It means it takes one month to move in one degree.
- *Rahu* and *Ketu* always move in the reverse direction and take 18 months to cross each sign of *zodiac*.
- The Sun and the Moon are never retrograde motion, it means that they never move in the reverse direction.
- Other planets move direct in their motions. But due to obstruction of certain invisible forces, these planets become stagnant for sometimes. Then, they regain their natural speed. During the period of their stagnation, they appear to be

retrograded. This phenomenon of going backward is called retrogression.

Constellations (Nakashatras)

As discussed earlier, that zodiac is sectioned by twelve signs (*Rashis*). It is further subdivided by *Nakshatras* (constellations). The first *Nakshatra Aswini* and first point of *Mesha rasi* start on same point in *zodiac*. Each *Nakshatra* consists of 13 degree 20 minutes (13°20"). In other words, it is a stretch of one *Nakshatra.* A *Nakshatra* consists of four parts which are called *padas* or *charan* in Hindi. Each *padas* or *charan* covers 3 degrees and 20 minutes (3°20") each. In this way, one zodiac sign (Rasi) contains two and one fourth (2 – ¼) *Nakshatras.* Like the Rasis, the *Nakshatras* are also ruled by various planets including *Rahu* and *Ketu.* The longitudinal span of *Rasi* and of a *Nakshatra* may be shown in the following table:[11].

	Rasis	***Nakshatras*** **with Charanas**	**Lord**	**Span in Degree and Minutes**
1.	*Mesh* (Aries)	*Aswini* (1, 2, 3, 4)	*Ketu* (Tale of Dragen)	0° to 13°–20'
		Bharani (1, 2, 3, 4)	*Shukra* (Venus)	13°–20' to 26°–40'
		Krittika (1)	*Ravi* (Sun)	26°–40' to 30°–00'
2.	*Varishava* (Taurus)	*Krittika* (2, 3, 4)	*Ravi* (Sun)	0° to 10°–00'
		Rohni (1, 2, 3, 4)	*Chandra* (Moon)	10°–00' to 23°–20'
		Mrigsira (1, 2)	*Mangal* (Mars)	23°–20' to 30°–00'
3.	*Mithuna* (Gemini)	*Mrigsira* (3, 4)	*Mangal* (Mars)	0° to 6°–40'
		Aridra (1, 2, 3, 4)	*Rahu* (Head of Dragen)	6°–40' to 20°–00'
		Punarvasu (1, 2, 3)	*Guru* (Jupiter)	20°–00' to 30°–00'
4.	*Katka* or *Karka* (Cancer)	*Punarvasu* (4)	*Guru* (Jupiter)	0° to 3°–20'
		Pusha (1, 2, 3, 4)	*Sani* (Saturn)	3°–20' to 16°–40'
		Ashlesha (1,2,3, 4)	*Budh* (Mercury)	16°–40' to 30°–00'

5.	*Sinha* (Leo)	*Magha*(1, 2, 3, 4) *Poorva – Phalguni* (1, 2, 3, 4) *Uttar – Phalguni* (1)	*Ketu* (Tail of Dragen) *Sukra* (Venus) *Ravi* (Sun)	0° to 13°–20' 13°–20' to 26°–40' 26°–40' to 30°–00'
6.	*Kanya* (Virgo)	*Uttar – Phalguni* (2, 3, 4) *Hasta* (1, 2, 3, 4) *Chitra* (1, 2)	*Ravi* (Sun) *Chandra* (Moon) *Mangal* (Mars)	0° to 10°–00' 10°–20' to 23°–20' 23°–20' to 30°–00'
7.	*Tula* (Libra)	*Chitra* (3, 4) *Swati* (1, 2, 3, 4) *Vishakha* (1, 2, 3)	*Mangal* (Mars) *Rahu* (Head of Dragen) *Guru* (Jupiter)	0° to 6°–40' 6°–40' to 20°–00' 20°–00' to 30°–00'
8.	*Vrischika* (Scorpio)	*Vishakha* (4) *Anuradha*(1,2,3,4) *Jyeshtha* (1,2,3, 4)	*Guru* (Jupiter *Sani* (Saturn) *Budh* (Mercury)	0° to 3°–20' 3°20' to 16°–40' 16°–40' to 30°–00'
9.	*Dhanu* (Sagittarius)	*Moola* (4) *Purvashada* (1,2,3,4) *Uttarashada* (1)	*Ketu* (Tail of Dragen) *Sukra* (Venus) *Ravi* (Sun)	0° to 13°–20' 13°20' to 26°–40' 26°–40' to 30°–00'
10	*Makara* (Capricorn)	*Uttarshada* (2, 3, 4) *Shravan*(1, 2, 3, 4) *Dhanishta* (1, 2)	*Ravi* (Sun) *Chandra* (Moon) *Mangal* (Mars)	0° to 10°–00' 10°–20' to 23°–20' 23°–20' to 30°–00'
11	*Kumbha* (Aquarius)	*Dhanishta* (3, 4) *Shatabhisha* (1, 2, 3, 4) *Poorvabhadra* (1, 2, 3)	*Mangal* (Mars) *Rahu* (Head of Dragen) *Guru* (Jupiter)	0° to 6°–40' 6°–40' to 20°–00' 20°–00' to 30°–00'
12	*Meena* (Cancer)	*Poorvabhadra* (4) *Poorvabhadra* (1, 2, 3, 4) *Revati* (1,2,3, 4)	*Guru* (Jupiter) *Sani* (Saturn) *Budh* (Mercury)	0° to 3°–20' 3°–20' to 16°–40' 16°–40' to 30°–00'

It is clear that under *Mesha* rasi, there are four *padas* or *charanas* of *Aswini*, four charanas of *Bharini* and one charana of *Krittika*. If the longitude of the Moon, or the Sun or any other planet is *Mesha* – 15°–20', it falls in Ist *Charana* of *Bharini* which extends from 13°–20' to 16°–40'. If the longitude of the planet is 15°–20' *Vrishchika* 3°–45', it falls under the first *Pada* or *Charana* of *Anuradha* which extends from 3°–20' to 6°–40'. The position in respect of the first example is that (if the *Moon* in *Mesh*) *Mesh being the 'Rasi'* of an individual or a native, the Rasi lord is *Kuja* or *Mangal* and the *nakshatra* being *Bharini*, its lord is *Shukra*. In the second example, the *Rasi* being *Vrishchika* the *rasi* lord is *Kuja* and *Nakshatra* being *Vishakha*, the *nakshatra* lord is *Guru*. Thus, within one *rasi* there will be influence of two planets, namely of the rasi lord as well as of the *nakshatra* lord. Accordingly, the effect of these planets will be in the birth chart/horoscope of an individual or a native. The calculation of latitude/longitude and *charnas* of Nakshatras can be analysed with the help of *Panchanga* or *Ephemieris*.

Meaning of '*Panchanga*'

'*Panchanga* is meant by five *Angas*.[12] It generally consists of five parts of astrology i.e., *Tithi*, *Var*, *Nakshatra*, *Yog* and *Karam*. Besides, some other information is also covered such as: *Vikram Samvatam, Shaka Sambvata, Ritus* (seasons), *Solar* months, Lunar months *Ayanasm Dinman*, Sun rise and set, Moon rise and set, Latitude longitude, *Lagnas*, festivals, transit of planets etc.

Ritus or Seasons

There are six seasons in one year namely – *Vasantha* (Spring) falls in the lunar months of *Chatra* and *Vaisakha*, *Greeshma* (Summer) (*Jyeshtha* and *Ashada*), *Varsha* (Rainy season (*Sravan and Bhadras*), *Sharad* (Autumn) (*Ashwin* and *Kartika*), Hamant (Winter) (*Mrigshir* and *Pausa*), *Sishir* (Winter) (*Magha* and *Phalguna*).

Solar Month

A solar month begins from the date when the Sun enters into a particular sign. So, according to twelve rasis, there are twelve Solar months as under:

1. The month of *Mesh Rasi* (it means, the Sun enters in *Mesh Rasi*) (April 20 to May 19).
2. The month of *Vrishabha* (May 20 to June 19).

3. The month of *Mithuna* (June 20 July 19).
4. The month of *Kataka* or *Karka* (July 20 to August 19).
5. The month of *Simha* (August 20 September 19).
6. The month of *Kanya* (September 20 to October 19).
7. The month of *Tula* (October 20 to November 19).
8. The month of *Vrishchik* (November 20 to December 19).
9. The month of *Dhanu* (December 20 to January 19).
10. The month of *Makra* (January 20 to February 19).
11. The month of *Kumbha* (February 20 to March19).
12. The month of *Meena* (March 20 to April 19).

In the above table, the approximate dates are given. Sometimes, these dates may vary in a particular year by a day or two, either the beginning or end of the month.

Lunar Month

The name of each lunar month is given according to the constellation which falls on the full moon day of the particular month. The Solar month may extend to 30 or 31 days, due to the Sun takes about a month to traverse a sign (*Rasi*) while the lunar month is generally of 27 to 29 days during which the Moon, who is the fastest moving planet, travels through all the signs and constellations of the zodiac. Hence the solar month is the period during which the Sun stays in a particular sign (*Rasi*) and the lunar month is the period during which the Moon completes her round through all the twelve signs of *Zodiac*. The twelve lunar months are as under:

Chaitra-March – April

Vaisakh-April – May

Jyestha-May – June

Ashada-June – July

Sravana-July – August

Bhadra-August – September

Aswin-September – October

Kartika-October – November

Mrigshir-November – December

Pausa-December – January

Magha-January – February

Phalguna – February – March

Shukla and Krishna Pakshas and Tithis[13]

It is a matter of fact that there are two sides of Moon; one is decreasing size and other is increasing size and other is increasing size. On the New moon day, we find that the Moon looks like a semi-circular disc. Then, every day the semicircular disc becomes thicker and bigger until after the 15th day of the new moon day we find the Moon full of light in a complete circle. This is the full moon, i.e., known as *Poornima* or *Purnmasi.* And these 15 days from New Moon to Full Moon are known as *Shukla Paksha* or the bright half of the lunar month.

After the Full Moon Day, the Moon starts decreasing in light or starts in reverse process and the circle of light gets smaller and smaller until it completely disappears. This day is known as *Amavasya* and the weakening Moon during this period is called in astrological terminology as 'Decreasing Moon'. These 15 days from Full Moon to New Moon are known as '*Krishna Paksha*' or the dark half of the lunar Month. In this way, there are thirty Lunar days. These are known as 'Tithis'. The New Moon Day is the first Tithi and Amavasya is the 30th tithi. But in common practice, new Moon Day is the first *Tithi* of *Shukla Paksha,* and the 15th Tithi of *Shukla Paksha* is *Poornima.* Then the 16th lunar day is called as the first Tithi of *Krishna Paksha* and so on until the Amavasya is 15th *Tithi* of *Krishna Paksha.* In actual practice the thirty lunar days may be equal to 27 to 29 solar days.

Ayanas

On the basis of the movement of the Sun, the year is divided astronomically into two parts i.e., *Uttarayan* and *Dakshinayan.* It is also known as *Devayan* and the *Pitrayan.* The Uttarayan (between 22 December to 21 June) period from *Makar Sankranti* to *Kark Sakranti* is considered good for self and upliftment of the soul. Most of the social and religious rituals are supposed to be performed during this period. The *Dakshinayan* (between 22 June to 21 December) period from *Kark Sankranti* to *Makar Sakranti* is important to strike a balance with one's ancestors or *Pitras.*[14]

Dinman and Ratriman

The whole day (i.e., 24 hours) is divided into two parts on the basis of rotation of earth on its axis i.e., the *Dinman* and the *Ratriman*. *Dinman* is the period from Sunrise to Sunset, while *Ratriman* is the period from Sunset to Sunrise.

The *Dinman* and the *Ratriman* are further divided by *Ghari*. The whole day contains 60 *Gharies* which is equal to 24 hours. *Ghari* is divided by *Pala* which is further divided by *Bipala*.

Besides aforesaid terms, some other information regarding such astronomical terminology is required for the process of casting a horoscope as follows:

Longitude

Longitude is the arc line drawn from the North Pole to the South Pole to mark the distance or location in degrees of a particular place from a central place which is '*Greenwhich*'. All cities or places are located either to the west or the east of '*Greenwhich*'. For instance, the longitude of Delhi is 77°–13' east. It means that Delhi is 77°–13' east of Greenwhich.

Latitude

Latitude is the arc line to mark distance or location in degrees and minutes of a particular place in north or south of the *Equator*. For instance, the latitude of Delhi is 28°–39' north. It means that the location of Delhi is 28°–39' north of Equator.

Sidereal Time

The time, which is taken by the earth complete to one full rotation, is called as "*Sidereal Time*". It is not exactly 24 hours but goes on changing according to increase or decrease in the days and nights. It is called *vernal equinox time* and it is a measure of earth's rotation to the equinox which has a very small retrograde motion. At the *Greenwich Observatory*, there is a special clock which indicates the sidereal time for each moment of the day or night. In India, there is an observatory at Jaipur, which has a clock to indicate the sidereal time. It is made by Sawai Jai Singh.

The workss concerning the astronomical part of astrological science have been discussed in Chapter I. A long list of astronomers in ancient India is also mentioned. Astronomers like Aryabhat,

Varhamihira, Brahmgupta, Bhaskara I, Bhaskaracharya II and others have given us the astronomical information, however, Varhamihira has also discussed the astrological aspect.

All above mentioned astronomical terms are required to cast a horoscope. On the basis of planetary position in horoscope, the future of an individual is predicted. To cast a horoscope, besides the aforesaid, the date, time, and place of birth of a native are required so that the planetary position on the particular date may be decided. The 'time' is important to know '*Lagn* at the particular time. Place of birth is required to know the latitude and longitude. Hence, the scientific part of a horoscope is based on astronomical configurations, while the predictive part of it is simply an art.[15.]

Casting of the Horoscope

The horoscope, made on the date, time and place of birth can reveal the past, present, and future of a person. A complete horoscope may be written into many pages with all the minute mathematical details. Ancient sages had laid down the principles on which different planets give particular results.[16]

For the purpose of making a birth chart or horoscope, first of all, the date of birth of an individual is needed. According to Hindu system of astrology a day is counted from Sunrise of one day to Sunrise of other day. Secondly, the time of birth is needed, whether it is A.M. or P.M. is to be ascertained. There is a controversy about the exact time of birth.[17] Some are of the opinion that the exact time is when the head or limb of the child appears. Others opine that the time of birth is when the head comes out fully. There is yet another view that the exact time of birth is the moment when the child is completely severed from the umbilical cord of the mother and becomes an independent entity. The place of birth is also necessary to make a birth chart. It is needed to determine the Lagna at a particular place correctly, and to know the latitude and longitude of the place.[18] For the purpose of the determination of the ascendant or Lagna the *Indian Standard Time* (IST) is to convert into *Local Mean Time*. There are so many methods to know this information.

Astrology, whether it is *Phalit* or *Ganit* is a vast subject. Every calculation is based on a formula.

The *Lagna* is also called the First *Bhava* or house. For example, *Lagna* has (3) no. it means *Lagna* is *Mithun Rasi* (Gemini). The Second

Bhava or house has (4) no. means *Kark* (Cancer) and third *Bhava has* (5) no. means *Sinha* (Leo) and so on. In this way, all twelve Bhavas or houses have *Rasis* in sequence. Then, it is to determine that the planets are in which Rasis in transit at that particular time of birth. For example, if a native i.e., *Vivekanand* was born on 12 January 1863 at Calcutta at Sunrise. His horoscope is as follows. His '*Lagna*' is *Sagitarius* and Sun is ruling there, it means Sun was in transit in *Sagitarius Rasi* and *Venus* and *Mercury* were in *Capricorn* and so on.[19]

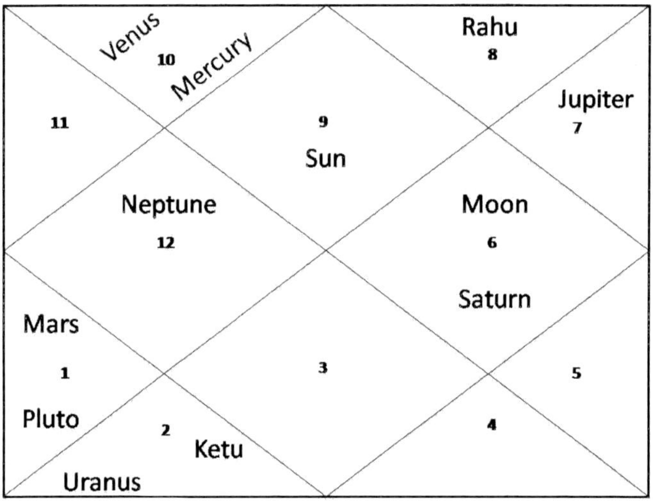

Here, the degree of every Rasi, Nakshatra, and planet is also calculated. This is known as "*Graha Spashta*". After determining the position of all Rasis and Planets, the *Vimsomtary Dasa* is calculated on the basis of Rasi and Nakshatra in which moon is posited. Nakshatra's Lord is the lord of starting *Bhavas* has their own significance and denotes the different aspects of life.

In a horoscope, houses No. 1, 4, 7 and 10 are called *Kendras* (Quadrants, angle); 5 and 9 *trikonas* (trine); 2, 5, 8 and 11 *Panaphara* (cadent) and 3, 6, 9, 12 as *apoklimas* (suceedent) House 3, 6, 10 and 11 are *Upachayas* which means house of growth, Planets when posited in Kendra are strongest – next in order are those posited in *trikonas, Panaphara, apoklimas.* House 3, 6, 8, 12 are bad houses (*Dusttanas*). Any planet in these houses destroys the significance of the house which it owns.

Significance of Houses (*Bhavas*)

To analyse the significance of houses or *Bhavas* is a vast subject. It can be discussed in more than hundreds of pages. So, a brief idea of significance of a *Bhava* is considered here.

In analysing *Bhava*, the following factors may be considered carefully:[20.]

1. The strength of the house itself.
2. The strength, aspects, conjunction and location of the lord of the house.
3. The natural qualities of the house, of its lord and the planets in it or having aspects.
4. Whether the influence has been altered by any yogas occurring in any particular house or houses.
5. The exaltations and debilitations of the house lords are equally important.
6. The situation – favourable or adverse – of the house lord or the lord in whose house the particular house lord is situated, in the Navamsa.
7. The age, position, status and sex of the subject.
8. Each sign has certain planets well disposed or ill-disposed. For instance, for those born in Aries, the Sun is good. The relation between the house lord (Mars) and the Sun is very important

All these must be properly examined before any prediction.

The first house in Hindi is called *Tanu* (body), the second is *Dhana* or *Kutumbha* (wealth or family). The fourth as *Sukha* (Happiness), the fifth as *Suta* (children), the sixth as *Ripu* (enemies), the seventh as Bharya (life partner) the eighth as Aayu or *Mrityu* (Longevity or death), the ninth as *Dharma*, the tenth as *Karma*, the twelfth as *Vyaya* (Loss or expenditure).[21] Hence, all thc twelve houses (*Bhavas*) denote the different aspects of life.

Planetary *Avasthas* and Strength

Due to their continuous movement, planets get certain states of existence, which is called '*Avasthas*'. And each *avastha* produces its own result. The various avasthas are *Deepta* or bright, *Swastha* (healthy), *Mudita* (happy), *Shanta* (calm), *Shakta* (powerful), *Peedya* (unhappy), *Deena* (helpless). *Vikala* (distress), *Khala* (bad) and *Bheeta* (in fear). These *avasthas* represent their names according to their meaning.[22]

Each planet is supposed to get a particular strength when it is in a particular position. These strengths, known as *Shadbalas* in Hindu astrology, are of six kinds namely, *Sthanabala, Digbala, Chestabala, Kalabala, Drigbala,* and *Naisargikbala.*[23] These balas signify the influences as their names are.

There are other positions of planets known as exalted and debilitated positions (*Uchch* and *Nich*).

Scope and Effects of Astrology

The scope and utility of Astrology in an individual's life as well as Nation's life is enormous. Astrology gives proper directions in an individual's marital affairs, education, health, diseases, material prosperity, spiritual attainment etc.[24] According to *Arnold Meyer*, a scientist and a member of the British Association for the Advancement of Science and author of *The Circulation of Matter, Electronics and Stars* "Since Astrology deals more particularly with the effects of heavenly bodies upon mankind, it does not require much imagination to appreciate the fact that this conjunction of the Sun and moon does definitely affect a child born during conditions of this nature. From within our own bodies, we have innumerable glands whose work is the secretion of hormones. These are forever adjusting themselves in harmony with our chemical changing environment without and are responsible for our emotions, desires, mental balance, rate of growth and length of life on this planet".[25] According to V. Gore, "It is but common sense to say that the planetary positions of the Sun and Moon which affect the sea-water causing tides are bound to affect all the store of fluids on the surface of the earth or contained in vegetable kingdom or in human beings".[26]

According to famous astro-scientist Dr. B.V. Raman, Editor, *The Astrological Magazine*, "Astrology was considered as the mother of all disciplines, both scientific and humanistic, because it was founded on the broad awareness of the laws that governed cosmos whose creature man was. Man's kinship with stars was rendered into an eminently practical of social and individual behaviour. It was a pattern for both fulfillment and betterment in consonance with the laws of heritage and environment. Thus, the ancient sages of India who fashioned astrology as a scientific humanism were dealing with the eternal varieties of human condition and inexorable laws of nature.[27]

He further states that 'A trifling change in weather through solar causes brings neuralgia, headache, bronchitis, sore eyes, fever, smallpox, cholera, dysentery, plague, and a host of other diseases too numerous to detail. War mania is a striking illustration of planetary influences. Our temper and moods depend upon the secretions of ductless glands. Fear as a matter of endocrine secretions, indecision is a matter of thymus; genius is a matter of thyroid. Sun's cycles of behaviour have their corresponding effects on these glands and their secretions and consequently on human behaviour.... Planetary vibrations of varying characters are continually exerting an influence which is taken up by our sensory nerves with the resulting bodily reactions, mental attitudes, and moods. Therefore, it is possible that solar, lunar, and stellar energies supply the cells through the media of the nerves, their motivity. Different planetary vibrations – astrologically designated as yogas or aspects – supply different sensory stimuli, according to the vibrations differ in wavelengths, intensity, frequency etc.[28.]

'The effects of sunspots and cosmic rays on human life', a basic principle of astrology is accepted by the modern scientist like *Prof. Gorges Lakhovsky*, the Russian biologist and physicist. He was perhaps the first modern scientist to openly state his belief that radiation from stars and planets can affect the future destiny of an individual at conception and birth, i.e., the great theory of the *Maharishis*. It is noted that *Varahmihira* propounded this truth two thousand years ago.[29]

B. V. Raman further quoted from Arnold Meyer[30] that due to spring tides there is suddenly overflow and flood in public buildings. The reason for this is that when the Sun and the Moon are in conjunction, they are both concentrating their forces on the same part of the globe at the same time; this added together, accounts for the abnormal conditions. So, under normal conditions, there is always a high tide at London, fifty minutes after the Moon has passed the meridian, i.e., the position, the Sun occupies everyday at noon, Greenwich time.[31]

Hindu astrologers have given predictions for each day of the Lunar month, related to the medicine, environment, metallurgy, agriculture etc. For example, the eighth day of lunar month is known as "*Ashtayam Vyadhinashastu*" or "*Ashtami Vyadhi Nashini*". It means that the eighth day removes the disease or cures the ailments. On this day the Sun and the Moon, being 90° apart, diminish each other's attractions on the fluids. The blood in the human beings remains in an undisturbed state from the outside influences and any medicine newly started on this day is bound to be more effective if it is properly chosen.[32]

We all are aware that the Hindus enjoined some restrictions in regard to food etc. a few hours prior to the actual occurrence of an eclipse and during the duration of the eclipse. Recent studies in connection with radio signals reveal a relatively low ionisation density at the time of the corpuscular eclipse. It is, therefore, possible that electrical disturbances taking place at the time of sunspot activity have some effect on the delicate fibers of our nerves and brain cells, resulting inn a change of our temperament and behaviour.[33] There are old belief in the villages of India that tree should not be cut near the time of the New Moon otherwise the sap will dry quickly. And that "the maize was found to grow best when planted two days before Full Moon".[34] *Dr. Kolisko* has shown the influences of planets on metals. She has proved that each solution had its characteristic forms and colours when it is experimented. But there is no change when solar eclipse occurs.[35]

An interesting association between meteorological fact and astrological views are noted by *Mr. John Nelson*, an engineer in the *R.C.A. Communications Department of U.S.A.* He has found that the benefic aspects of planets are pacifying to the ionosphere, while malefic aspects disturbing to it. Hence, astrologers also predict wars, revolutions, and political disturbances when *Jupiter*, *Saturn*i and Mars are in conjunction i.e., the same degree or mutual angles of 90° and 180 ° involving certain constellations. The combined influences of *Mars, Venus,* and *Mercury*, if closely placed with Saturn-Jupiter team, create magnetic disturbances on the earth.[36] So, it naturally creates the disturbance in the delicate and complex systems in the living organisms on the earth, subsequently regulate and stimulate thought and feelings and action.

B. V. Raman also refers[37] Sevente Arrhenius, a Swedish scientist, who proved by statistical investigation of 25,000 cases that is a correlation between the frequency of human births and the revolution of the Moon in the ecliptic. As a matter of fact, he has shown that menstruation occurs in a large number of women at one particular point in the lunar month. It means that menstruation usually occurs when the Moon arrives at a certain fixed point in the horoscope. *Varahmihira* also clearly mentions in *Brihat Jataka* that when the Moon is in an *Upachaya* from the *Lagna* and due to the interaction of Mars and the Moon, the menses of a woman sets in every month.

Hence, it is obvious that the influence of planets upon mankind is undoubted. A horoscope can reveal an accurate picture of the individual's psyche, such as his temperaments, his likes and dislikes, aptitudes, his moods, his abilities and weaknesses and strong traits. It can help in guiding the choice of careers in industrial institutions to employ the workers. Astrology reveals the general tendencies inherent in certain types of persons due to the position of stars and planets at their birth. We can use them in life to make the best of our endowment.

Endnotes

1. V. Raman, *Planetary References on Human Affairs*, UBS Publishers & Distributors, New Delhi (1992), pp. 43-44.
2. Sandipan Chaudhuri, "Scientific Rationale of Astrology", *Journal of Asiatic Society*, Kolkata, 2005, p. 78.
3. Ibid., p. 79.
4. Dr. Nemichand Shastri, *Bhartiya Jyotish*, Bhartiya Gyan Peeth Prakashan, New Delhi 1983), pp. 2-5.
5. Gauri Shankar Kapoor, *Learn Astrology*, Rajan Publication, New Delhi (2004), pp. 13-14.
6. Ibid., also see V. Raghuraman, *Vedic Nadi Astrology*, Sterling Publisher (P) Ltd., New Delhi (1996), pp. 2-5. Also see *Jaimini Sutram*, Prof. P.S. Sastri (Tra.), Rajan Publication, New Delhi (1992), (1992), pp. 1-6.
7. Ibid., pp. 3-4.
8. Gauri Shankar Kapoor, *op. cit.*, pp. 13-14.
9. V. Raghuraman, *op. cit.*, pp. 5-6; also see Jamini Sutram, *op. cit.*, pp. 8-10.
10. Umesh Puri Gyaneshwar, *Prachin Bhartiya Phalit Shastra*, Randhir Prakashan, Haridwar (1996), pp. 60-61.
11. Jamini Sutrain, *op.cit., pp. 15-16.*
12. Swami Krishna Satyarthi and R. C. Verma, *Bhartiya Jyotish Avam Lal Kitab*, Hare Krishna Trust, Chandigarh (1996), p. 17.
13. *Divakar Panchanga Samvat* 2067 (Jullunder).
14. Pandit Ajay Bhambi, *Be Your own Astrologer*, Wisdom Tree Darya Ganj, New Delhi (2004) p. 02.
15. Sandhipan Chawdhari, *Scientific Rationale of Astrology*, op. cit., p. 86.

16. Pandit Ajay Bhambi, *Be Your Own Astrologer*, op. cit., p. 7.
17. Gauri Shankar Kapoor, op. cit., pp. 52-53.
18. A ready racknor "Table of Ascendants by Lahiri is available to know Latitude, Longitude, Lagna, Sidereal time, Local mean time etc.
19. Pandit Ajay Bhambhi, op. cit., pp. 308-09.
20. B. V. Raman, *How to Judge A Horoscope*, Motilal Banarasidas Publishers Private Ltd., Delhi, (2002), Vol. I, p. 5.
21. Gauri Shankar Kapoor, op. cit., p. 17.
22. Ibid., pp. 85-86.
23. Ibid., pp. 87-88.
24. Sandipan Chaudhari, op. cit,. p. 80.
25. Ibid., p. 81 (quoted), also see B.V. Raman, op. cit., pp. 61-62.
26. Ibid. (quoted), also see B.V. Raman, op. cit.
27. Ibid., p. 81, Also see B. V. Raman, Planetary Influence on Human Affairs", op. cit., pp.10-16.
28. B. V. Raman, op. cit., pp. 55-57.
29. Ibid., p. 56.
30. Arnold Mayer, the author of "The Circulation of Matter, Electrons and Stars" and "Astrology's Place in the World of Science", is a scientist and a member of the British Association for the Advancement of Science., is a scientist and a member of the British Association for the Advancement of Science.
31. B.V. Raman, op. cit., p. 60.
32. Ibid., p. 63.
33. Ibid., p. 70.
34. Ibid., p. 71.
35. Dr. Kolisko, "Agriculture of Tomorrow", as quoted by B. V. Raman, op. cit., pp. 71-73.
36. Quoted by B. V. Raman, op. cit., pp. 77-78.
37. Ibid., pp. 80-81.

CHAPTER 3

Development and Impact of Astrology and Astronomy during Mughal Period (A.D. 1526 – A.D. 1605)

Owing to the liberal and broad - based attitude of the Mughals, all branches of Hindu culture such as architecture, literature, painting, music and moreover, Hindu sciences like astronomy, astrology, medicine etc. flourished; not only flourished, but an impact and synthesis can be seen in these fields.

The present work is an attempt to depict the development and impact in one field only i.e., the science of astronomy and astrology. It flourished and developed in medieval period of Indian history. Although few fanatics Muslim and Sultans had not encouraged this subject, but the common people always accepted and were influenced by it as Barani, a contemporary historian, mentioned[1] in the time of Allauddin Khalzi. In Mughal period, as we find in contemporary writings, emperors were highly influenced by this science. It appears that they were acquainted with this science before their advent in India, as we find a long list of astronomers and astrologers of Central Asia in Abul Fazal's *Ain-i-Akbari.*[2]

Astronomical tables bearing various names are mentioned by Abul Fazl, such as: *Adani, Tavlasani, Asabai, Kirmani, Daylami, Elkhani.* Besides these tables various canons are also mentioned in *Ain-i-Akbari.* These canons are *Shahryaran, Nasiri, Mulakhkhas, Dastur, Murakkab, Miklamah, Asa, Shatsalah, Hasil, Mufrad* and *Gurgani.*

Hence, we find how the Mughal emperors were curious to know about the astronomical phenomenon. Their basic assumptions about astronomy were derived from Aristotle and Ptolemy, though over the centuries, much had been added to the Hellenistic heritage by observations. Their ancestor Ulugh Beg (15th century) had built a celebrated astronomical observatory and left a book of tables (*zij*) which remained authoritative in all its essentials for *zij* compilations in India. The Mughal astronomers used astrolabes, sun dials, sand glasses and water clocks for accuracy. Side by side with the Hellenistic and Arab heritage, the Mughals were also becoming familiar with Indian astronomical and mathematical tradition.[3]

Among the famous astrologers of the period the names of Maulana Chand, Maulana Alyas of Aradbil, Amir Fath-ullah-Shirazi (Azad-ud-daula) Jotik Rai, Kanjar Beg, Nurud-din-Muhammad Tarkhan, Imam-Abdul-Mohammad of Ghazni etc. find frequent mention in the contemporary sources. Abul Fazl, himself seems to be an astronomer. He knew all astronomical calculations, as is clear from his analysis of Akbar's horoscopes. Description of planetary positions during the occurrence of comets and eclipses are very impressive and shows his deep knowledge of astronomical phenomenon.

Babur (1526 A.D. to 1530 A.D.)

Lanepoole has stated that "Babur's place in history rests upon his Indian conquests, which opened the way for an imperial line, but his place in biography and in literature is determined rather by his daring adventures and preserving efforts in his earlier days and by the delightful memories in which he related them. Soldier of fortune as he was, Babur was a man of fine literary taste and fastidious critical perception. In Persian, the language of culture, the Latin of Central Asia, as it is of India, he was an accomplished poet and in his native Turki, he was master of a pure and unaffected style alike in prose and verse".[4]

Babur is remembered as a conqueror and an empire builder. It is often forgotten that he was extremely versatile, interested not only in constructing gardens and palace, but also in music, Persian and Turki poetry, sufism, fiqh and calligraphy. He invented a style known as *Khatt-i-Baburi*, in which he edited the Quran. He was a cultured prince and enjoyed the society of poets and scholars. There were so many poets and learned men who adorned his court such as Shaikh Abdul Wajd, Maulana Ali Jan, Maulana Ali Khan, Tardi Beg Khaksar, Maulana Shamsuddin Farghari, Maulana Sams-Talib, Shaikh Zain, Maulana Baqai, Maulana Shibabu-ddin and Mir Jamaluddin.[5] But we never find any reference of astronomer or astrologer who adorned his court in comparison to Humayun's court. Although an astrologer, Muhammad Sharif, who came to India from Kabul, is found to have made a prediction. Babur himself writes in his autobiography 'Baburnama' that "On Sunday, the 15th of the first Jumada, Khwaja Muhammad Ali came from Khwast bringing a saddled horse as an offering and also *tasadduq* (*Khams*) money. Muhammed Sharif, the astrologer, and the Mir-Zadah of Khwast came with him at Kabul.[6]

He again states[7] that Qasim-i-Hussain, Ahmad-i-Yusuf, Qawwam-i-Aurdu Shah with 500 men came to India from Kabul. Muhammad Sharif, the astrologer of ill augury came with them too, Baba Dost was also along with them. As Babur further mentions that (before the battle of Khanwah) the army was anxious and afraid by reason of past occurances and vicissitudes, wild words and opinions, this Mohammad Sharif, the ill-augurer, though he had not a helpful word to say to me, kept insisting to all he met, "*Mars is in the west in these days, who comes into the fight from this (east) side will be defeated*". Timid people, who questioned the ill-augurer, became the more shattered in heart. We gave no ear to his wild words, made no change in our operation, and got ready for war".

This story is also mentioned by Harold Lamb in his book "*Babur the tiger, first of the great Moguls*".[8] Although Babur did not change his plan for war according to the prediction but he alongwith his army was shaken by the situation. And he had to motivate his army declaring 'Jehad' against Hindus and he also declared to abondon the wine.

Babur, after the victory in the battle of Khanwah, mentions that "With what ill omened words Muhammad Sharif, the astrologer had frightened me! Yet he came at once to congratulate me! I emptied my inwards in abuse of him, but in spite of his being heathenish, ill-omened of speech, extremely self satisfied, and a most disagreeable person, I bestowed a lakh rupees upon him because there had been deserving services from him in formertimes, and after saying he was not to stay in my dominions, I gave him leave to go".[9] Thus it is obvious that Babur was not demoralised by an astrologer due to his brave and courageous nature and he was not completely involved in it, but he had been availing the services of above mentioned astrologer as he himself admits. Muhammad Azhar Ansari[10] writes that Babur was shrewd enough not to hear the prediction of an astrologer before the battle of Khanwah and wise enough not to order for his death.

Babur was very much acquainted with zodiac signs and also knew the months corresponding to different zodiac signs. He illustrates it in his description of the climate of Hindustan. He states[11] that the summer months are *Chait, Baisakh, Jeth* and *Asarh* corresponding to zodiac signs: Pisces, Aries, Taurus, and Gemini. Those of the monsoon are *Sawan, Bhadon, Kuar,* and *Kartik*, corresponding to Cancer, Leo, Virgo and Libra. The winter months are *Aghan, Pus, Magh,* and *Phalgun*, corresponding to Scorpio, Sagittarius, Capricorn, and Aquarius. He also knew the astronomical division of time as he has further written that the people of India divide the day and night into sixty parts, each of which is called a *Ghari*. Besides this, the night, and the day each are divided into four parts each of which is called a *Pahar*.[12]

Babur has also mentioned many times that when the sun entered Aries,[13] they proceeded against their enemies, because sun is exalted in Aries zodiac sign that is auspicious moment. He further writes[14] that once lost a battle against the Uzbaks because the stars were in Uzbak's favour. Here, the dates of battles of Panipat and Khanwah can be compared.

Thus, Babur was acquainted with the subject but not involved or influenced like Humayun. However, we do not find any instance that he condemned astronomy and astrology in his autobiography.

Humayun (1530 A.D. to 1540 A.D. and 1555 A.D. to 1556 A.D.)

Humayun had a remarkable inclination towards natural sciences, and he had a good knowledge particularly about astronomy and geography. Later these subjects were intimately connected with his favourite studies i.e., magic and divination. In later life, he is said to have written mystical dissertations upon the nature of elements, and it is certain that he was always attracted towards occultism.[15] In the science of astronomy and mathematics, he was without a rival. Learned, erudite and great men were always in his company.[16]

William Erskine[17] mentions that he liberally patronised those who were eminent in these sciences. Again, he writes critically that astronomical knowledge was directed chiefly to the frivolous or pernicious doctrines of astrology and the occult sciences. And the course of his policy, as well as the actions of his ordinary life, was too often regulated by an absurd and childish attention to signs, omens, and superstitious observances. Nizamuddin Ahmad writes he never, in entering or leaving house or mosque, put his left foot first and if he observed any of his attendants doing so, he called him to go back and advance again from left side.[18]

A triffling incident[19] which occurred when Humayun was about ten years old is worth recording, not merely because it serves to illustrate the boy's bent of mind, but because it exercised a considerable influence upon his future career. In the year, A.D. 1517-18 when Babur was engaged in an expedition against Qandhar, he left Humayun as an incharge of the Kabul government. One day as the prince was riding about in the forests, hills, gardens and meadows, the fancy came into his mind to take an omen. Calling his teacher, Maulana Masihuddin Ruhulla, he told him that he intended to ask the first three people he met what their names were and to take an omen from their replies. Maulana suggested that only one person would be sufficient, but the prince persisted in his intentions and replied that he had a secret inspiration to this effect. After they had gone a little distance, they saw a man about forty years of age, who, on being asked his name replied that he was *Murad* Khwaja (Desire). After him another person came with an ass loaded with firewood. When they inquired his name, he answered '*Daulat* Khwaja' (Prosperity). Upon this the inspired Humayun said that "if the name of the next person that comes be *Saadat* Khwaja, it will be a strange and beautiful coincidence and the star of joy (*Murad*) will ascend from the horizon of auspiciousness (*Saadat*)". At that very moment a man (a boy in Khwandamir's account) appeared, who was grazing some cattle and when they asked him what his name was, he replied, "*Saadat* Khwaja". The servants in attendance were astonished at this marvel and all felt assured that the lord of auspicious fortune would by Divine favour attain the lofty rank. Humayun was highly delighted and not only remembered the omen as long as he lived, but also allowed it to influence his judgment on important occasions. Ishwari Prasad writes that it was probably about a couple of years after this incident that Humayun, between twelve and thirteen years old, was released from his tutors and sent to undertake his first important charge.[20]

Marriage with Hamida Banu Begum

In 1541, after paying a visit to his cousin Yadgar Nasir Mirza for three days, Humayun reached Pater, about twenty miles west of the Indus, and met his brother Hindal. It was during this visit to Pater that Humayun's marriage with Hamida Banu Begum (would be mother of Akbar) was settled. In those days Hamida Banu Begum often used to be in Mirza Hindal's residence (*Mahal*).[21] Humayun was attracted by her beauty, as he saw her. He wished to marry her despite the fact that she was only fourteen years old. Hindal greatly objected to the idea of marriage and a quarrel took place between them. But Dildar Begum, mother of Hindal, appeased both the brothers. According to Gulbadan, Dildar persuaded Hamida Banu for the marriage. After forty days, at last, she agreed to the proposal. In September 1541, the Emperor took the astrolabe in his own hands, and selecting the auspicious hour, sent Mir Abul Baqa to solemnise the marriage accordingly.[22] The influence of astrology can be seen here as the marriage with Hamida Banu Begum took place according to the calculation of planetary position.

Birth of Akbar – an astro child

In Akbarnama,[23] Abul Fazl has mentioned a number of miraculous secret annunciations and holy manifestations which occurred before the birth of prince Akbar. Though no other contemporary writer has mentioned these occurances in such a manner, Abul Fazl gives the detailed description of these events which occur during Humayun's exiled life. He has tried to depict the secret divine and spiritual power which was behind his emperor Humayun in a philosophical way. Astronomical and astrological terms are being used with many superlative adjectives. The purpose of these adjectives is to prove that Emperor Akbar possessed a divine personality. In this description, it is supposed that a divine light would be born and enlighten the whole world. Abul Fazl writes that after receiving an intimation of the advent of the glorious light through the miraculous occurance, Humayun used to pray with invocations.

One of his dreams can be mentioned here. Abul Fazl writes that on 4th Rabi-ul-awwal, 947 of the lunar eras (Friday, 10 July 1540), Humayun had dreamt after paying his devotion to God, that God was bestowing on him an illustrious successor, whose greatness shone from him forelock and the lightening of whose splendour was flashing from his temple.[24] This dream occured about a year before Humayun's marriage with Hamida Banu. The marriage took place, according to Gulbadan Begum, on Monday, 9th Jumada-l-awwal 948. She says the dream occurred at Lahore and Ahmad-i-jam himself appeared in a dream to Humayun, when Humayun was in great distress on account of the conflict with Sher Khan, and bade him not to lose heart, because he would have a wonderful son whom he was to call Jallal-ud-din Mohammad Akbar. Bibi Konor was pregnant at that time, and it was thought that she would have a son, but she bore a daughter Bakshi-i-Banu.

Another occurance[25] was that one day, near the time of the auspicious birth of Akbar Hamida Banu was riding on a camel. On the way, her eye fell on a mango-garden. Due to her inclination to have sub-acid drinks and sour sweet fruits, she bade her cousin brother Khwaja Mu'azzam to fetch some mangoes. He brought and was putting them into her hand, at that moment, he saw a light upon her glorious brows like that from a mirror. He asked if she had a mirror on head. But she replied negatively. Then Khwaja looked narrowly and saw that her shining forehead was lighted by the light of God. He marvelled at the light eternal and mentioned the circumstances to several of the confidential courtiers. His statement was that the glory of the divine light streamed so from the shining brows that he had not strength to gaze steadily at it.

Another anecdote[26] was mentioned by Humayun's nurse, who was the venerable mother of Khan-A'zam Mirza Aziz Kokaltash. She related that one morning she felt that a great light approached her and entered her bosom. And she also felt that the world warming sun had fallen into her breast. So, she was astonished greatly and shaken with joy and ecstacy.

One instance[27] was also mentioned by Mir Abdul-hai Sadr. He related that one morning, Humayun was bowed down in reverie. After a moment, he raised his head and exclaimed "Praise be to God the Gracious, the lamp of our royal family has been relit". Then, Mir asked him the meaning of his giving thanks to God. He replied that last night he saw in dream a brilliant star that emerged from a certain quarter and rose higher and higher every moment. And as it ascended, its size and brilliance increased, until its light embraced the greater portion of the world. Then Humayun asked a holy man what the luminous body was? He replied that it was the light incarnate of Humayun's successor and that whatever part of the earth had been shone upon by this world – illuminating ray, would come under his dominion, and be civilized by the light of his justice. This dream occurs before two days the news came to him about the auspicious birth of Akbar.

It would not be out of place to mention here a story, told by Maulana Nuruddin Tarkhan, an astrologer and some others, who were in attendance on the court. According to this story just before the birth of Akbar, Humayun was recreating himself in a room, which had lattice windows, and the formula of the rectification (*Harf-a-namudar*) of the glorious birth was before him. The *namudar* was a device for obtaining the date of birth. The device is used to calculate the time when will a birth take place. It seems that *namudar* was also used to discover the nature of the coming child and its sex. Abul Fazl mentions that Ulugh Beg gives three types of *namudars* viz. – Ptolemy's, Herme's and Zoroaster's.[28] Relating to the story Abul Fazl further writes that suddenly rays of divine light shone from the lattices. Humayun explained the meaning of the phenomenon that the good news would be ahead.[29]

In 1542, the queen Hamida Banu was in an advanced state of pregnancy. So, Humayun decided to go towards Amarkot. Both Jauhar and Gulbadan describe the sufferings of the royal party. According to Jauhar, Humayun's party consisted only of sixteen persons. Abul Fazl writes that there were about twenty people including some domestic slaves and learned men like Mulla Tajuddin and Maulana Chand, the astrologer.[30] According to Abul Fazl, it was an extremely fortunate for Humayun that the Rana Birsal of Amarkot faithfully offered hospitality. The Rana received the emperor with distinguished courtesy and furnished him with all supplies as well as military aids of 2,500[31] horsemen. For seven weeks the emperor remained at Amarkot resting and refreshing himself.

Abul Fazl further states that before the auspicious moment mentioned above, the mother had felt a pressing urgency to bring forth the child. Maulana Chand, the astrologer, who, by the King's order, had been stationed by the chaste threshold in order that he might cast the horoscope was perturbed, as the moment was inauspicious. He said, "In a short time, a glorious moment will arrive, such as does not happen once in a thousand years. What an advantage if the birth could be delayed!" Those who were present made light of it and said "What is the good of your agitation, such things are not under control".[32.]

At this very instant the impulse to bring forth passed off and the astrologer's mind was set at rest somewhat by the transit of the unlucky moment. The ostensible cause of this supreme blessing was that a country midwife had been just brought in to perform her office, and as her appearance was repulsive, the holy soul of Hamida Banu felt disgusted and her even temper was rebuffed and so the urgency for perturition (process of giving birth to child) left her. But when the chosen time came, Maulana became disturbed, lest it should accidentally pass by. The confidants of the harem said to him, "Her Majesty (Hamida Banu) has, after much suffering, got an interval of relief and is now slumbering. It would not be right to awaken her. Whatever Almighty God, in his good pleasure, has determined, must happen". Just as they were speaking, the pains of travail came upon and awoke her and in that auspicious moment, the unique pearl of the vice-regency of God (*Khilafat*) came forth in his glory.[33]

According to Gulbadan Begum, three days after his Majesty's departure and in the early morning of Sunday, the fourth day of the revered Rajab 949 H; there was born his imperial Majesty, the world's refuge and conqueror, Jalalu-d-din Muhammad Akbar Ghazi. The moon was in Leo. It was of very good omen that the birth was in a fixed sign, and the astrologers said a child so born would be fortunate and long lived.[34]

Hence it may be explained here that when the moment of birth of child is decided according to the auspicious planetary position and the birth is taking place deliberately according to the calculation of stars, this type of child is called, in the term of astrology, as an 'astro child'. The birth of Akbar was decided according to auspicious planetary position. That's why Akbar was an astro child.

Abul Fazl has explained the horoscope of emperor Akbar. He also discusses his planetary position according to the different views of Indian and Greek astrologers. The analysis of his horoscope will be discussed later on.

We further find references to the impact of astrology felt in context of court and daily life in Humayun's reign period. Khwajah Nizammuddin Ahmad mentions that Humayun was very much influenced by astrology. He used to wait for auspicious moments even to start a journey.[35] We find another instance about the influence of stars felt in battlefield also. Abul Fazl writes[36] that after the expedition to Badakhshan had been planned the imperial army set off 'at an auspicious hour on Monday, 5th Jumadab-al-awal, 955 (12th June 1548)' and encamped at Alang Calak, – one kos from Kabul. After two or three days, they moved to Qara Bagh. He further narrates that Hazi Muhammad Khan and Qasim Hussain Sultan came and did homage. At this stage, M. Ibrahim 'under the guidance of an auspicious star' came and paid his respects.

Abul Fazl further refers to an omen, which Humayun believed as revealing his victories. He writes that before proceeding to

Badakhshan Humayun was standing in the room. Suddenly, he took an omen that "if this white bird (referring to cock which was always in the room) come upon my shoulder and crow, it will be a sign of victory." As soon as he had this thought, the auspicious bird came flying and flapping its wings perched on his shoulder and cast an auspicious shadow over the head of fortune. Abul Fazl has given considerable space to the description of some of Humayun's remarkable inventions and regulations. From the beginning of his career, Humayun's mind exercised strange inventions. Based on the story of three men whose names were *Murad* Khwajah, *Daulat* Khwajah and *Saadat* Khwajah (as earlier discussed), Humayun founded his affairs, on joy (*Murad*), dominion (*Daulat*) and auspiciousness (*Saadat*). And he divided all the servants rather all the inhabitants of his dominions into three classes. He called architects, painters, musicians, and singers "*Ahl-i-Murad*" because they were the delight of the entire world. He called his brothers, relatives, his officers, his *vazirs*, and all his soldiers as "*Ahl-i-Daulat*", because it was clear that without the help of these persons, the ladder of dominions and fortune could not be climbed. He called the philosophers, the *ulama*, the chancellors, (*Sadra*) the sayyids, the shaikhs, the Quzis, the poets and the other learned men, the judges, nobles, and skilful persons as "*Ahl-i-Saadat*", because the honouring of these auspicious persons, and the association with them were a means of gaining everlasting auspiciousness.[37]

Similarly, he classified the days of the week[38] into or as the *Ahl-i-Daulat, Saadat* and *Murad.* Saturday and Thursday belonged to *Ahl-i-Saadat* as on these two days, his attention was drawn to the regulators of knowledge and devotion. The reason for appropriating those two days to the *Ahl-i-Saddat* was that Saturday is assigned to Saturn, which is the patron of *shaikhs* and ancient families. Thursday is Jupiter's day and that is the star of learned men and of other noble orders. Sunday and Tuesday were assigned to the *Ahl-i-Daulat* and on these days, royal affairs and the management of world government were transacted. The reason for thus assigning these two days was that Sunday denotes the sun, whose rays regulate rule and sovereignty, while Tuesday is Mars'day which is the patron of soldiers. Monday and Wednesday were days of joy (*Murad*). On these days boon companions and favourites and others of the *Ahl-i-Murad* were treated with special favour. The point in selecting these two days was that Monday is the Moon's Day, and Wednesday is Mercury's. Both of these have a special connection with household matters (*Amur-i-biyutat*), Friday (*Juma*) in accordance with its name, applied to all objects and on this day all the classes of humanity, participated in the royal bounty on Friday.

Another invention of Humayun was that of three golden arrows which were an indirect reference to the three divisions of *Saadat*, *Daulat* and *Murad*. Each of these was assigned to one of the leaders of three classes in order that he could supervise the work. Khwandamir, the chief chronicler (*Mir Muwarrikh*) has recorded in his *Qanun-i-Humayuni*,[39] that the arrow of *Saadat* was entrusted with absolute authority to the most excellent of the masters of learning and perfection – Maulana Farghali. All affairs of Sayyids, Shaikhs, Ulama, Qazis and removal of those entrusted with the works of religion and the assignment of stipends were all in his charge.

The arrow of *Daulat* was entrusted with Amir Hindu Beg. He was an incharge of all affairs of the officers, *vazirs*, and all government segments, i.e., clerks, those entrusted will civil affairs, the fixing of the pay of soldiers and the appointment of the household servants.

The arrow of *Murad* and the works of architecture were assigned to Amir Waisi. He had to look after the buildings and the arrangements of matters of pomp and pageantry and to care for the perfection of the things of splendour and glory.

Another invention was the distribution of arrows into twelve classes which denote the twelve signs of zodiac. Each order of men was assigned an arrow. The arrangement was as follows:

1. The twelfth arrow, which was of the finest gold, was reserved for the royals i.e. for Humayun and Akbar.
2. The eleventh arrow was for the brothers and other kinsmen and the sons of kings.
3. The tenth arrow was for the *Sayyids*, the *Shaikhs* and the *Ulema*.
4. The ninth was for the great officers.
5. The eighth was for the intimates (*Maquarraban*).
6. The seventh was for other intimate associates.
7. The sixth was for the heads of clans – according to Khwandamir, the *harram* and the well behaved female attendants.
8. The fifth was for the distinguished young volunteers.
9. The fourth was for the cashiers.

10. The third was for the soldiers.

11. The second denoted to artificers, perhaps used for civilians – such as shopkeepers and like others.

12. The first denoted to the doorkeepers, watchmen and the like.[40]

His another invention[41] was the division of the department of State into four classes corresponding to the four elements, namely, fire, air, water, and earth. Abul Fazl writes that for the transaction of the business of each of these four departments, a *Vazir* was appointed. The artillery and the arrangement of armour, arms and other things were attached with the Fire (*Aatashi*) Department. Khwaja Abdul-Mulk was appointed to be *vazir* of it. The wardrobe (*Karqiraqkhana*), the kitchen, the stable and the necessary management of the mules and camels were attached with the Air (*Hawai*) Department. Khwajah Latif Ullah was in charge of it. The arrangement of *sharbatkhana*, the wine-cellar (*Sucikhana*) and of canals was attached with the Water (*aabi*) Department. Khwaja Hasan was appointed as *vazir* of it. The affairs of agriculture, buildings, and the administration of exchequer lands (*Sabt-i-Khalisat*) and buildings were put under the Earth (*Khaqi*) Department. The *vazir* was Khwaja Jalalu-d-din Mirza Beg.

Another of his inventions[42] was a tent (Khirga) which had twelve partitions corresponding to signs of the zodiac. Each mansion (burj) had lattices (*pinjaraha*) through the interstices of which there shone the light of the stars of dominion.

There was another tent which represented the heaven of the fixed stars. This surrounded the other tents and as the crystalline sphere (i.e., the heaven of Heavens) is undotted (with stars) so this tent was without lattices. Khwandamir explains[43] that the outer tent was distinct from the inner one and could be used separately. The inner tent which represented the twelve signs of the zodiac was perhaps the tent mentioned by Gulbadan Begam and called *Mihr-amiz* i.e., associated with the sun.

Another invention was the "carpet of mirth" (*Basat-i-nishat*). This was a round carpet corresponding to the orbits of the spheres and the elemental spheres. The first circle which corresponded to the crystalline sphere was white; the second blue (*Kabud*); the third black like saturn; the fourth, which was the house of Jupiter, was light brown (*Sandali*); the fifth, which was related to Mars, was ruby coloured; the sixth, which was the house of the Sun, was golden; the seventh, which was the house of Venus, was bright green; the eighth, which was the station of Mercury, was bluish (Susani i.e. lilly or iris coloured). For the nature of Mercury is composite and when blue and rose are mixed, the result is Susani. The ninth circle, which was the station of Moon, was white. After the circle of the Moon, came the region (i.e., in globe or sphere) of fire and air that is of earth and water. The inhabited quarter of the earth was divided into seven climes. He himself occupied the golden circle (i.e., the one denoted the Sun) and there he adorned the throne of *Khilafat*. Each section was ordered to sit in accordance with one of the seven planets which was appropriate to it in the circle which corresponded therewith. Thus, the Indian officers sat in the circle of Saturn, while the Sayyids and the *Ulema*s sat in the circle of Jupiter.

Khwandmir[44] has described this carpet. He says that it appears to have been of enormous size, for each of the seven circles had 200 grades so that 1400 persons could sit in it. Abul Fazl[45] further explains the meaning of mirth. He says that the people who occupied the circle had to use dice, each side of which was represented by a human figure in a different position. According to each one's throw, he assumed a position which corresponded to the figure that turned up. In this way, this was a means of increasing mirth.

Another excellent device was the wearing of clothes each day corresponding to the colour of the planet on that day. Thus, on Sunday, he wore a yellow robe, which is an appropriate colour to the sun. On Monday, he wore green, which is appropriate to the Moon and so on. But Khwandmir says that when the moon was near the full, Humayun wore white. In this way, the astrological impact can be seen in the most of his inventions.[46]

Humayun was always fond of the company of men like Shaikh Abdul Qasim Astrabadi, Mulla Nuruddin and the famous astronomer Maulana Illyas. As we came to know that when he married Hamida he consulted the astrolab himself and when Akbar's horoscope was presented to him, he examined it within closed doors and danced with joy. He himself fixed an auspicious hour, in consultation with famous astrologers and for starting the schooling of Akbar. But when the master moment arrived, Akbar had disappeared for sports. In spite of all endeavours of search on the part of royalty, no trace of him could be found.[47]

Sidi Ali Rais, the Turkish admiral, was asked by the emperor to calculate solar and lunar eclipses, their degree of latitude and their exact date in the calendar. And he also asked to assist his astrologers in studying the course of the sun and about the points of the Equator.[48]

There is an instance that indicates or proves that Humayun had belief in the influence of astronomy. At the very day, when accident of Humayun took place, he came out on the terrace of the library after having discussion with Pahlwan Dost and Maulana Azad, who had come from Kabul, and he was thinking about the promotion of officers at the moment when Venus would rise on that night, and he wished to observe it. It was a practice with him that when Venus rose and the moment became auspicious, he would hold a grand assembly and make promotion of officers.[49]

William Earskin and Ishwari Prasad mention that by the time of his death he had a plan to construct an observatory and had collected the necessary instruments for that purpose.[50]

Horoscope of Akbar with Different Opinions of Greeks and Indian Astrologers

Abul Fazl gives four horoscopes of Akbar.[51] The first and fourth, however, appear to be substantially the same. Both were made by Mohammadan servants of Humayun – the first by Maulana Chand and fourth by Maulana Alyas of Ardabil. The horoscope drawn by Maulana Chand was according to the "New Tables" i.e., those of Ulugh Beg Mirza who was Timer's grandson. The horoscope drawn by Maulana Alyas was cast according to the Ilkhani or imperial table i.e., those made by Nasiruddin Tusi at Maragha – in the reign of Hulaga Khan cir. 1272 A.D.

The second horoscope was made by Jotika Rai, who was Akbar's astrologer. The exact date of drawing the horoscope is not found, but it was drawn after many years of Akbar's birth and after the first and fourth horoscopes had been drawn.

The third was made by Fathullah of Shiraz. It was not drawn earlier than 991 (1583) A.D. because he did not come to Akbar's court till that year. Abul Fazl tells us that it was in the first year of Fath-ul-lah's service that Akbar asked him to compare the horoscopes and reconcile their discrepancies.[52]

Description of the Horoscope[53] by Greek Astrolabe (at the time of birth of Akbar)

Maulana Chand, the astrologer was possessed of great acuteness and thorough quickness in the science of the astrolabe, in the scrutinizing of astronomical tables, the construction of almanacs and the interpretations of the stars. He was deputed to be in attendance of Hamida Banu. When leaving the fort of Amarkot, Humayun appointed him in order that he might observe the happy time and ascertain exactly the period of birth, He reported in writing to Humayun in the camp, that according to altitude taken by the Greek astrolabe and by calculations based on the "Gurgani" tables (Canon of Ulugh Beg), the figure of the nativity was as described in the diagram No. I.

Before describing the calculation of stars given by Abul Fazl, diagram of the horoscope of Akbar, which was cast by Maulana Alyas of Ardabil, should be mentioned. It is also illustrated by Abul Fazl in his Akbarnama.[54] Maulana Alyas of Ardabil had calculated the stars according to the Ilkhani Tables. Maulana Alyas held high rank among mathematicians and was one of Humayun's courtiers.

Birth Chart of Akbar

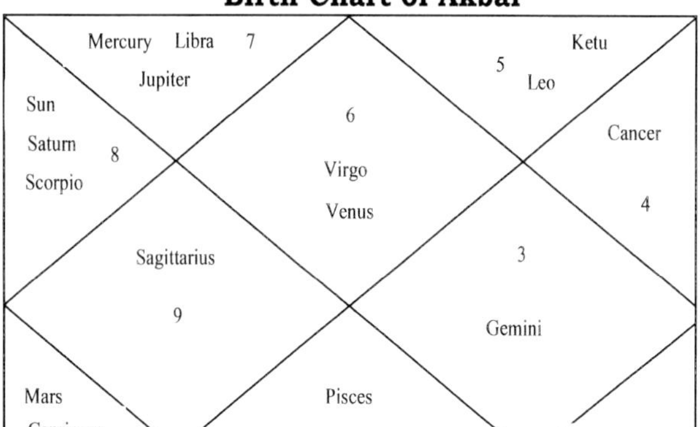

Date of Birth –
Sunday, 5 Rajab
949 A.H.
= 15th October, 1542
Time – Circa 2 A.M.
Place - Amarkot

Diagram No. I (By Maulana Chand)

The translator of Akbarnama, Ms. Beveridge has not given full description, instead, she has only copied the sketch of horoscope as follows: –

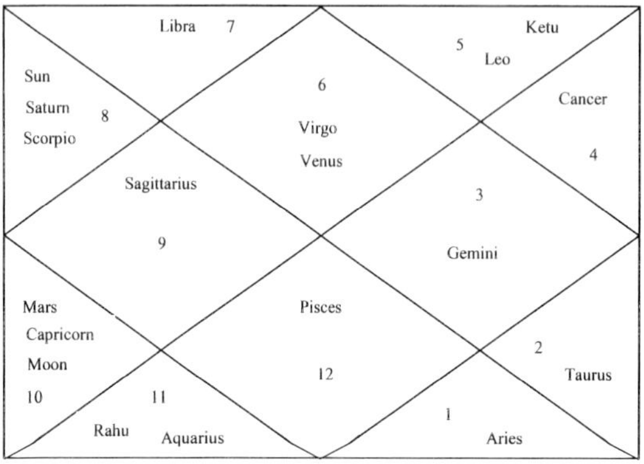

Diagram of Horoscope by Maulana Alyas of Aradbil

This diagram is partly mentioned in the text, otherwise is similar to the diagram drawn by Maulana Chand.

Interpretation of Horoscope (According to Maulana Chand)

Abul Fazl has given the interpretation of planetary position of the horoscope, which was cast by above mentioned two astrologers. He describes that the ascendant of horoscope is virgo that is bicorporal sign. Here, it should be mentioned that astrologers divide the signs into three groups of four each – Aries, Cancer, Libra, and Capricorn are tropical signs. Taurus, Leo, Scorpio and Aquarious are fixed signs. Gemini, Virgo, Sagitarious and Pisces are bicorporal signs. Thus, the fixity of the horoscope is indicated by two reasons. One is that the cusp, (i.e., transition of a zodiac sign from one house to the next house) of Ascendant is 7° and so belongs to the first third part of the sign (as one sign contains 30° in a house) denotes fixity as astrologers assume. The other is that Virgo is an earthy sign (these are four groups of signs corresponding to the four elements – earthy, airy, watery, and heavenly) and fixity is the property of the earthy element. Badaoni mentions[55] that on the festival of the 8th day after the sun enters into the sign, Virgo, Akbar used to show himself marked on the forehead like a Hindu and had strings of jewels tied on his wrists by Brahmins. Apparently, this was because of his birth anniversary.

Moreover, Mercury, the Lord of the Ascendant, in this glorious nativity is combined with the Greater Fortune i.e., Jupiter. Mercury is a planet, which stands for good luck (better luck) Venus, the lesser fortune, is in Mercury's House (Virgo) and Mercury is in Venus's house i.e., Libra. It signifies wisdom, knowledge, dexerity and ingenuity. And both by interchange of Houses and by sign, Libra is in the second House which is connected with the means of livelihood and the support of life.

Mercury bestows on the Native's amplitude of perfect reason and understanding so that he adorns the universe with the light of intellect in the affair of this life and the next and opens knots, whether spiritual or temporal, with deep understanding. As Venus is renowned for auspiciousness and prosperity, and signifies joy and pleasure is in the First House the Ascendant. Venus keeps everready the things of joy and gladness and the materials of magnificence and glory. It is a remarkable circumstance that the exchange between the lord of the house of wealth (Venus) and the lord of ascendant (Mercury) signifies personal and circumstantial felicity and bestows a life of power and pleasure.

Jupiter – the greater fortune – who signifies justice, integrity, magnanimity, firmness of soul and civilisation, is in the *second house* and it is also a lord of fourth house that keeps perfection of power and pleasure closely associated with the glorious condition. The double-natured Mercury has acquired extreme auspiciousness, by reason of his vicinity to the Greater Fortune and has heaped felicity upon felicity. It signifies that the Native will become the apex of mankind, and he indicates assemblages of the masters of understanding and reason and of the lords of perception and penetration. He will apply his genius to founding magnificent buildings such as have rarely been constructed in the times of former princes and in those choice mansions he will pass his time in varieties of joys and happinesses and in all manner of ease and independence. Thus, three happy influences are combined i.e., the happy influences of Jupiter, the happy influence of Venus and the happy influence of mercury. This is something very uncommon.

The great light (Sun), the benefactor of the Universe and moderator of the affairs of mortals and the special bestower of glory, power, pomp, and prestige, is in the *Third House* and in a fixed sign i.e., Scorpio, signifying the grant of dignity, glory, greatness, and magnificence. As it has come out of his malefic sign and its face is set towards its exaltation, it has made the Native's glory increase, day by day and as it is in the opposition to the Ninth House (Taurus) that is of travel, victory and conquest will always be upraised on the march, while he himself protects mankind from the confusions and calamities of the age and is the light-giver of the world. As the Third House is Scorpio, it is significant of Scorpian-kinsmen. The combination of sun and Saturn gives support to those of alien relatives suffering from calamities and disasters.

Abul Fazl calls fourth angle instead of fourth House. He writes that there are four angles or cardinal points namely, the First, Fourth, Seventh and Tenth House of a horoscope. These four angles can be called the central house of a horoscope. These houses are the most important houses in a figure. So, the fourth angle is Sagittarius and is the house of the final issue of things. Jupiter, its lord, is contiguous to the ameliorated Mercury and in his own term and triplicity whatever the Native designs to undertake will be accomplished with greatest ease, and the terminations of his works will be prosperous.

The Fifth House is the house of offspring and is Capricornus, a sign inactive for many children. Mars, the soldier's planet, is in the fifth house and it is a *Kadkhuda* of the Ascendant which is the centre of the laws of life. Here, Abul Fazl[56] has given the meaning of '*Kadkhuda*', as seems, that *Kadkhuda* corresponds to the term "Lord of the geniture". It is a glorious thing that this warlike planet is in its house of exaltation and by face triplicity has endowed the Native with long life and has given him the enjoyment of many sons and grandsons. His sons, too, will be fortunate and capable. He will have world-traversing, victorious soldiers. Experienced philosophers have laid stress on the power of Mars in the horoscopes of princes. In Akbar's horoscope Mars is in the House of exaltation (Capricornus) and has other dignities. This signifies glory and greatness, lofty rank, victory and dominion and his glory will be greater and better from his youth upwards. The Moon is the intermediary between the heavens and the earth because it is nearest to the earth. It is also the distributor of light from the heavenly bodies to the earthy ones. It is also the hyleg (longivity) which is the tabernacle of the soul and guardian of the body in the Fifth House. It is with mars also a cause of continual health, soundness of constitution and bodily strength.

The Sixth House is Aquarius and signifies Armies, that is used to defeat the enemies Saturn, the lord of Sixth House is the dominant and it is in the Third House which is that of allies and helpers. The Dragon's Head (Rahu) is there and signifies soldiers of loyal and devoted clans and also protectors from enemies.

The Seventh Angel i.e., the Descendant is Pisces Jupiter as Lord, at the seventh degree with aspect of Venus. It gives chaste veiled ones who are constant in pleasing service and respect, and it makes the Native happy and prosperous by their good offices.

The Eighth House is Aries, Mars is its lord. And its good influence has been aforesaid as it is an exalted position. It signifies the Divine protection in position of fear and hidden dangers. As the Eighth House denotes misfortune and danger.

The Ninth House (Taurus) is that of travel. As its regent (Venus) is posited in the Ascendant – Virgo, it holds in readiness, tranquility and pleasure in distant journeys and makes them a cause of increase of territory.

The part of Fortune is in the Tenth angle which is that of dominion and prosperity. Its lord, the auspicious Mercury is in trine[57] to it. As the Greater fortune – Jupiter is also in trine to it, this signifies majestic, sovereignty, perfect reason, and justice and brings the world's treasures into the powerful grasp of the Native.

The Eleventh House is having Cancer sign and is that of hope. Its Lord is the crescent of the Moon. It is in the fifth House of the horoscope with exalted Mars. So, it is a cause of safety and of the attainment of desires.

The Twelfth House is having Leo sign and its lord is Sun. It is that of Enemies. The Dragon's tail (Ketu), being posited in it, makes the enemies of eternal fortune downcast and contemptible. Its lord, the Sun being posited in the Third House, viz., that of allies and helpers, will bring many opponents to repentance and the path of submission and devotion. A wonderful thing in this horoscope is that the Tenth house that of dominion and sovereignty is in Gemini of which the lord of the Ascendant (Mercury) is the regent. It is established that every lord of the Ascendant desires to promote his own signification, but that he may be frustrated by obstacles in his power.

Horoscope of Akbar, according to the methods of Indian Astrologers

Abul Fazl reproduces the horoscope emperor of Akbar according to the calculation of Indian astrologers[58]. He writes that according to them, his Majesty's auspicious horoscope falls under Leo, which is a fixed sign and is significant of perfect supremacy, victory, energy, and superiority. The Sun, more than all the other objects in the universe, is the dominant and this is a clear indication that the native will be victorious and paramount over famous sovereigns and mighty rulers. The pillars of his sovereignty and government will gain stability and strength, day by day, and the regulations of his exaltation and glory will be carried out firmly and with permanence.

Abul Fazl has further given details of the horoscope of Akbar, cast by an Indian astrologer, Jotik Rai,[59] (which seem to be a title not the name) as follows: –

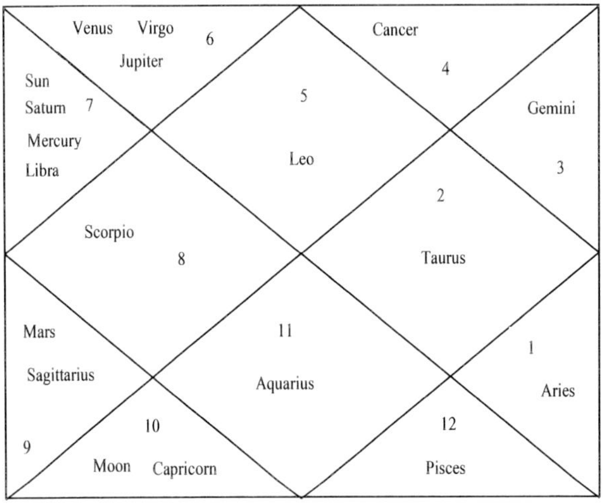

Diagram of Horoscope of Akbar, cast by Jotik Rai, an Indian astrologer.

Abul Fazl has indicated that the Indian astrologers are not far from the truth when they assert that his noble horoscope belongs to Leo. Gulbadan Begum also mentions that birth of Akbar falls in Leo sign.[60] According to the Indian astrological calculation, the Native of this Ascendant is wealthy, victorious over enemies, forgiving towards offenders, ruling according to just and equal laws, and accomplishing his purposes by force of his own reason and by firmness in his own opinions. He will be fond of travel and will reap benefit from it. And he is lord of excellent and obedient children. The conjunction of Jupiter and Venus in second house makes the Native a guide in various arts and sciences.

As the Greater Fortune, Jupiter is in the house of Mercury, he will be endowed with beauty of form, proportional admixture of the elements, gravity of speech, social graces, lofty understanding and sublime apprehension in theology and divine worship will be adorned with well doing and with ability to accomplish everything in accordance with propriety.

Venus in Virgo provides for the increase of beauty and elegance. As the sun is in Third House, the native will accomplish whatever great undertaking he desires to compass. He will be powerful, and his brethren will not attach to him. People will be united and agreed in love of him. As Mercury is in the Third House, he will be talented and well versed in business and disliking idleness, a subduer of difficulties and a slayer of enemies. He will be famed throughout the world as Mercury is in Libra. As Saturn is in the Third House, he will enjoy repose and much tranquility, and will have attached servants innumerable, but he will act according to his own personal coverage. As Saturn is in Libra and in exaltation, he will be master of the treasures of the world and as Saturn is under the shade of the venerable, world warming Sun, his boundless treasures will last for lengthy periods and will remain unaffected by prolonged usage of them. The Sun, Saturn and Mercury are in one sign. He will, therefore, be friend cherishing foe-subduing, well knowing the laws of amity and inimity. Mars, being in Sagitarins, mankind will glorify him. Mars is in the house of his friend i.e., Greater Fortune. This powerful friend Jupiter puts away the sorrows and the apprehensions of the native. He will be happy and joyful. And by power visible and invisible, essential, and accidental, he becomes Great of the Greats and King of Kings. The glory of his renown embraces the world, and the fame of his majesty extends from shore to shore. Many princes and rulers will be subject to him and being afraid of him, will be obedient and submissive. The Moon is in the Sixth House, he may have powerful enemies, but they will not approach him, and they will always endeavour to gain his friendship. As the Moon's detriment is in Capricorn, the weakness of his enemies is signified.

Abul Fazl has given some sundry rules of Indian astrology. He also describes the diagram '*Nuhbahr*' i.e., *Navamansh* according to Indian astrology. *Nuhbahr* means the dividing a sign into nine parts of 3°20 each and assigning a planet to each part.[61] This description shows Abul Fazl's deep knowledge of Indian astrology.

Description of the Horoscope, cast by Amir Fath-u-lah of Shiraz.

Abul Fazl writes that the learned astronomer Amir Fathu-l-lah, one day told Akbar that the horoscopes were discrepant and expressed the hope that he would examine them according to the true *namudar* (a device to know the time of birth) and weigh them in the trutine of inquiry. The honoured Mir, having, after complete investigation deduced the horoscope from the Persian rules and Greek canon, found that the birth was in Leo. In his opinion, this was the most reliable horoscope. He gives its figure here, together with some specimens of the prognostication.[i62.]

As Shirazi has explained the planetary positions of the horoscope, the cusp of the glorious Ascendant is 28°36" Leo. The angles (central houses) are in Fixed Sign and as the cusp of the fortunate starred Ascendant is in the Sun's house, no planet is its dominant.

Mir Sirazi says[63] that Jupiter is lord of the triplicity in companionship with the Sun and with Saturn in attendance. He has calculated the planetary position according to the diagrams of Darijan (Dreskkan), *Nubbahr* (*Navmansh*) and *haftabahr* (*Saptamans*). He describes that there are the face and *darijan* of Mars, the *Nubbahr* of Jupiter and *haftabahr* of Mars, twelfth of moon and detriment of Saturn.

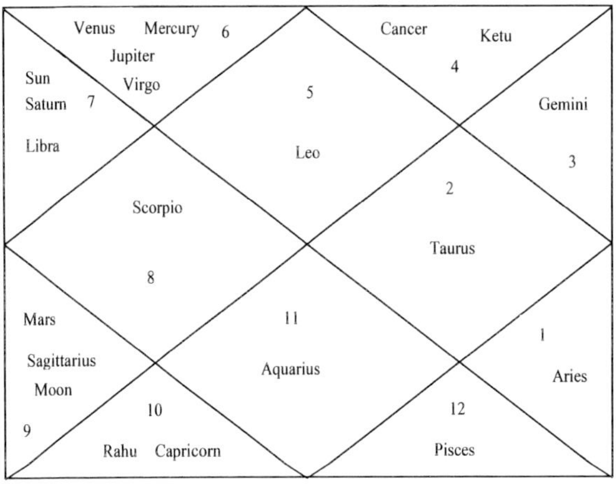

Horoscope[66] cast by Fathu-i-lah of Shiraz.

He has described all planetary position in transition (Cusp) such as Venus is in 26"23"37 virgo. The cusp of second house is 28"43 virgo, although it is the house and exaltation of Mercury. The cusp of Third House is 28'1 Libra, cusp of fourth house is 27'21 scorpio, the fifth house is 27'11 Sagitarius, and other houses are also in cusp.

The hyleg (the prorogator of life) in this horoscope is firstly, the point of anterior conjunction, secondly the part of fortune and thirdly, the Ascendant. As regards the hyleg, the lord of geniture is Saturn and then Jupiter, as regards the part of fortune Jupiter comes first, then Saturn as regards the Ascendant, the Sun comes first than Mars.

Thus, we find that both Maulana Chand and Maulana Alyas put the birthtime under Virgo. The Indian astrologers probably put the birth in Leo because it is the sign of the Sun, between whom and Akbar, there was supposed to be a mysterious connection, as Abul Fazl has mentioned so many instances[64] about this mysterious connection before the birth of Akbar.

According to Abul Fazl,[65] the difference between the Indian astrologers and Maulana Chand amounts to 17°. But apparently, Fathula-Shirazi did not adopt the Indian calculation, which indeed he probably could not read. He was a Persian. According to Blochmann,[66] he superintended the translation of Ulugh Beg's table, though these were originally written in Persian, probably he might have explained these tables or Abul Fazl's remark implies that Ulugh Beg's tables were written in a foreign language i.e., Arabic or Turkish. According to D'Herbelot, they were first written in Arabic.[67]

Fathu-l-lah Shirazi based his calculation on the Greek and Persian Tables not on the Indian and found the cusp of the Ascendant to be 28°36 Leo. It should also be pointed out that the Houses or compartments of the figure are Mundane Houses so there are overlapping signs.

An Auspicious moment for the beginning of schooling chosen by "Humayun."

Humayun was a great scholar of Astronomy and Astrology, as has been discussed earlier. He assumed the influence of this science in his daily life. He was a master of so many disciplines. He had also deputed many tutors to teach his son.

Abul Fazl mentions[68] that Akbar was taken to school on 7th Shawal of the year, 20th Nov' 1547. He was four- year, four month and four days. Asamuddin Ibrahim was deputed as his teacher.

Abul Fazl further writes[69] that a strange thing was that his Majesty Jahanbani, who was acquainted with celestial sciences and versed in the mysteries of the stars, had fixed, in consultation with acute astrologers and time-knowing astrolabe-canners, a special hour for the initiative of Humayun's instructions. Such moments might happen once during cycles and lifetimes, but when the master-moment arrived, Akbar had attired himself for sport and had disappeared. In spite of all endeavours and search by Humayun, no trace of him could be found.

However, Humayun made many efforts for the education of his son. But it could not happen as it is corroborated by Jahangir's description[70] about him as an unlettered man. It seems probable too that Akbar never knew how to read and write.

The Horoscope of the auspicious Accession of Akbar

Abul Fazl has described the planetary position at the time of the accession of Akbar at Kalanaur. At that time, he was only 14 years old. It was decided that Akbar should immediately ascend the throne. Due to untimely demise of his father, Abul Fazl writes[71] that astronomical observers, and heaven-conjoined interpreters of the Almagest, who watched the influential constellations with the astrolabe of science, cast the horoscope of a particular moment from the pages of celestial tables and assured that there was help of glorious grace and union of the fortune and dominion.

The Sun had reached the auspicious house of Pisces and had bent his sublime aspect towards his house of Exaltation, in order that he might make the four pillared throne of Aries radiant with the auspicious accession.[72] A great feast and assembly were organised in the *Idgah* of Kalanaur such as suggested by the celestial writers. At that place, in a felicitous hour, near noon of Friday, which was according to opinion, the second of Rabi-as-sani 963 of the lunar year (14th Feb. 1556) he sat on the throne with the grace of 'God'. On the same day, the recipient of sovereignty was exalted by the title of Shahinshah. Bairam Khan became the 'Vakil-a-Sultanat'. The date and time of accession had been scrutinized by the astronomical observers, and the horoscope of accession was prepared by Imam-Abu-l-Muhammad of Ghazni, who was one of the great masters of astronomical prognostication. Abul Fazl has given the horoscope,[73] which was cast by him as follows. Although he had suggested that the Ascendant in Scorpio was good so that the Tenth angle may be Leo, the house of the sun.

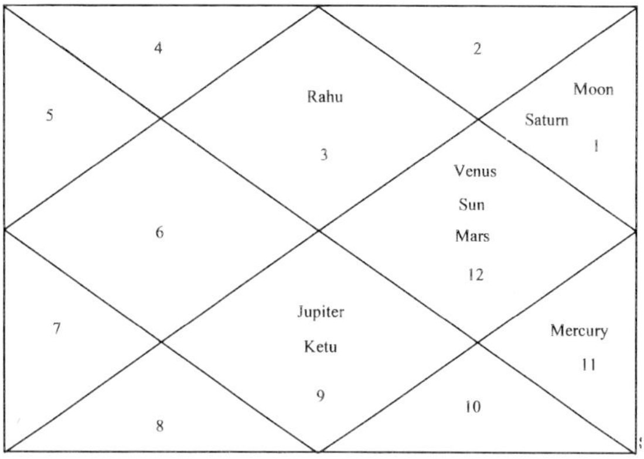

Accession of Akbar at Kalanaur on 14th Feb 1556 Friday noon

Abul Fazl also gives the description of horoscope. He says that various delightful points arise from the consideration of this auspicious horoscope. The first is that in the tenth Angle, which is the house of sovereignty, the sun is showing an increase of light. Now the main point for consideration regarding the hour of an accession, is the auspiciousness of the tenth house.

The second house, which is that of property, is cancer and the moon, which is the regent of the house, has attained in the eleventh house, which is that of hope, income, and public support.

The third house, which is that of kinsmen and connexions, is Leo, and its dominant, the sun, is in the tenth angle. All the relatives will be obedient to orders and submissive to the commands of the Shahinshah.

The fourth house is Virgo, which is called the terrestrial angle, and is conversant with the final results of actions and with possessions. The dominant (Mercury) is in the ninth house which is that of travel. This is proof of excellent eventualities and of the stability of conquests.

The fifth house is Libra, which is that of children, enjoyment and presents. Its Regent Venus is in Pisces, the house of exaltation. It proves that auspicious children will be worn to the king by affection and favour and will grow up in the shadow of dominion and grace.

The sixth house is Scorpio, which is that of slaves and servants, and of diseases. Its Regent, Mars, is in the house of sovereignty (the tenth). This indicates equability of temperament, numerous faithful slaves, and devoted servants. Though Jupiter is in Sagittarius, yet by virtue of equal distribution on houses, he is imparting blessings to the sixth house.

The seventh house, Sagittarius, the western angle, and the opposite of the ascendant. It is the house of enemies. As by the equal distribution of houses, it is void of an auspicious star, there is strong evidence that the enemies of the State will be overcome.

The eighth house is Capricorn which is conversant with heritages. As its dominant (Saturn) is in the eleventh house, this is proof that hereditary blessing will be attached to the perfect conditions of his personality.

The ninth house is Aquarius and has to do with knowledge, faith, and travel. Mercury is the lord of the Ascendant as Regent of Gemini. He has a kind aspect to the Ascendant and causes the acquisition of the lights of wisdom. He tells of sincere inquiry into the affairs of realm and religion, soundness of plan in matters of travel and conduciveness thereof to the confirmation of dominion.

The tenth house, Pisces, is called the tenth angle, and is the house of sovereignty and of masters. The Sun, Venus, and Mars are there. The days of sovereignty will always pass pleasantly, and the owner of the horoscope will have daily increasing sources of splendour and glory. Masters of high rank will attain their desires through his good fortune.

The eleventh house, Aries is associated with hopes and with sincere friends. It is the Sun's house of exaltation, and the swiftly moving Moon is waxing there. Every hope that arises in the holy soul (Akbar) will be fulfilled quickly and thoroughly and friends will become successful from being associated with his great fortune.

The twelfth house is Taurus and is the house of enemies. It is void of stars and Mars is in aspect from the tenth house. The enemies of realm and religion will be suppressed by the sharp sword of Mars.

The Moon was in Aries, the Sun's house of exaltation. The astrologers had declared that in accession horoscopes, the Moon, which is the intermediary for conveying light from the superior (Sun) heavenly bodies to the inferior (other planets), should be in Aries. They had considered this a circumstance greatly to be relied upon. The Sun is in conjunction with Jupiter. The regent of the tenth (Jupiter) is in the seventh house. The Lord of the ascendant is in Ninth house.

These combinations indicate that the victorious troops will be well disciplined and that there would be increase of the royal splendour and glory. The part of 'Good Fortune' is strong for it and is situated in Leo, which is the sun's house, and its Regent is in tenth house. Jupiter, who is strong evidence of loyalty, is in the seventh in his own house (Sagittarius) and is most auspicious. The affairs of the state shall advance and prosper. And Mercury has a friendly aspect to the Moon. All these were clear indications that things would turn out for the best, that fortune would increase, and desire be attained.

Abul Fazl writes[74] that the interpretation of the good points in this horoscope, and the wonders of it, are beyond the power of description. Acute scrutineers of celestial tables and canons and scrutinieers of astrolabes, know by thought and the intelligence how few of such great and greatness conferring houses, in which so many everlasting blessings are unfolded, have occurred since the unknown time of the heavens and the constellations.

Maulana Nurud-din-Tarkhan, an astronomer of the age, also approved of the auspiciousness of the time of accession.

Akbar (1556 A.D. to 1605 A.D.)

Establishment of New Era and Year

Akbar established the new divine era from the date of his auspicious accession. The beginning of this great era took place with effect from the ensuing new year. The principle of the calculations rested on true solar months and years. H.M. the Shahinshah designated this grand epoch as the *Tarikh-Ilahi* (Divine Era). The names of the months of the era were made identical with the famous names of the Persian months but were adorned in addition by the title *Ilahi* (Divine) i.e., Farwardin, Divine month. The names of the days were the same as those of the current thirty Persian days.

Amir Fath-Ullah-Shirazi, whose title was Azad-ud-daula, laid the foundation of the edifice of New Era. Although the foundation took place in 1584 A.D., yet the new Era began with the accession of Akbar. The copy of the firman was composed by Abul Fazl and was issued to the dominions after the establishment of this auspicious Era.

This firman contains some changes that were made for the calculation of dates in almanacs, which was commonly used among the people of India and which in their language are called '*Patra*'. It further adds that "we find in these almanacs, the beginning of the lunar month from the opposition (of sun and moon) that is, from the season of advancing darkness! In the Hindi language this is called '*Kishnpacc*'. So, those darkened ones, out of pure formalism, ignorance and excessive eccentricity and error, have based their month upon darkness! In addition to the fact that the folly of this empty and baseless arrangement is too clear for argument, it has been reported to us by orthodox religious teachers, and has been shown by them from their old authoritative books, that in ancient time the lunar month began with the lighting up of the moon, which is called in their tongue '*Shuklpace*', and that this rational practice ceased from the time of *Bikramajit*, on account of the prevalence of the heterodox and of the disorder and confusion. Accordingly, an order had been promulgated that astrologer`s almanac-makers, and casters of horoscopes, throughout the territories, shall base their calendars on the pure method of the 'Shuklapae'. As a precautionary measure, in order to make things simple and easy, a calendar was prepared and sealed with the sacred seal and was sent to them so that they might take it as a model".[75]

Thus, it is obvious that the new era was established with New Year that took place near the date of accession. It was according to solar year, that was also called *Nau-roj* in Persian. The solar year began with the changing position of sun from Pisces sign to Aries sign, because, in Aries Zodiac sign, the sun becomes exalted. At the time of accession, the sun was in Pisces Zodiac sign and was towards Aries sign. Soon after the accession, it had entered its exalted position in the Aries sign.

Celebration of anniversary of Akbar's accession

Akbar always celebrated the anniversary of his accession. Akbar considered the beginning of the first Divine year after accession, when Sun entered into Aries, an exalted position. Therefore, Abul Fazl writes[76] that "Twenty-five days after the auspicious time of the accession, viz. on Wednesday, 28 Rabi – as sani 963, there was the world-illuminating New Year and the Sultan of the East confronted Aries with his world-adorning banners".

Abul Fazl further writes[77] about the beginning of second year Ilahi in similar manner. He says that "In the station of abundance, the reservoir of brilliancy for the terrene and terrestrials, and the adorment of time and time's offspring, to wit, the sun, the benefactor of the universe, arrived at his house of exaltation and gladdened and refreshed the earth with the breath of spring. It would seem that Aries is called the house of exaltation because at that time the beings of earth are given exaltation and fresh life. Otherwise, the dignity of that bestower of exaltation on heavenly and terrestrial bodies is too high for any place to receive the title of the house of exaltation of that giver of light to all existence. In fine, this world-adorning light came from the fountain of Pisces to the abode of joy, in the night known as Thursday, after ten houses, and forty minutes of the astronomical night of Wednesday, the 27th Rabi-as-sani of the luner year 964 and the world illuminating new years day came to pass and the second year of the Divine Era began".

Here, we can elaborate the descriptions of all anniversaries of Akbar's accession narrated by Abul Fazl in his works. He always talked[78] about the exaltation of sun at the time of anniversary of accession.

Celebration of Birthdays twice in a year

Akbar celebrated his birthday anniversary according to solar and lunar day. On both days, he used to perform a ceremony of weighing. The weighing was practised twice on the day, according to the Hijra calendar and again on the solar day.[79] Abul Fazl narrates that "he proceeded towards Jaunpur on the day. When he reached the town of Nizamabad, the ceremony of weighing Akbar took place and there was a great feast. Mankind received delight from the Shahinshah's bounty and offered up prayers for his long life and reign". (But Ain-i-Akbari contains that the weighing ceremony took place at Jaunpur).[80] He was weighed[81] against 8 articles and sometimes 12 articles.

It means that he never failed to perform this ceremony, whenever he was even out of his capital.

Auspicious Moment for the entry in Capital

Whenever Akbar went out from his capital, he used to return or enter his capital at an auspicious moment according to the planetary position. On 13th May 1573, Akbar arrived at Ajmer. After visiting the holy shrine, he proceeded towards the capital. In the space of one day and two nights he completed that long journey and arrived at the town of Bacuna (Bajuna) which was eight *kos* from Fatehpur. Jotik Rai, the astrologer, stated that after three days there would be an auspicious time for reaching the capital. So, Akbar remained in that town for three days.[82]

Another instance may be mentioned here. In 1592, when Prince Danial was to set out on his campaign of Qandhar and Akbar was to proceed to Kasmir,[83] it was reported by the astronomer that due to fall of about 300 little stars from west to east, they should return and set out again at a chosen hour. Therefore, Shah and Shahzada had to go back.

In 1601, Akbar left Sarangpur and proceeded towards Ranthambhor. He stayed at Biana on the way. It was only after the favourable hour came, that he entered his capital Agra.[84] Also Akbar postponed his visit to Fatehpur to see his new-born son Salim due to the belief prevalent among Hindus that "when God bestows an auspicious child after long expectation, he be not produced before the honoured father till after a long delay".[85.]

Belief in astrology in Battlefield

Abul Fazl mentions so many instances of battlefields when Akbar took decision according to the guidance of astrologers. Abul Fazl gives description of wars betraying the belief in the influence of stars as follows:

> 'In 1563, Akbar paid his attention towards the management of Kabul. So, he had appointed Munim Khan Khana with Mohammad Hakim to solve the problem of Kabul and were sent there'. Abul Fazl writes[86] that when "Khan Khana marched to besiege Jalalabad, the news arrived that M. Hakim and the army of Kabul had come. Jabir Bardi Beg, who had been an officer of Firdaus Makani, and had become a darvish, and who was accompanying the army, was sent to Mirza, in order to settle the affair without battle. If it could not be done, it was decided that the battle should take place next day, as the star was in front".

In 1580-81, there was a rebellion of officers in Bengal, and it was a very disturbing occurance for the emperor Akbar. Abul Fazl narrates that in the beginning of twenty fifth year, the rebellion's suppression was predicted by the astrologers. He writes[87] that, "In as much as awakened hearts and active brains read the writings of the stars on the forehead of the beginning and perceived the beautiful conclusion from the preamble, the lights of the daily increasing dominion of the august cycle brightened hearts and eyes. They (the astrologers) conveyed the news of the ruin of the seditious and of the suppression of the rebellion".

There is another instance in 1581 A.D. when Akbar received news of the coming of Mirza to Panjab. Abul Fazl writes[88] that "The astrologers under Akbar's directions held a meeting to determine the auspicious moment. Akbar paid some attention to the arrangement of the affairs of the capital. And to keep a watch over the eastern provinces, he decided to go himself to Punjab".

Abul Fazl further mentions another instance of the belief in the influence of stars when the war against Sultan Mozaffar Gujrati took place in 1583. He writes[89] that 'as the soldiers of Gujrat had joined battle with Mozaffar, M. Khan arrived with a large force and produced tranquility. Meanwhile, near Mirtha, Khwajagi Tahir came to him. About 31st December 1583, the army halted at Pattan. The soldiers were incorporated and there was rejoicing, and a council was held. Some foolish propositions were brought forward. Some said that they should remain there until the Malwa troops arrived. Some said that to march before Akbar should advance towards that quarter would be to transgress the rules of farsightedness. Some thought that the only thing to do was to march on quickly in reliance on the daily-increasing fortune without regard to external arrangements. By the guidance of the star, and glory of Fortune, all agreed to this view, and resolution of acting in unity were taken'.[90.]

Another instance is pointed out by Abul Fazl, when in 1583, the news of the Gujrat disturbances reached Akbar. The emperor inquired[91] from Amir Fath Ullah of Shiraz about the circumstances of Gujrat and about the final result. Amir Shirazi was an astronomer acquainted with the minutest details of science. He was not only a compendium of astrology but of philosophy also. He did research and reported that it appeared that in this year two battles would be fought, and that the imperial servants would be victorious. As he reported so did it turn out and there was a fresh currency of recognition (of Akbar's and Fath-Ullah's merits).

Abul Fazl also mentions[92] some references of the Sadhana of the sages of India. In this connection, he mentions a brahman named Shiv Dat who lived in Srinagar. The brahmin predicted as he was acquainted with a Spirit also, about the conquest of Akbar over Kashmir. This event occurred about 1586 A.D. Thus, Abul Fazl writes that "when the news of the conquest reached the sublime court, there was an increase of thanksgivings to God and the deserving servants were exalted by various favours. The truth of the statements of the Hindu astrologers were revealed".[93.]

Similarly, in the context of Akbar's Deccan campaign of 1595, Abul Fazl writes, 'As the unpleasant reports arrived one after the other, he (Akbar) determined to proceed there. By wondrous fate, there was some rain on that day. The Indian astrologers represented that whenever the sun was in one of the latter four signs and there was some rain, the despatch of the advance camp should be postponed to another hour". Accordingly, Akbar postponed the departure of advance camp and, meanwhile, he enjoyed hunting.[94]

Belief of Auspiciousness for the foundations

Akbar also believed in the auspicious time to lay the foundation of town and buildings. Abul Fazl refers to the auspicious time for every foundation laid by Akbar. Some instances may be given as follows:

On 23 Sept. 1570, Akbar set out with the intention of obtaining the blessings of Khwaja-Muninad-din to Ajmer. And he spent some days in devotion at the shrine and distributed gifts among the attendants. At this same auspicious time, an order was issued for repairing and enlarging the fort of Ajmer. Accordingly able architects laid the foundation and in an auspicious hour, began to construct the noble building with stone and lime.[95]

The foundation of the fort of Atak Benaras (that was also called as Katak Banaras) is also mentioned by Abul Fazl. He writes that near the end of May 1588, 'after passing of two pahars, two gharies, the foundation was laid by the holy hand with the name of Katak Banaras'.

In 1595, after much inquiry, a place was found near Akmahal and the foundation of a city was laid in a fortunate hour and in a short time there was a choice city, to which the glorious name Akbarnagar was given.[96]

Account of the appearance of Star Zo Zoaba – Comet.

The appearance of a 'Comet' in space was a very disturbing phenomenon for Akbar. He immediately called upon the renowned astrologers to read about the influence of this star on his empire. Abul Fazl, who was acquainted with the subject of astronomy, describes this great phenomenon in detail. He writes[97] that on 5th November 1577, at the time when sun was auspiciously placed in 'Scorpio', this celestial sign appeared in Sagittarius in the west. It appeared in many western countries but inclined to the north. It had a long tail, and, in some countries, it was visible for five months.

He further adds that the astrologers and those acquianted with the subject, represented that in some of the inhabited parts of India, grain would be dear and they (astrologers) mentioned the particular places where this would occur. They also predicted that ruler of Parsia would die, and that there would be the confusion in Iraq and Khurasan. And it would not leave any worst effect on Akbar's dominion. After some time, the news was reported to Akbar that Shah Tahmasp had died, Sultan Haider had been put to death and Shah Ismail had come to power.

Nizam-ud-din Ahmad also mentions that following the emperor's order astronomers came up and their opinions were that its (Comet's) effect would not be felt in the country of Hindustan, but in all probability, that would be in Kurasan and Iraq.[98] He further writes that there was very great disorder in the country of Iran.

After twenty years, in the beginning of the year 1597, a comet again appeared, and astrologers predicted that there would be dryness and scarcity. As the famine occured in the same manner, Akbar appointed able men to every place to give food to the needy ones.[99] The famine lasted about six months and many persons died of hunger.

Abul Fazl gives[100] an account of the comet, in general. He describes the astronomical and geographical basis of appearing the comet that will be discussed later on.

Shireen Moosvi, a renowned historian, has given a full account of Comets appeared in Mughal period. She says[101] that during the one and a half centuries that cover the period of the Great Mughals (1556-1707), seven appearances of Comets are recorded, being remarkable in the sense of being distinctly visible to the naked eye. The years of their appearances were 1556, 1577,1607, 1618, 1661, 1680 and 1689. The comets of 1577 and 1618 are reported to have been bright enough to be seen even in daytime. The comet of 1577 was of singular significance and Keplar made observations on it.

The appearance of the comet of 1577 is also recorded by Arif Qandahari,[102] writing mainly in 1579 and by Abul Fazl, from whom, we have two accounts. His contemporary Badauni also reports the appearance of this comet. Arif records that on the night of Thursday, 25 Shaban 985 (7 Nov. 1577), a bright star appeared in the west inclining towards the south with numerous tiny stars flowing from its top, making it look like a Cypress tree; it remained visible for four gharis (1 hour 36 minutes) in the cities of Agra, Delhi, and Lahore. It disappeared in the month of Shawwal of the same year (12 December 1577 – 9 January 1578) and became known as the long tailed-star (*Sitara-i-dum-i-daraz*).

Arif Qandahari's description does not particularly give the impression of any apprehensions or nervousness shown by the court on the appearance of this Comet. He reproduces some verses from an ode composed on the occasion by one of Akbar's court poets, Sheri, where the Comet is treated as a remarkable sight, comparable with similar things of value and splendour in the world. According to Abul Fazl's earlier draft, it was in November 1577, when Akbar was just lying down the foundation of a new fort, Mot Manoharnagar, not far from Fatehpur Sikri, that a spectacular comet made its appearance after sunset in the west (but inclining to the north) and remained visible till two hours before dawn. This strange spectacle shook the hearts of the people, for the appearance of this unfamiliar Comet was regarded as an extremely bad omen. The historian Badauni also writes that Shah Ismail of Iran was assassinated and the evil influence of this comet became evident in that country.

Shireen Moosvi further writes that emperor Akbar, at this time barely thirty- five years of age, took the matter more seriously. And he directed his minister Raja Todarmal to invite astronomers to carry out research on the matter and to predict the consequences. And the astrologers predicted no damage to India. Then, Akbar distributed the generous gift to the astrologers, muslims or brahmins for playing their due part.

In Akbarnama, Abul Fazl takes the opportunity of the appearance of this comet to sum up the knowledge of comets and meteors that had been assembled by his time. He considers this phenomenon as belonging to the realm of physical sciences (*hikmat-i-taba*) and testifies the existence of monographs on them, including Greek treatises and an alleged work of Ptolemy that sets the distance between the sun and a comet as eleven signs apart. Abul Fazl seems to consider meteors and comets as of terrestrial origin and says that they are created by the action of solar light on the elements of the earth. Abul Fazl adds that the Indian astronomers had identified more than a hundred comets while the Greeks had determined seven categories but held the *Zuzanab* and *Zuzuaba* to constitute the major and most ominous kinds of comets. He attributes to the Greeks for the statement that the *Zuzuaba* appears in the east in dawn, the *Zuzanab* in the west at sunset.

Eclipses

Shireen Moosvi writes that it is rather surprising that out of the 56 eclipes of the sun (39 in the reign of Akbar and 17 in that of Jahangir) only one solar eclipse during Akbar's reign and two in the reign of Jahangir are recorded.[103] The account of two eclipses is given by Abul Fazl. Unlike the appearance of comets and the fall of meteorites, eclipses could be predicted well in advance. The Indian astronomers, since ancient times, well understood the phenomenon notwithstanding the prevalent myths and superstitions. But among Indians a solar eclipse was taken to be a bad omen and a total or annular one especially so. Akbar, notwithstanding his commitment to rationality, was not immune to these superstitions.

Moosvi further adds that the earlier account contained in the first draft of the Akbarnama reveals that he was quite concerned over the effects of the predicted eclipse of the sun. Since the belief was that if, at the time of the eclipse, clouds obscured the sun, the evil effect would be nullified, the emperor called upon the Brahmans to perform their rituals for gathering the clouds at the required moment. But the Brahmans failed and retired abashed. Barely half a ghari (12 minutes) had remained and the sky was still clear. The emperor himself now prayed to the Almighty, then the clouds duly came, bringing rain and obscured the sun at the moment of eclipse. Despite the eclipse, there remained ample brightness, a testimony to the fact that the eclipse was not complete. But owing to the clouds obscuring the view, the embarrassment of the astronomers at their prediction of a total eclipse not having been fulfilled, was also mitigated.

Endnotes

1. Iqtidar H. Siddiqui, *Medieval India: Essays in Intellectual Thought and Culture*, *op. cit.*, Vol. I, p. 88.
2. Abul Fazl, *Ain-i-Akbari*, Eng, tr. Jarrett, New Taj Office, New Delhi (1989), Vol. III, pp. 4-15.
3. Irfan Habib (ed.), *Akbar and his India – Science and Superstition under Akbar and Jahangir: The Observation of Astronomical Phenomena* by Shireen Moosvi, Delhi Oxford University Press, Calcutta (1997), p.109.
4. Staley Lanepoole, *Babur*, Clarendon Press: Oxford, p. 10; also see, S.M. Edward, *Babur Diarist and Despot*, Haritage Publication, New Delhi (1977), p. 103.
5. Mohibbul Hassan, *Babur*, Manohar Publication, New Delhi (1985), p. 192.

6. A. S. Beveridge (tra.), *Baburnama*, London (1921), p. 399.
7. *Ibid.,* Vol. II, p. 551.
8. Harold Lamb, *Babur the Tiger, first of the great Mughals*, Great Britain (1962), pp. 53-61.
9. Beveridge (*tra.*), *Baburnama, op. cit.,* p. 576.
10. M.A. Ansari, *Social Life of the Mughal Emperors*, op. cit., p. 180.
11. M. Thaekston (ed. and trans.), *Baburnama*, Free Gallery of Art: Washington D.C., USA (1996, 2002), p. 350.
12. *Ibid.,* p.351.
13. *Ibid.,* p.322; also see Beveridge, *tra.*, *Baburnama, op. cit.,* p. 557.
14. Ibid.
15. Ishwari Prasad, *The Life and Times of Humayun*, Orient Longman, Bombay, Calcutta, Madras (1955), p. 6.
16. Khwajah Nizamuddin Ahmad, *The Tabaqat-i-Akbari*, tra. B.N. De. Bile Inds., Calcutta (1927-33), Vol. II, p. 138.
17. William Erskine, *History of India under two first Sovereigns, Babur and Humanyn*, Idarahe-e-Adabiyat-i-Delhi, Delhi (1973), Vol. II, p. 531.
18. Nizamudin Ahmad, *op. cit.*
19. Beveridge, tra., *Baburnama, op. cit.,* p. 643. Also see, Ishwari Prasad, *op. cit.,* p. 6.
20. *Ibid.*, p. 7.
21. Beveridge (Trans), *Humayun Nama –Gulbadan*, Muhammad Ahmad Idarah-i-Adabiyat-Dellh (1972), p. 149.
22. *Ibid.,* p.151.
23. Abul Fazl, *Akbarnama*, Beveridge (Tra.), Asiatic Society of Bengal and Manmohan Satish Kumar Rare Books, Delhi (1972), Vol. I, pp. 34-49.
24. *Ibid.,* p. 42.
25. *Ibid.,* p. 44.
26. Abul Fazl, *Akbarnama, op cit.,* pp. 44-45.
27. *Ibid.,* pp. 46-47.
28. Ibid.
29. Ibid. pp. 45-46.
30. Ishwari Prasad, *op. cit.,* p. 217.
31. *Ibid.,* p. 218.
32. *Ibid.,* pp. 56-57.
33. *Ibid.,* p.57.
34. Gulbadan Begum, Humayunnama, pp. 157-158.
35. Nizammuddin Ahmad, *The Tabaqat-i-Akbari*, op. cit., p. 155.
36. Abul Fazl, *Akbarnama, op. cit.,* Vol. I, p. 525.
37. *Ibid.,* pp. 521, 522 and 643; also see, Ishwari Prashad, *op. cit.,* p. 642-48.
38. *Ibid.,* p. 644.

39. Elliot and Dowson, *History of India, as told by its own Historians*, London (1977), Vol. V, Aligarh Reprint (1952), p. 116.
40. Abul Fazl, *Akbarnama, Op.cit.*, Vol. I, pp. 645-46.
41. *Ibid.,* pp. 646-47; also see, Nizamuddin Ahmad, *op. cit.*, pp. 157-58.
42. *Ibid.,* p. 649.
43. Ibid. Also see, Khwandamir's *'Qanun-i-Humayuni'*, p.122.
44. Khwandamir' *op. cit.,* p. 206; Abul Fazl, *Akbarnama*, *op.cit.*, Vol. I, p. 650.
45. Ibid.
46. Ishwari Prasad, *op. cit.,* pp. 640-42.
47. *Ibid.,* p. 519.
48. Ishwari Prasad, *Life and Times of Humayun*, *op. cit.,* p. 657.
49. Abul Fazl, Beveridge, Trans., Akbarnama, *op. cit.,* Vol. I, p. 657.
50. William Earskin, *Life of Humayun*, p. 531; Ishwari Prasad, *Life and Times of Humayun*, *op. cit.,* p. 370.
51. Abul Fazl, Akbarnama, *op. cit.,* Vol. I, pp. 70, 86, 97 and 118.
52. *Ibid.,* p.125.
53. *Ibid.,* p. 70.
54. *Ibid.,* pp. 70, 86, 97 and 118.
55. Al-Badaoni, Muntakhabru't-Tawarikh, W.H. Lowe (tra.), *Idarah-i-Adabiyat-i-Delhi*, Delhi (1899, 1973), Vol. II, p. 269.
56. Abul Fazl, *Akbarnama*, *op. cit.,* vol. I, p. 77 (Note).
57. 'Trine means an aspect of 120° between two planets.
58. *Ibid.,* pp. 85-88.
59. Abul Fazl, Blockman (Trans.), *Ain-a-Akbari*, p. 404.
60. Gulbadan Begum, 'Humayun Nama', S. Beveridge (Tran.), *Idarah-i-Adabiyat-i-Delhi*, Delhi (1972), pp. 157-58.
61. Abul Fazl, *Akbarnama*, *Op. cit.*, p. 90 (See Footnote).
62. *Ibid.,* p. 97
63. *Ibid.,* pp. 99-105.
64. *Ibid.,*
65. *Ibid.,* pp. 126-27.
66. Abul Fazl, *Ain-a-Akbari*, H. Blockman (tra.), New Taj Office, Delhi (1989), p. 104.
67. Abul Fazl, *Akbarnama*, Beveridge, (Trans.), *op. cit.,* Vol. I, p. 126.
68. *Ibid.,* p. 519.
69. Ibid.
70. Jahangir, *Tujuk-i-Jahangir*, Alexander Rogers (Tra.), Munshiram, Manohar Lal Publishers Pvt. Ltd., Delhi (1968), Vol. I, p. 316.
71. Abul Fazl, Beveridge (Trans.), *Akbarnama*, *op. cit.*, Vol. II, p. 4.
72. *Ibid.,* p. 3.

73. *Ibid.,* pp. 10-14.
74. *Ibid.,* p.14.
75. *Ibid.,* pp. 20-22.
76. *Ibid.,* p. 32.
77. *Ibid.,* p. 78.
78. Abul Fazl, *Akbarnama, op. cit.,* Vol. II, III, pp. 101, 124, 137, 210 (Vol. III) and pp. 281, 316, 401, 416, 481, 493, 512, 525 (Vol. II).
79. Abul Fazl, *Ain-i-Akbari,* H. Blochman (tra.), *op. cit.,* p. 266.
80. Abul Fazl, *Akbarnama, op. cit.*, Vol. II, p. 397; *Ain-Akbari,* Jarett (tra.), Vol. II, p. 164.
81. Abul Fazl, *Akbarnama, op. cit.,* Vol. III, p. 699.
82. *Ibid.,* vol. II, p. 54.
83. *Ibid.,* p. 942.
84. *Ibid.,* Vol. III, p.1192.
85. *Ibid.,* Vol. II, p. 505.
86. *Ibid.,* Vol. II, p. 291.
87. *Ibid.,* Vol. III, p. 437.
88. *Ibid.,*Vol. III, p. 495.
89. *Ibid.,* pp. 631-32.
90. *Ibid.,* p.632.
91. *Ibid.,* p. 643.
92. *Ibid.,* pp.773-74.
93. Ibid.
94. *Ibid.,* p. 1044.
95. *Ibid.,* Vol. II, p. 516.
96. *Ibid.,* Vol. III, pp. 1042-43.
97. *Ibid.,* pp. 315-16.
98. Brajendra Nath (Trans.), *Tabaquat-i-Akbari –Nizamuddin Ahmad,* p.506.
99. Abul Fazl, *Akbarnama, op. cit,* Vol. III, p. 1064.
100. *Ibid.,* pp. 311-315.
101. Shireen Moosvi, "Science and Superstition under Akbar and Jahangir: The Observation of Astronomical Phenomena", in Irfan Habib (ed.), *Akbar and His Times,* op. cit., pp.
102. Arif Qandhari, *Tarikh-i-Akbari,* pp. 231-32. Muinu-ud-din Nadvi, Azhar Ali Dehelvi and Imtiyar Ali Arshi (eds.).
103. Shireen Moosvi, op. cit.

CHAPTER 4

Astrology and Astronomy under the Mughals: A.D. 1605 to A.D. 1750

Jahangir (1605 A.D. to 1627 A.D.)

With the Hellenstic and Arab heritage, the Mughals were also becoming familiar with Indian astronomical and mathematical traditions.[1] Jahangir was deeply influenced by the Indian astronomical and prognostical sciences. He himself was a great scholar and had a literary bent of mind. He wrote his Memoirs, known as '*Tujuk-i-Jahangiri*' in Persian.[2] He loved to converse with *pandits* and Hindu ascetics.[3]

Jahangir provides very interesting descriptions pertaining to the impact of astrological and astronomical sciences in his Memoirs. He has also described Comet and eclipses. He was very much influenced by Pt. Jotikray, a Hindu astrologer of his time. Now, we must trace out the narrations which indicate his belief in the impact of astrology upon him.

Jahangir writes[4] in the very beginning of his Memoirs that 'with the grace of God, when one sidereal hour of Thursady, *Jumada-s-sani* 20th, A.H. 1014 (October 24th, 1605), had passed, he ascended the throne in the capital of Agra'. He further mentions about the fact of his birth that in 'on Wednesday, 17th Ravi-ul-awwal, 977 A.H. (August 31st, 1569), when seven *ghari* of day had passed and the zodiac sign Libra (*Mizan*) had risen to the 24th degree, he (Jahangir) was born'.[5] Here it is notable that at the advice of a Hindu astrologer Jotikray, Akbar deferred seeing the prince for thirty-one days – this belief is still prevalent in India that a son born after a period of long waiting would bring luck to the family if the father avoids seeing him for a lunar month. After the expiry of the period when the stars and the moon were in astrologically propitious position, Akbar went to Sikri for the blessings of Shaikh Salim Chisti.[6] Jahangir describes even a transit of sun on the day of *Nauruz*. He was very much aware of the fact that from the first day of the *Nauruz* to the 19th degree of the

Ram i.e. a zodiaq sign of Aries and the sun passed from the constellation of the Fish (Pieces) to the house of Honour in the constellation of the Ram (Aries).[7] This moment was also chosen by the astrologers.[8] It means that he understood the process of the transition of Sun with astronomical perspective. He always liked Akbar, performed weighing ceremony on his birthday according to solar and lunar years.[9] Jahangir further provides some information about the same ceremonies[10] of Princes. He narrates that it was the rule of Akbar to have himself weighed twice every year according to solar and lunar year and to have the princes weighed according to solar and lunar year. Thus, the same practice was adopted by Jahangir. On the 16th birthday of Khurram (Shahjahan) according to lunar year, the astrologers and astronomers predicted that according to Shahjahan's horoscope a most important period would occur regarding Prince's health. He further adds that the order was released to weigh the prince according to the prescribed rule against gold, silver and other metals and distributed among *faqirs* and the needy persons.

Jahangir was aware about the division of Hindu into four castes i.e., *Brahmin, Kshatriyas, Vaishya,* and *Shudra.*[11.] Each caste had its own festival such as *Rakhi, Vijaydashami, Diwali* and *Holi* respectively. He even discussed the month of the festival and its zodiac sign (means the sign in which sun is placed). He narrates that *Rakhi*, the festival of the Brahmins occurs in the month of Tir (*Sawan*) when sun is in the constellation of *Cancer, Vajyadashmi*, the festival of the Kshatriya, falls in the month of Shahriwar (*Ashwin*) when sun is in the zodiac sign of Virgo. The third festival *Diwali*, the festival of Vaishya, occurs in the month of Mihr (*Kartik*), when sun is in the constellation of Libra and the fourth caste Shudra was having the fesvital of Holi in the month of Isfandarmuz (*Phalgun*) when the sun is in the constellation of Pisces.

Jahangir further provides information of the occurrence of comets, fall of *meteorites* and eclipses. He has also discussed the astronomical reason behind the occurrence. Shireen Moosvi opines that Jahangir's interesting description of the comet of 1618 seems to be based on careful observation.[12]

Jahangir gives an account[13] of a luminous vapour in his Memoirs. He writes that some days before, on 18 Aban, 13 regnal years (i.e., 3 November 1618), a luminous vapour in the shape of a pillar appeared at three *gharies* before sunrise. At this moment, Jahangir was at

Ramgarh. He further narrates that every night it rose one *ghari* earlier. At its full form, it took the shape of spear thin at the ends and thick in the middle, curbing like a sickle. Its rear was towards the south, the front towards the north. Jahangir mentions that at the time of his writing, it rose full one *pahr* (one fourth of the night) before sunrise. Astronomers observed its shape, by using their astrolabes, and ascertained the difference of appearance and it extended over 24 degrees. While it moved in the Universe, it was initially a scorpio, a zodiac sign, then moved into another zodiac sign, i.e., Libra. As the Comet faded sixteen days after the recording by Jahangir, a star appeared in its position with faded tail two or three yards long.

Shireen Moosvi writes[14] that "the way Jahangir describes about this comet, shows little trepidation on his part at the appearance of this ominous sign. He informs us that the astrologers in their books called this type of comet spear like (*harba*) and had recorded that its appearance means weakness of the rulers of Arabia and the victory of their enemies against them". Mùtemad Khan gives[15] the same detail of the comet, but describes its other ill effects, such as it caused an unprecedented plague epidemic which had anticipated its appearance by a year and lingered on for many years. He even considers the rebellion of Khurram (Shahjahan) in 1622 A.D., a consequence of this comet's appearance, and so concludes that there was much bloodshed and no household remained unaffected by its apperance.

Eclipses

Jahangir mentions two solar eclipses and one lunar eclipse in his Memoirs. He gives the date of the first eclipse as 28 Ramazan A. H. 1028 (14 December 1610) and the other one as Sunday, 9 Rabi, I, 1024 corresponding to 8 April 1615. Jahangir though has not given the detailed description about the solar eclipse of December 1610; he has only mentioned the remedies to wave off the evil effects of eclipse. He further writes that he weighed himself against precious metals and gave away these and other articles and animals in alms at Agra and at other places.[16]

Another solar eclipse which occurred in 1615 A.D. is discussed more elaborately by Jahangir. Perhaps, it was a near total eclipse. He writes that the eclipse began 12 *Gharis* after sunrise, beginning from the west. At the maximum extent of the eclipse, four fifths of the sun was covered as seen from Agra, and the eclipse lasted about 8

Gharis. Precious metals, animals and cereals were distributed among the needy and poor people.[17]

Jahangir also mentions one lunar eclipse,[18] which was a total eclipse and occurred on Saturday, 13 Shawwal A.H. 1018 (20 January 1609). It began 4 *Gharis* after sunset and gradually moon was covered, and it lasted for 5 *Gharis* of the night. He further mentions that on this occasion, he weighed himself against gold, silver, cloth, grain and these things and animals`worth rupees 15000, were distributed among the poor people to remove the evil effects of eclipse.

Thus, the above descriptions show Jahangir's beliefs and his interest in astronomical sciences. Jahangir's strong beliefs in astronomical phenomenon can be seen even in his daily life, as was in the case of his father and grandfather. He always used to start journeys according to the auspicious position of stars. He even used to enquire about auspicious moments even for his hunting excursions and to enter the capital Agra after his journey. He always used to consult astrologers for auspicious moments before moving to battlefield. Pandit Jotikray was one of his court astrologers. Jahangir was very much impressed with the astrological knowledge of Jotikray like his father Akbar. Pandit Jotikray had been felicitated for many times by Jahangir for his services. Here, some related references can be cited from his Memoirs.

One of the instances relates to Sunday, the 17th of the Divine Month of Farwardin, 15th regnal year of Jahangir.[19] Shah Shuja, a son of Prince Khurram, was playing in the royal palace. There was a window with a screen in front of it looking towards the river. While playing the prince went towards the window to look out and accordingly fell down. As per chance, a carpet was laid down below the wall by carpet spreader. The prince's head struck the carpet from the height of ordinary ten yards. But by the grace of God, no harm happened to his limbs that was amazing. Jahangir further writes that for God's grace and for the act of goodness, he ordered to distribute alms to deserving and poor people of the city. Jahangir also admitted[20] that three or four months before this event, Jotikray, the astrologer, who was one of the most skilled in astrology, had predicted from the prince's horoscope that "next three or four months would be unpropitious to him and probably he might fall down from some high place, but no calamity would touch his life". He writes that his prognostications had repeatedly proved correct.

Another occurrence is mentioned[21] by Jahangir in his 16th regnal year i.e., 1621 A.D. He narrates that in those days, Shah Shuja again was in trouble as he had an eruption so violent that he was not even able to drink the water. All the astrologers were unanimous that he would not live, as it had been recorded in his father's horoscope that his son would die this year. But, on the contrary, Jotikray said that no calamity would be for his life as Jahangir had a great affection for Shah Shuja, and no trouble or distress had been recorded in Jahangir's horoscope in that year. Thus, no calamity would happen to Shah Shuja, but some other child would die. Jahangir writes that Jotikray's prediction proved true. Shah Shuja remained safe but another son, that Shahjahan had by the daughter of Shah-Nawaj Khan, died at Burhanpur. Jahangir admitted that a number of predictions made by Jotikray had turned out correct. As a reward, Jahangir ordered Jotikray to be weighed against money and thus, Rs.6,500 were given to him as reward.

In the 17th year of his reign, Jahangir mentions [22] another instance which shows his beliefs in the impact of astrology. He writes with astonishment that when a pearl worth Rs. 14,000 or 15,000 was lost in the *harem*, again, Jotikray represented that it would be found in two or three days. Sadiq Khan Rammal and a female, who were soothsayer also predicted the same thing. It happened in the same manner, and on the third day, a Turkish girl found it in the oratory and handed over it to Jahangir. Jahangir announced rewards to all the three astrologers.

Choice of an Auspicious Hour in Daily Life

Jahangir himself admits at several places in his memoirs that an auspicious hour was often sought by him before doing some important work. He always used to consider the auspicious hour to decide any important matter, to enter his capital, or to depart for a battlefield or any other like object. He never forgot to consult an astronomer for it. While he was pursuing his rebellious son, Khusrao, Jahangir could not consult his astronomer. He writes[23] that he was not held back even for ascertaining the auspicious hour etc. and could not take rest until Khusrao was captured. But Jahangir could not resist the temptation of taking astrological advice on the way as he further writes that after he had set out from the capital, he asked Hakim Ali, who was learned in the subject, how the hour of the departure had been, whether it was propitious or not. Hakim Ali replied affirmative.

Jahangir always entered his capital Agra or any other city in an auspicious hour.[24] He even used to postpone his arrival time to Agra due to inauspicious time. He used to fix hours for hunting according to calculation of planets.[25] He used to make appointments of his officers in auspicious moments. To site an example he writes, at one place in his memoirs that 'at the hour when *Mushtari* (Jupiter) was propitious, he appointed Mir Qasim, son of Mirza Murad as the chief paymaster and news-writer'.[26] Similarly, he at another place writes that on the auspicious day, an order was given to issue royal *firman*. It was issued for the appointment of revenue collectors for the transfers of Jahangir Quli Khan and Ibrahim Khan Fath-Jang to Bihar and Bengal respectively.[27]

Jahangir had immense reliance on the predictions made by the Hindu astrologer, Jotikray. Jahangir never went out, be it an excursion, a hunt, or a military campaign without Jotikray. Jotikray used to follow him in a palanquin in almost all his visits or march to various places. Jotikray used to give the time and date of pitching tents, crossings of rivers and bridges, entering the cities and indeed of every major event. Jahangir consulted him about the propitiousness of time for all his public engagements. Army commander also took Jotikray's assent before carrying any proposal to the emperor. Jahangir's desire to be always on the right side of the Sun, the moon and the stars gained strength by the proved infallibility of Jotikray's predictions. Nurjahan, too depended on his advice. The Brahmin astrologer never exploited his knowledge for personal gain. Jahangir considered him a guru, a saint san parallel.[28]

Jahangir also had faith in good and bad omens. Thus, he cites an example of Mutaqid Khan, a *Mansabdar* who had bought a house at Agra and spent some days in that place. But the house proved unfortunate for him.[29] Jahangir writes about an established custom to know the prosperity or bad luck attached to a house. He also confesses that prosperity and bad luck depended on four things, a wife, a slave, a house, and a horse. He also considered some days auspicious and other inauspicious, thus Wednesday was called *Kham Shambah* and Thursday *Mubarak Shambah*.[30]

Terry, a European traveller, writes, "Jahangir's confidence in astrologers was very great. Neither any journey was undertaken, nor any resolve made, nor any undertaking begun unless the astrologer was consulted".[31] Pelsert remarks that the emperor kept Brahmin astrologers at his court, "whose forecast had often proved to be correct".[32] .

Shahjahan (1627 A.D. to 1657 A.D.)

The history of Shahjahan can be derived from the Badshah-Nama of Abdul Hamid Lahori and from other Badshah-Namas and Shah *Jahan-Namas.*[33] Being proud by nature, Shahjahan was very anxious to see that the annals of his reign were handed down to posterity in glorious language.[34] Hence, he appointed various official historian to write *Badshahnamas* and *Shajahan-Namas*. Abdul Hamid Lahori was one of the official historians. He came up to the expectations of Shahjahan. According to Muhamad Shadiq, he was a follower of Abul Fazl's style of writings.[35] He himself accepted it in the preface of his writings. So, he has given a description of the emperor's horoscope as well as a brief review of the proceedings of Shahjahan's accession to the throne.[36] It seems to be based entirely on the pattern of Abul Fazl's writings.

Shahjahan too took a keen interest in astronomy and astrology. He had his court astrologers, who used to give him advice. His minister, Asaf Khan, proposed to make the year of Shahjahan's accession the beginning of another new era, called '*Tarikh-i-Illahi Shah Jahani*'. Accordingly, a royal command was issued to Mulla Farid Ibrahim Dehlavi to prepare a new *Zij*. Mulla Farid did not have sufficient time for fresh observations, so his *Zij* was to be based on the table of Ulugh Beg, which however, was subjected to many corrections and improvements.[37]

Shahjahan believed in the influence of astrological and astronomical sciences in his daily life. He used to take decisions according to the calculation of the position of stars like his grandfather Akbar. Abdul Hamid Lahori has given a detailed analytical description of the planetary positions of Shahjahan's horoscope, but he has not reproduced the copy of the exact horoscope in *Badshahnama.*[38] According to the description of Shahjahan's horoscope, which was drawn up by Mulla Ala'u-i-Mulk of Tun in Khurasan. Shahjahan was born under the libra sign, the sign under which the Prophet was born.[39] Abul Fazl also writes that the horoscope of Shahjahan under the Libra zodiaq sign. But according to Hindu astrologers, Shahjahan was born under the Virgo zodiaq sign as ascendant. Munshi Devi Prasad mentions his horoscope as follows:[40.]

The date of his birth is mentioned as Samvat 1748 *Shaka* 1513 *Magh Sudi*, Wednesday, *ghati* 37-53 (Rabi-usmani, 1000 Hizri). The difference in terms of *Ghari* and *Pahar* can be noted in the descriptions of horoscope given in *Akbarnama* and *Badshahnama*. The birth time, according to *Akbarnama*, is 4 hours, 24 minutes of the day, while it is 5 hours, 14 minutes, and 20 seconds according to *Badshahnama*.[41]

Lagan Chart

According to Hindu Astrologers

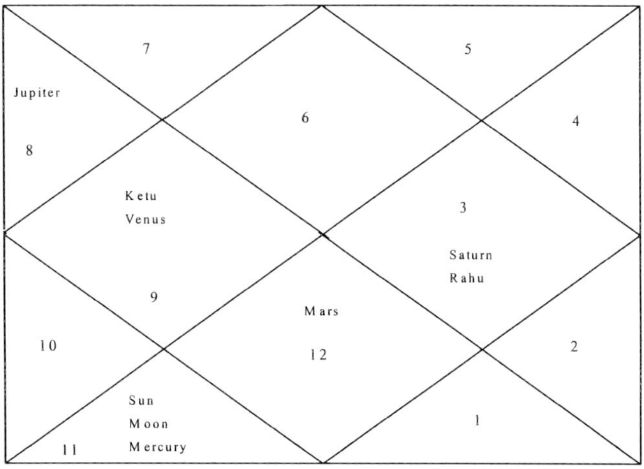

According to Muslim Astrologers

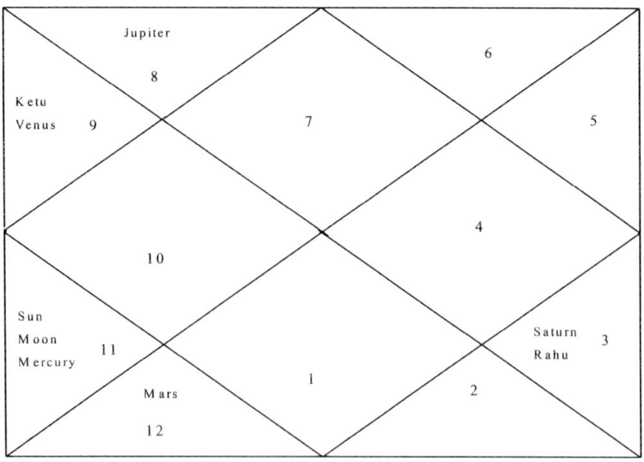

The impact of astrology was also considered with regard to matrimonial alliances. Shahjahan consulted Muslim as well as Hindu astrologers for performing the matrimonial proceedings. The auspicious moment for the *Nikah* of Dara Sikoh was fixed as two *pahar* and six *ghari* of the night. Shahjahan also ordered Makrmat Khan to fix the time of marriage of Shahzada Mohd. Shuza. And both Hindu and Muslim astrologers had fixed 22 Feb. 1633 as the auspicious date for the marriage of Shah Shuza.

Another instance of the impact of astrology is mentioned in '*Shahjahanama*'. In the month of October 1648 A.D., when Shahjahan had gone for prey, he received two letters, one from Khwas Khan of Kandhar and another from Gairat Khan of Bihist. Both informed about the expedition of the King of Iran to conquer Kandhar and arrival of his army at *Meshad*. As soon as Shahjahan heard this news, he ordered astrologers to calculate the auspicious moment and accordingly, an order was sent to Qazi Afzal (who was a *hakim* of Dara Shikoh) to stop Shahkuli who was proceeding towards Lahore. Shahjahan according to astrological calculation, also ordered Aurangzeb to proceed towards Lahore. Shahkuli was an ambassador of the Shah of Iran. Later on, Shahjahan, considering to astrological calculation, also ordered Aurangzeb to proceed towards Kandhar.[42]

In February 1652 A.D. Shahjahan planned to proceed toward Kabul. The auspicious moment was calculated, according to planets, as the 15th of Feb. 1652, Sunday at night. Shahjahan also suggested the same moment to prince Aurangzeb to march from Multan to conquer Kandhar. Accordingly, Aurangzeb left Multan at the fixed moment.[43]

Shahjahan, like Akbar, used to perform weighing ceremony on his birthday according to solar as well as lunar months. He also used to promote his higher officials and distribute precious jems, metals and cloths among the needy people on this occasion.[44] On his solar birthdays, the emperor was weighed against twelve things, once against gold and eleven times against other articles such as silk, silver, perfumes, rice, milk, salt etc.[45] He was also very particular about his horoscope and auspicious hours also took his seat on the Peacock throne at a proper time fixed by astrologers.[46]

It is noteworthy that *Zij-i-Rahimi* and *Zij-i-Shahjahani* were composed by Fariduddin Masud b. Ibrahim Dehlavi under the patronage of Shahjahan.[47] *Zij-i-Shahjahani* was the first Indian *Zij* which was translated in 1630 into Sanskrit under the title

'*Siddhantasindhu*' by the Hindu Court astronomer of Shahjahan, Nityanand, for the emperor's minister Asaf Khan. Nityanand also wrote another astronomical treatise in Sanskrit i.e., '*Sarvasiddhantraja*' in 1639 A.D.[48] The *Parasiprakasa*, also known as *Samskrta Praasiba-Raclina*, is a Persian-Sanskrit Dictionary of astronomical or astrological terms composed by Malajit in 1643. Malajit was bestowed with the title of 'Vedangaraya'.

Aurangzeb (1658 A.D. to 1707 A.D.)

Aurangzeb was a great puzzle to his contemporaries; we are hardly in a position to understand him correctly.[49] Lane-Poole describes Aurangzeb as 'a puzzling compound of contradictions'. Bernier found him 'reserved, subtle and a complete Master of Arts of dissimulation. He was an idealist Sunni Muslim and had an orthodox bent of mind. He was a follower of the doctrines of the Imam Abu Hanifa and established the fundamental doctrines of Kauz.[50] We do not find even a single instance of his life, which can show his indulgence in astronomical and astrological sciences. But it seems that in early years of his age, though he was not under influence of such beliefs, he never tried to condemn these sciences. He seems to have followed all rituals practiced by his ancestors.[51]

One of the instances can be mentioned here: On 15th Feb. 1652, Shahjahan planned to proceed towards Kabul, as per the auspicious moment calculated astrologically. So, Aurangzeb was also ordered by his father to leave Multan to conquer Kandhar. Aurangzeb had to leave Multan at the fixed moment. He never seems to be opposed to or condemned his father's beliefs.[52] He also did not condemn the weighing ceremonies on lunar and solar birth dates.

Aurangzeb's first coronation took place on 22 July 1658. He took his seat on the throne of the Empire of Hindustan after saying his prayers and at an auspicious time[53] and his second coronation was celebrated on 5 June 1659. With the passage of time, he identified him with the Islamic fanaticism.[54] First of all, he banned the celebration of the '*Noroze*' festival in the court. This festival was supposed to be the first day of the new year by Parsians, because on this day the Sun enters into Aries, a zodiac sign, indicating the 'exalted position of Sun'. We have seen that his ancestors used to celebrate this day with grand festivity.[55] Hence, it implies that he was reluctant to give importance to such astronomical events.

However, in spite of staunch fanaticism Aurangzeb could not shake off the old custom entirely. He admitted in his writing that he weighed himself against gold on his birth days and distributed it amongst the poor.[56] Sometimes, he showed a firm belief in his horoscope. Aurangzeb wrote that the pages of his horoscope composed by Fazil Khan, have all been verified by actual experience.[57]

During this period, people in general were superstitious and had belief in things supernatural. Aurangzeb himself could not escape from such beliefs. He used to worship the so- called footprints and hairs of Prophet Mohammad.[58] Aurangzeb also believed in myth and rituals. Manucci records some rituals, which were observed by Aurangzeb to do away with some evil effect. He writes that after ascending the throne, he continued the practice of sacrificing *pimiento* (pepper) which he had begun while serving in the Dceean as a prince. While performing the rite he would take a handful of *pimientos* (pepper) and having offered a prayer, threw it on some live charcoal, and it was allowed to smoke for some moments. Then, the charcoal and the pimiento were taken out and thrown on some mound. It was performed on every Friday.[59]

The above references indicate that in spite of Aurangzeb's fanaticism, he was not averse to contemporary astrological practices.

Sawai Jai Singh II (A.D. 1686 to 1743) and His Astronomical Contribution

Sawai Jai Singh II of Jaipur, born in 1686, succeeded the throne at the age of thirteen in 1699 A.D.[60] It is true that he neither acquired much fame as a military commander, nor was he ever a pillar of the empire as were his predecessors like Raja Mansingh and Mirza Raja Jai Singh I.[61] However, he could make Jaipur the busiest centre of learning of those times. He, in fact, had a versatile and amazing power to plan for peaceful arts and astronomical sciences, in the middle age of anarchy in India.[62] In his time, many foreign astronomers from Baveria, France and Portugal, frequently visited his court. These astronomers used to bring along with them maps, charts and latest works on astronomy published in Europe.[63]

The Indian astronomy, at his time, has developed into two branches – Hindu astronomy and Muslim astronomy, and both were different in method, scope, and utility. The major aspects that were considered relevant to the astronomy of the time were first, there was the need for a calendar to predict time for agricultural operations, festivals, and religious functions, as most of the religious functions are connected with the lunar calendar. And secondly, there was a need for fixed dates for the purpose of administration, which could be based on solar calendar.[64]

Thus, Jai Singh gives three main reasons[65] for preoccupation with astronomical observations. The first was the inaccuracy of the existing calendars, namely the Gurgani, Ilkhani and Ilahi calendars. These calendars were the result of the efforts of Tusi, Ulugh Beg and Mulla Chand respectively.[66] Secondly, since the "affairs of religion and administration of the empire" depended upon the correct calendar, there was a need to revise the calendar. Lastly, Jai Singh points out the prevalent disagreements on the time of rising and setting of planets, the beginning and end of seasons, and the timing of eclipses of the sun and moon. For the purpose, he tried to persuade Mughal emperor Muhammad Shah to agree to the reform of the calendar and to reintroduce the secular calendar like Akbar. He also built astronomical observatories at five principal cities of Hindustan. He also conceived and carried out a scheme of scientific research for the purpose that is still a notable example.[67] In the words of Tod, "the observatories, he erected, are monuments that irradiate a dark period of Indian History".[68] He took every means to achieve the success in his objects. He tried to study Hindu, Muslim, and European methods impartially. He collected astronomical books and translated a few of them. He sent some of his staff workers to foreign countries to collect information. He also invited some Europeans, who were interested in astronomy, to Jaipur. First of all, he built a large observatory at Delhi and made careful observations there for seven years with a view to the preparation of a new star catalogue. Subsequently, he built some other observatories at Jaipur, Ujjain, Benaras and Mathura.

Here, it is important to know about the sources of Jai Singh's astronomical knowledge. It is evident in the contemporary works of Jai Singh, that he was acquainted with Ptolemy's Almagest, also known as "Syntaxis or Al Majista in Arabic translation. He also studied the astronomical tables of Ulugh Beg, some treatise on astrolabe, Lathire's '*Tabulae Astronomicae*' and Flamsteed's *Historia Coelesties Britannica*, also some western mathematical works such as Euclid's Elements and other available material at that time.[69]

Jai Singh was ably assisted in his work by Samrat Jagannath, a Maratha Brahmin, who was invited by Jai Singh in his early days from Maharashtra. Jagannath had a good knowledge of Arabic, Persian and Sanskrit. Jai Singh translated Ptolemy's Syntaxis into Sanskrit with the assistance of Jagannath under the title '*Siddhanta Sara Kaustubh*'. Jagannath was also the author of the '*Samrat-Siddhanta*' as well as the *Rekha Ganit*, a translated work from the Arabic of Euclid's Elements of Geometry. He was held in high esteem by Raja Jai Singh.[70]

Pundit Kewal Ram was another learned Gujrati Uddambri Brahman, who collaborated with Jai Singh. Pundit Kewal Ram was the author of a number of Sanskrit books i.e., *Jiv Vinod*, *Vibhag Sarni* (logarithmic tables), *Mithya Jivachhaya Sarni*, *Drig Paksh Sarni* (a translation of la Hire's tables), *Tara Sarni* (Ulugh Beg's Tables) and *Brahma Paksh Niras*. Another trusted colleague of Jai Singh was Pundaric Ratnakar, who came from Maharashtra. He was the author of *Jai Singh Kalpadrum*. All these learned men were rewarded generously with gifts of land and money by Raja Jai Singh.

It is very interesting to note that while Jai Singh was busy with these projects, a revolution took place in European astronomy. The remarkable works of Copernicus, Keplar, Tycho Brahe Galileo, and Newton had great significance in the field of astronomical sciences.[71] Jai Singh might not have been untouched with this new knowledge. He had collected all material related to the subject from distant lands. He also procured all available sources of astronomy from Muslim lands through Muhammad Sharif and Muhammad Mehdi. On the other hand, he contacted with the Portuguese to be acquainted with the European astronomy. As a result, Padre Manuel de-Figueiredo was sent from Goa to Jaipur in 1730 A.D. Then, he was sent to Europe to procure books and instruments for Raja Jai Singh. He was accompanied by Padro da Silva Leitao from Goa. Jai Singh also invited two French Jesuits to his capital Jaipur. Jai Singh also obtained the maps and globes of the '*Feringhese*' from the British at Surat. Another two Bavarian Jesuits, Father Andre Strobel and Antoline Gabelsperger were also at Jaipur. Two priests came from Chandernagar to Jaipur at Jai Singh's request.[72]

Jai Singh's chief astronomer Jagannath says that Jai Singh was clever in exhibiting new methods with globes and other instruments and he had made observations of the stars with the help of certain learned mathematicians and astronomers. Some instruments related to an observatory;[73] is mentioned as follows:

1. *Nadi Yantra* (Sun-dial)
2. *Gola Yantra* (Sphere)
3. *Digamsa Yantra* (azimuth instrument)
4. *Dakhshino Digbhitt* (Mural Quadrant)
5. *Vritta Shashtamsaka* (an arc of sixty degree placed in the meridian)
6. *Samrat Yantra* (an equinoctial dial) 'the best among the instruments'
7. *Jaya Prakash*, the crest jewel of all instruments

Jai Singh also prepared a set of asronomical tables, known as "*Zij Muhammad Shahi*" after the name of Emperor Muhammad Shah which is divided into three parts.[74] The first part deals with a Calendar, the second with practical astronomy and the last with planetary motion.

The first part consists of four chapters, and it discusses various calendars which were prevalent in India, viz., the Indian, Islamic, Christian and his own, i.e., Muhammad Shahi. It also contains a method to convert the data of one calendar to others. This was very important historically as well as to know the correctness of dates under different calendars, which created confusion in those days.

The second part deals with astronomy. It discusses the problems of practical astronomy and spherical trigonometry, such as the inclination of the ecliptic, determination of coordinates of heavenly bodies, method for determination of the meridian, latitude and longitude and the measurement of the distances between planets and stars.

The last part of the book is extremely remarkable as it throws light on the nature of planetary orbits. It states that the orbits of the planets are elliptical, in contrast to the accepted notion of orbit as being circular. It also states the heliocentricity of the system, in contrast to the common beliefs of those days.

A Soviet scholar, Sobirov, analyses the contribution of Jai Singh in his work.[75] He narrates that the study of the works of Sawai Jai Singh shows that his scientific school gave not only a new direction to the growth of the mathematics and astronomy but also resulted in a number of fundamental discoveries.

On the basis of the planets and their satellites, a telescope, made at Jaipur, seems to be used by Jai Singh.[76] He had collected a large number of artisans at Jaipur, who were making a number of instruments for him. There was a foundry and mint at Jaipur Jantar Mantar and the pavilion of mirror at Amber testifies to the skill then available in mirror making. The optical glass for the telescope could be easily made with the help of such a skill.[77]

Jai Singh's observatories were undoubtedly the best built in India till his time and many of his instruments were indeed unique. G.P. Kaye says[78] that these observatories and the various instruments constructed by Jai Singh are an appropriate monument to "one of the brightest intellects of India".

But Bindraban informs us in his '*Safina-Khushgo*', "now a days Mulla Abul Khair popularly known as Khair Allah is unrivalled in astronomy, engineering, and other branches of learning. On several observatories, Sawai Jai Singh spent twenty lakh rupees in twenty years under the supervision of Abul Khair.[79]

Astronomical Development in Mughal India

During the Mughal period astronomy was considered to be the most important subject of mathematical sciences. In astronomy, the Muslim tradition of instrumental technology survived in India until the middle of the eighteenth century. Lahore seems to have been the centre for making astrolabes where a single family produced astrolabe makers, generation after generation from the time of Humayun to Aurangzeb. Thus, Sheikh Allahadad flourished in Humayun's time, his son Mulla Isa in Akbar's, his son Qaim Mohammad in Jahangir's and Qaim's son Zainuddin Muhammad in Shahjahan and Aurangzeb's time.[80] Numerous astrolabes and celestial globes were manufactured by the Lahore family.[81] Syed Sulaiman Nadvi has brought to light the family of astrolabe makers at Lahore, who were active in the field from the reign of Humayun to Aurangzeb.[82] More than one hundred instruments, signed by seven members of this family belonging to four successive generations have been discovered nowadays. In the entire history of scientific instrumentation in the Middle Ages, there has been no other family comparable to this one in the long continuous family tradition, in immense work production and in innovative technical designs.

S. R. Sarma[83] has given an account of the achievements of this family as well as the function of the astrolabe and celestial globe. He writes that the astrolabe and celestial globe are two most important astronomical instruments invented in Hellenistic antiquity. These two instruments were adopted by Islamic world, where they were preserved, elaborated upon, and disseminated westward to Europe and eastwards to India.

The astrolabe, known as '*Asturlab*' in Arabic, is a versatile instrument for observation and computation. Here, the great circles and other circles, the star positions etc., are drawn on a plane of two dimensions by a method called stereographic projection which was known already to Hipperchus in the second century B.C. The astrolabe consists of two principal parts. First the rete, known as *Ankabut*' in Arabian, which is an openwork circular disc, containing stereographic projection of the ecliptic and of the position of some prominent fixed stars. The second part, called tympan or plate or disc, known as *Safiha* in Arabian, represents the sky as seen from the observer's latitude. It contains stereographic projections of the equator, the tropics and equal altitude curves, known as *al-mucantera* and *azimuth* lines in Arabic. There are also curves to measure time, in seasonal hours, or in equal hours. Some Islamic astrolabes contain additional curves to indicate the prayer times. The rete and the set of tympans are accommodated in the hollow space of thicker disc with a raised rim, which is named appropriately as a mater, known as '*Unum,*' in Arabic. On the inner side of the matter, there is usually a geographical gazetteer. The matter is surmounted by a crown like triangular projection called '*Kursi*', to which are attached a shackle, a ring, and a cord for suspending the astrolabe. Often the *Kursi* and the rete are highly decorated. The back of the matter, known as '*Zahr,*' in Arabic is divided into four quadrants. Each of these contains various trignometric scales and astrological tables. This is the observational part of the astrolabes. It also measures the altitude of the sun in daytime, or the altitude of some prominent fixed star at night. When the rete is adjusted according to these values, it simulates the starry heavens upon the observer's place. Then, one can read off from the dialing the time, and also note the times of prayer. The ascendant for the particular moment can also be directly read off and the other points on the ecliptic, can also be read-off without resorting to complicated calculations. The knowledge of these points on the ecliptic is essential for casting the horoscopes, or for determining the auspiciousness or otherwise of given moment. More important, the astrolabes work as an analog computer, and can be used to solve a number of trignometrical problems. These astrolabes can be used in land surveying for determining the heights or depths of objects and calculating the distances. Further, S.R. Sarma writes that it was thought that the person who held the astrolabes in his hands, was in fact, holding the secrets of the universe. Therefore, any person who owned or understood the astrolabe, was highly esteemed throughout the medieval world.

The celestial globe was relatively a latecomer to India. Although it was a standard instrument of teaching astronomy in the *madrasas*, it was not mentioned in Indian context until the time of Humayun. He adopted using both the astrolabes and the celestial globes. Two interesting anecdotes speak about his interest in these instruments. But no celestial globes manufactured at the time of Humayun survived either.

The celestial globe, known as *Al-Kura* in Arabian, consists of a spherical globe made usually of brass on which the celestial equator, ecliptic, tropics, and other circles are plotted. Upon this grid are marked the positions of about 1020 fixed stars either according to the coordinates given by Ptolomy in his *Almagest* or by Ulugh Begh in his tables or by any other subsequent astronomer. Often, the figures of the twelve signs of the zodiac and also the figures of another thirty- six constellations, like the bear, as conceived in the Hellenistic and Islamic traditions, are drawn with greater ingenuity. The celestial globe is mounted on a stand consisting of a horizontal ring and a vertical ring, these two acting as the local horizon and meridian respectively. When the axis of globe is adjusted according to the local latitude, the hemisphere visible above the horizontal ring would resemble the starry sky above the viewers' latitude. Thus, the celestial globe makes an excellent teaching instrument.

Most of the earliest surviving astrolabes and celestial globes are linked with Lahore family. The patriarch of the family was called Allahdad. Two astrolabes, made by him, survive today. The first is dated 1567 A.D. and the second is not dated. But both are signed by him as "Ustad Allahdad Asturlabi Lahuri'. Through the astrolabes, signed by Allahdad's descendents, we can also trace the history of this family from 1567 to 1691. Allahdad's son Isa is known through three astrolabes produced between the years 1600 and 1604. He had two sons, Qasim Muhammad, and Muhammad Muqim. The instruments made by Qasim Muhammad are dated from 1609 to 1637. Consequently, this period coincides with the reign of Jahangir.

Qasim was, in fact, patronised by Nawab Abul Hasan, brother of Nurjahan Begum. He made six astrolabes and four celestial globes. Two of these astrolabes were made jointly in association with his brother Muqim. He is said to have perfected the art of casting celestial globes in one piece through wax process. About 37 astrolabes were made by him in between the year 1609 to 1659.

Ziya-al-Din Muhammad, the son of Qasim Muhammad, was the most prolific and versatile member of this family. During 1645 to 1680, he seems to have produced about 32 astrolabes and 16 celestial globes. Hamid and Jamal-al-Din were two sons of Muqim Muhammad. Both of them had made a great contribution in the production of astrolabes and celestial globes during the period of 1666 to 1691. After this period, a gradual decline can be seen in the quality of production. But we can say that every instrument manufactured by the members of this family exhibits fine workmanship in metal and a high degree of artistic excellence. As A. J. Turner also rightly puts it, "The multiplication of complexity and a delight in the unusual seem to be typical of the astrolabe-makers of Lahore".[84]

Some instruments had engraved names of nobles, that indicates the support or patronage of the nobles also. One of the earliest celestial globes made by Qasim Mohammad in the reign of Jahangir in 1622 was patronised by Nawab I'tiquad Khan, a brother of Nurhajan Begum. He also designed an exquisite astrolabe for Nawab Abul Hasan, another brother of Nur Jahan Begum. Perhaps this is the only astrolabe where calligraphy is fully incorporated into the design of the rete. Ziya-al-Din, son of Qasim designed an unusual celestial globe for Muhyi-al-Din Muhammad Aurangzeb Bahadur Alamgir and a universal astrolabe for Nawab Iftikhar Khan, a *faujdar* of Jaunpur in 1679 and 1680 respectively. Some of these magnificient instruments were acquired by the astronomer Prince Swai Jai Singh in the early 18th century.[85]

A prominent instrument maker outside this family was Muhammad Sahib of Thatta, who produced three astrolabes and four globes between the years 1665 to 1677. But the average achievements of the Lahore family overshadowed those of others.

The astrolabes, produced in fine workmanship by the family of Isa b. Allahdad in Lahore in the reign of Jahangir, was used by the astronomers of Maharaja Sawai Jai Singh II (1686-1743) at his observatories in Delhi, Jaipur, Ujjan, Varanashi and Mathura.[86]

Though Jai Singh's principal astronomer was Jagannath, he made full use of European and Islamic ideas. In particular his massive masonry quadrants and dials, constructed to get maximum accuracy, closely follow the precedent set by the Samarkand observatory of Ulugh Beg.[87]

The Development of *Zij* Astronomy in Medieval India

As mentioned earlier in Chapter I, the '*Zij*' is derived from the Persian word *Zig* meaning thread, especially warp and woof of a carpet. Due to similarities between warp and woof of a carpet with astronomical tables, the books on these tables are named *Zij*. In Arabic its plural forms are Aziya and *Zij*at. This word has entered Greek and Latin languages as *Zich* or *Ezich*.[88]

It has been discussed earlier that there were three types of *Zijes*:

1. *Zij-e-Rashadi* (direct tables) based on actual observations.
2. *Zij-e-Hasabi* (calculated tables) obtained by correcting observational tables for errors, precession, etc.
3. *Zij-e-Tas-hil* (simplified tables) which were the simplified versions of other tables-like the one which could deal with the Moon alone.

A brief discussion of the transmission of Islamic Astronomy into Medieval India, may be attempted here. A specific feature of Islamic Astronomy was the effort to develop observational/practical astronomy rigorously, which led to the compilation of about 250 *Zijes*; the astronomical-mathematical tables used for the positional astronomy of the Sun, Moon, planets and then known 'fixed' stars.[89] To that purpose, a number of famous observatories were established in Islamic countries which may mention here briefly:[90].

> The *Zij* period began in Baghdad under the auspices of the Abbasid Caliphate. To place the astronomical development of the period in the political context, we may note the sequence of the early Abbasid Caliphs: Al-Saffah (750-54), Al Mansur (754-74), Al-Mahdi (775-85), Al-Hadi (785-86), Harun Al-Rashid (786-809) and Al-Mamun (813-33).

As already discussed in earlier chapter that the *Zij* Astronomy first started with the translation of the Sanskrit and Greek texts into Arabic. The name of an Indian astronomer Kankah-al-Hindi was recorded by the Arabic bibliographical tradition but not known to Indian sources. He was probably the author of "*Ktab-Kankah Al-Hindi*" giving an astrological history of the Abbasids up to the reign of Al-Manum. Kankah was perhaps an astrologer who migrated from India to Baghdad. '*Brahmasphuta-Siddhanta*' and '*Aryabhatiyam*' were translated into Arabic as *Zij-Al-Sindhind Al-Kabir* by Al-Fazari and *Zij* Al-Arbhar respectively. Al-Mamun set up observatories in Baghdad and Damascus. The first Astronomical tables were prepared by translation from Sanskrit by Muhammad-ibu-Musa Al-Khwarizmi. His tables constituted a landmark in the history of astronomy and mathematics. One of the greatest *Zij* astronomers was Muhammad ibu-Jabir-ibu Sina Abu-Abdullah-Al-Battani. His own observations extending from 877 to 918 figure in his 'Az-*Zij-as-Sabi*'. He was the first to introduce the *Siddhantic* half-chords (sines) for half angles into his tables. Umar-Al-Khayyam, now better known as a poet than astronomer, was the director of an observatory built by Malik Shah of Saljuki dynasty. His work came to be known as *Zij*-e-Khayyam. The Mongol ruler Halaqu Khan set up an observatory at Maragha in Iran in AD 1258 under the direction of Nasir al-din Al-Tusi (1201-74) from Khurasan. His observations resulted as a '*Zij*-e *Ilkhani*'. A hundred years later, it was amended by Ghyathuddin Jamshid bin-Masud Al Kashi (1429) under the title *Zij*-e-Khaqani and completed at Samarqand where Al Kashi was invited to assist Ulugh Beg (1394-1449), the most outstanding observational astronomer of the medieval times. His work became as famous as the '*Almagest*'. His star catalogue was the first independent catalogue after Hipparchus (2 century B.C.). It formed the basis of most subsequent catalogues, and was even used by Johan Flamstead (1646-1719), the first Astronomer Royal at Greenwich observatory.

In Indian context, Ulugh Beg was well known for the collateral and paternal ancestor of the Mughal Emperors, the common link being Timur. Ulugh Beg's work was also called *Zij*-e-Gurgani after Gurgan, a title used by Timur, Babur in his autobiography proudly noted that Gurgani *Zij* was then used throughout the world.

The *Zij* astronomy was introduced in India through Al-Beruni (973-1048), the author of '*Zij-e-Masudi*'. India's first *Zij* was prepared by Mahmum bin-Umar. His work was called *Zij-e-Nasiri* (1246-65). As discussed in Chapter I, the *Zij* astronomy took root in India under the patronage of Firoz Shah Tughlaq. He himself is known to be an expert in making astrolabes. One of these astrolabes was placed on the highest *minar* of his capital Ferozabad at Delhi.

All cultural activities in Delhi, including astronomy, came to a halt as a result of Timur's invasion. All such activities were resumed with the establishment of Mughal Empire in India. Babur's son Humayun was an expert in using astrolabes, globes, and other instruments of the observatory. His astronomer Maulana Chand used an astrolabe to determine the time of Akbar's birth. Some references are found in *Zij-e-Shahjahani* and *Zij-e-Muhammad Shahi* that Chand prepared a Tas'hil or gloss on Ulugh Beg's *Zij*. However, no copy of it is known to exist.[91] According to Abul Fazl, there were 86 different *Zij*es known in Akbar's time.[92] Shahjahan's court astronomer Fariduddin Masud bin Hafiz Ibrahim Munajjim computed his *Zij-e-Shah Jahani* based on Ulugh Beg's observations. He also gave detailed classification of all *Zij*es compiled till his time. This *Zij* was translated into Sanskrit by Nityananda (c. 1639). Interestingly, Shah Jahan even toyed with the idea of setting up an observatory and asked Mullah-Muhammad Jaunpuri to prepare the plans. The idea, however, was given up because all the funds had to be diverted to build the tomb for queen Mumtaj Mahal.[93] In 18th century, we find Raja Sawai Jai Singh's contribution in Astronomy. His astronomer was Jagannath, who translated Al-Tusi's Arabic recension of *Almagest* into Sanskrit under the title '*Samrata-Siddhanta*'. *Zij-e-Muhammad Shahi* (completed 1728) was also an important contribution of Raja Jai Singh.

A brief introduction of 11 traced *Zij*es of Mughal period may be given here:

(1) Zij-e-Muzafar Shahi:

This *Zij*, anonymous, and undated, was composed in the reign of Sultan Muzaffar Shah, the ruler of Gujarat and dedicated to him around C.1511 – 1525 A.D. This was the Persian *Zij*, composed in India at the beginning of the reign of Babur.

(2) Zij-i-Rahimi:

It was composed by Fariduddin Mas'kd Dehlavi in 1627 A.D. The author died before finishing this work and his brother Mulla Tayyab Ibrahim completed it. This *Zij* comprises a preface and four chapters. The author explained Hijra, Alexandria, Persian and Khatai calendar. It also consists of tables of *sine* (*Jayb*) function of the first and the second declination, and of the ascensious of the zodiaq signs for diverse latitudes. The last two tables are calculated for the latitudes of Samarquand, Agra, Lahore and Burhan based on Ulugh Beg's astronomical table.

(3) Zij-i-Shah Jahani:

This *Zij* is also known as *Karanama-ye Sahib Kiran-I Thani* composed by Fariduddin Mas'ked b. Ibrahim Dehlavi, the author of previous *Zij*. It was composed during 1629-1630. *Zij-i-Shahjahani* is the oldest astronomical tables which give some information on Illahi calendar which was introduced by emperor Akbar and was employed also during Shahjahan's reign. These tables were prepared under the patronage of Yamin-al-Dawlah Asif Khan of Iranian origin, who was a minister of Shah Jahan. This *Zij* comprises many tables for the first and the second declination including tables for correcting them, and tables for ascensions of the zodical sign etc. All the tables are based on Ulugh Beg's astronomical tables.

(4) Zij-i-Muhammad Shahi Hindi:

It was an astronomical table of the Indian emperor Muhammad Shah. The author of this *Zij* is not known[94] and it was composed during the reign of Muhammad Shah (reigned 1719-1748).

(5) Zij-i-Muhammad Shahi or Zij-i-Jadid Muhammad Shahi:

Its author is Raja Jai Singh Sawai, and it was composed during 1727-28 in the reign of Muhammad Shah. This *Zij* had been very important, especially in Iran. More than A hundred years ago, it was mentioned in many annual calendars that this *Zij* has been the basis of their own calendar calculations. Because of its importance, many commentaries were written on it. The authors of these commentaries are Khayrullah Khan Muhandis, Abdullah Khan bin Asmuddin Muhammad Khan, Dust Muhammad Munajjin and Shar Muhammad Khan.

Zij-i-Muhammad Shahi is the most important *Zij*. It contains many tables, such as table for transforming different calendars into one another, table for sine, for the first and the second declination, for ascensious for geographical longitudes and latitudes of about 340 different cities, elongation tables of planets, tables for the visibility of Moon and tables for peculiarities of stars. The last tables are based upon the parameters mentioned in Zij-e-Ilkhani. It had influenced deeply Mirza Baqir Mulla Bashi Mazan darani, who composed a *Zij* in Persian.

The following *Zij*es out of the traced 11 *Zij*es were composed during later Mughal Period.

(6) Zij-i-Mir Alami:

It was composed by Safdar Khan b. Muhammad Hussain Khan la. Muhammad Ismail Shirazi and dedicated to the Minister Mir Alam. But the exact date of its composition is not known. As Mir Alam died in 1808, so it must have been written earlier.

(7) Zij-i-Ashki:

It was composed in 1816 by Raja Kundan Lal Ashki b. Mannu Lal Dehlavi.

(8) Zij-i-Bahadur Khani:

It is also known by the other names *Zij*-i-Bahaduri[95] and Rasad-i-Tughiyani. This is the latest and the most important Persian *Zij* composed in India during 1841-1842 by Ghulam Hussain Jaunpuri. The author seems to have immigrated from Shiraz to India. Its another name is *Zij-i-Tughiyani*, that is named after a flood, because during the writing of this *Zij*, a great flood had occurred, and it had affected the author. Along with other tables it contains diverse tables for peculiarities of stars and tables for geographical coordinates of about 420 cities and localities. This *Zij* contains one preface and seven chapters. In the second chapter which is devoted to calendars, there are 16 explained calendars, some of which are not found in other similar *Zij*es.[96] This *Zij* is counted as a very important compilation for its astronomical information.

(9) Zij-i-Talpar:

It is composed by Sultan Ali Baluch Khan known as Talpar. It was completed in 1835 A.D.

(10) Zij-e-Nizami:

It is composed by Khwaja Bahadur Hussain Khan b. Bahadur Khan.

(11) Zij-e-Hindi:

It is a translation of an Indian work into Persian. The translator is Mirja Gul Beg Munajjim. According to him the title of the original work was '*Habindi*'.

Endnotes

1. Shireen Moosvi, "Science and Superstition under Akbar and Jahangir", in *Akbar and his India,* Irfan Habib (ed.), Oxford University Press, Delhi (1997), p.110.

2. *Jahangir's Memoirs*, Trans., Rogers Beveridge, Munshiram Manoharlal, New Delhi (1978), Preface, p. VI. Elliot and Dowson, Vol. VI, p. 360.
3. Jahangir's Memoirs, *op. cit.*, Preface, p. 10.
4. Jahangir, *Tujuk-i-Jahangiri*, Alexander Rogers (Trans.), Munshiram Manoharlal: Delhi (1978), Vol. I, p. 1.
5. Jahangir, *Tuzuk-i-Jahangiri*, *op. cit.*, p. 2.
6. Muni Lal, *Jahangir*, Vikas Publishing House, New Delhi (1983), p. 5.
7. *Ibid.*, pp. 48, 85,154, 191, 235.
8. *Ibid.*, p.206.
9. *Ibid.*, pp. 77, 111.
10. *Ibid.*, pp. 155, 230.
11. Jahangir, *Tuzuk-i-Jahangiri*, *op. cit.*, pp. 244-46.
12. Shireen Mossvi, *op. cit.*, pp. 114-20.
13. Jahangir's Tuzuk-i-Jahangiri, *op. cit.*, pp. 48-49.
14. Shireen Moosvi, *op. cit.*, p.115.
15. Mùtemad Khan, *Iqbalnama-i-Jahangiri*, Elliot Down (tra.) Vol. 3, Nawal Kishore: Lucknow (1870), p. 552.
16. Syed Ahmad (ed.), *Tuzuk-i-Jahangiri*, Ghazipur and Aligarh (1863-64), pp. 76-77 Eng. Tr. Beni Prasad and Beveridge, Delhi.
17. *Ibid.*, p. 138.
18. *bid.*, pp. 76-77.
19. Ibid., pp. 151-52.
20. *Ibid.*, pp. 152-53.
21. *Ibid.*, p. 203.
22. *Ibid.*, p. 235.
23. *Ibid.*, Vol. I, p.68.
24. *Ibid.*, Vol. I, pp. 137, 139, 166, 167, 182, 191, 249, 253, 276; Also see Muni Lal, '*Jahangir*', *op. cit.*, p. 241.
25. *Ibid.*
26. *Ibid.*, p. 209.
27. *Ibid.*, p. 373.
28. Muni Lal, *Jahangir*, *op. cit.*, p. 241.
29. Tuzuk-i – *Jahangir*, *op. cit.*, p. 235.
30. Muhammad Azhar Ansari, *Social Life of the Mughal Emperors*, Shanti Prakashan: Allahabad and New Delhi (1974), p. 180.
31. Terry, 220, quoted by Ansari, op. cit.
32. Pelsert, *Jahangir's India, 1977* and quoted by Ansari, op. cit.

33. Elliot and J. Dowson, *History of India as told by its own Historians*, Kitab Mahal Private Ltd: Allahabad (1964), Vol. VII, Preface.
34. Banarsi Prasad Saksena, *History of Shahjahan of Delhi*, Central Book Depot, Allahabad (1958). Introduction, p. IV.
35. *Ibid.*, Introduction, p. V, Also see K.A. Nizami's work, *On History and Historians of Medieval India*, p.153.
36. Elliot and Dowson, *op. cit.*, p. 3. Also see *Badshahnama* of Abdul Hamid Lahori, Vol. I, pp. 10-11.
37. O. P.Jaggi, *Science and Technology in Medieval India*, *op. cit.*, Vol. VII, pp. 53-54. Also see, Catalogue of the Persian Manuscripts in the British Museum, 2, 459, 60, quoted by Nadvi, Islamic Culture, 280.
38. Munshi Devi Prashad, *Shahjahanama*, tra. by Raghubir Singh and Manohar Singh, Rawat Publication Scheme, Jaipur (1990), p. 61.
39. Abul Fazl, *The Akbarnama*, H. Beveridge (tran.), *op. cit.*, (1972), p. 110 (Footnotes), (Also see *Badshahnama*, 201:5).
40. Munshi Devi Prasad, *Shahjahanama*, *op. cit.*, p. 61. The author had procured it from the astrological office at Jodhpur.
41. *Ibid.*, pp.61-62.
42. *Shahjahan Nama*, *op. cit.*, pp. 250-51.
43. *Ibid.*, p. 269.
44. *Ibid.*, pp. 269, 281, 300, 301.
45. M.A. Ansari, *Social Life of the Mughal Emperors*, Shanti Prakashan, New Delhi (1974), p. 120.
46. *Ibid.*, p. 180. Also see Elliot and Dowson, *The History of India as told by its Own Historian*, Vol. VII, p. 45.
47. Both Zijs are described in the chapter "Astronomical development in Medieval period of India".
48. David Pingree, "Islamic Astronomy in Sanskrit", 1978, *Journal of History and Arabic Science*, Vol. 2, (1978), pp. 323-326.
49. S. R. Sharma, *Crecent In India* (1954), p. 660.
50. David Pingree, "Islamic Astronomy in Sanskrit", *Journal of History of Arabic Sciences*, Vol. 2, pp. 323-326.
51. Elliot and Dowson, *op. cit.*, Vol. VII, pp.156-157.
52. Munshi Devi Prasad, *Shahjahan Nama*, *op. cit.*, pp. 250-51.
53. Khafi Khan, 'Muntakhabu-l-Lubab', quoted by Elliot and Dowson, op. cit., Vol. III, pp. 229.
54. J.N. Sarkar, 'Aurangzeb' Publication Scheme, Jaipur (1985), ed. by Raghubir Singh, pp. 74-75.

55. *Ibid.*, Also see *Ruka'at-i-Alamgiri* (Letters of Aurangzeb), by Jamshid H. Bilimoria (Trans.), *Idarah-I-Adabi-yat-1*, Delhi, Qasim Street: Delhi (1972), pp. 5-6.
56. Aurangzeb, 'Ruka'at-i-Alamgiri', op. cit., pp. 78-79.
57. M.A. Ansari, *Social Life of the Mughal Emperors*, Shanti Prakashan: New Delhi (1974), p. 180.
58. J.N. Sarkar, *'Aurangzeb' op. cit.*, p. 341.
59. Manucci Niccolao '*Storia do Mogor*', tra. W. Irvine, London, 1906, Vol. II, 2, I. O.P. Jaggi, *op. cit.*, p. 31.
60. G. R. Kaye, *A Guide to the Old Observatories at Delhi, Jaipur, Ujjain, Benaras*, The Academic Press, Gurgaon, Haryana (1985) (Reprint Published), p. 1.
61. M. F. Soonawala, *Maharaja Sawai Jai Singh II of Jaipur and His Observatories*, Jaipur Astronomical Society: Jaipur (1952), p. 1.
62. V.S. Bhatnagar, *Life and Times of Sawai Jai Singh*, Impex India: Delhi (1974), p.314.
63. *Ibid.*, p. 11.
64. A. Rahman, *Maharaja Sawai Jai Singh II and Indian Renaissance*, Navrang: New Delhi (1987), p. 11.
65. *Ibid.*
66. O. P. Jaggi, *Science and Technology in Medieval India*, *op. cit.*, Vol. VII, p. 54.
67. G. R. Kaye, *op. cit.*, p. 2.
68. James Tod, *Annals and "Antiquities of Rajasthan*", Routledge and Kegan Paul: London (1829), Vol. II, p.360.
69. G. R. Kaye, *op. cit.*, p. 3.
70. N. F. Soonawala, *op. cit.*, p.10.
71. *Ibid.*, p. 11.
72. G. R. Kaye, *Ibid.*, pp. 7-9, N. F. Soonawala, *Ibid.*, p. 11.
73. *Ibid.*, p. 4. Also see A. Rahman (ed.), *History of Indian Science, Technology and Culture*, Oxford University Press: New Delhi (2004), Vol. III, Part I, pp. 216-18.
74. A. Rahman, *op. cit.*, pp. 36-37.
75. G. Sobirov, *Samarkand Scientific School of Ulugh Beg, Dushanbe*, 1975 (in Russian) quoted by G. R. Kaye, *op. cit.*, p. 12, and A. Rahman, *op. cit.*, pp. 37-38.
76. A. Rahman, *op. cit.*, pp. 40-41.
77. *Ibid.*
78. G. R. Kaye, *op. cit.*, pp. 59-60.
79. O. P. Jaggi, *Science and Technology in Medieval India*, Vol. VII, Atma Ram & Sons: Delhi (1977), p. 54; Also see, Catalogue of Persian Manuscripts in British Museum, 2, 459, 60, quoted by Nadvi, *Islamic Culture*, p. 280.
80. O. P. Jaggi, *Ibid.*, p. 59.

81. S. R. Sarma, "The Lahore Family of Astrolabists and their average", *Indian History Congress (55th Session)*, Aligarh (1994), p. 287.

82. Syad Suleman Nadvi, "Some Indian Astrolabe Makers", *Indian History Congress IX* (1935), pp. 621-631.

83. S. R. Sarma, *op. cit.*, pp. 288-295.

84. A. J. Turner, *The Time Museum: Catalogue of Collections Part I: Astrolabes, Astrolabes-related Instruments Rock for 1985*, pp.25-26.

85. A. L. Basham, *A Cultural History of India*, Clarendon Press: Oxford (1975), p.158.

86. *Ibid.*

87. *Ibid.*

88. Farid Ghasemlou and Negar Naderi, "Persian Astronomical Tables Composed in India" (Article) written in *500 years of Tantrasangraha* by M.S.Sriram, Ramsubramanium and Srinivas, Inter University Centre, Indian Institute of Advance Study, Shimla (2002), p. 137.

89. S.M. R. Ansari, "Islamic Astronomy in India during 16th-18th centuries and its interaction with traditional Indian Astronomy, written in 500 years of Tantrasangraha", *op. cit.*, p. 145.

90. Rajesh Kochhar, "Pre Telescopic Astronomy in India" in D. P. Chattopadhaya (ed.), *History of Science, Philosophy and Culture in Indian Civilisation*, Vol. III, Part I, Oxford University Press: Delhi (1999), pp.187-193.

91. *Ibid.*, p. 191.

92. Abul Fazl, *Ain-e-Akbari*, Eng. tr. Jarratt, Vol. III, *op. cit.*, pp. 103-04.

93. Rajesh Kochar, *op. cit.*, p.192.

94. .M.R. Ansari, quoted by Ghansemlon and Naderi, *op. cit.*, p.140.

95. S.M.R. Ansari, "Ghulam Hussain Jaunpuri and his Zij-i-Bahadurkhani", *Studies in History of Medicines and Science* (New Delhi), Vol. XVI, nos. 1-2, New Series (1995-96), pp. 181-188.

96. S.M.R. Ansari, "On the Transmission of Arabic-Islamic Astronomy to Medieval India (1995)", *Archieves International d'Historire des Sciences*, Vol. 45, pp. 273-297.

CHAPTER 5

Impact of Astrology and Astronomy on Society, Literature, Education, Architecture and Painting in Mughal Period

The history of astrological beliefs in India goes back to early ancient period as we see that Vedic civilisation exhibits beliefs in the prognaustications and omens.[1] There was a landmark in the knowledge of astronomy and practice of astrology during early Vedic period of India. Calculation of the time was a part of sacred ritual of the Vedic Aryans. Religious sacrifices, that they performed, were of different types. While some of these were performed at a particular time of the day, the others were performed at full moon or new moon or when the days and nights were of equal length, and occasionally a sacrificial ritual lasted even for a year or more.[2] There was a class of men well versed in the art of recognizing and noting the position of the various stars and calculating the time of the performance of different religious sacrifices. *Yajurveda* mentions *naksatra-darsha* (star gazer) and *ganaka* (calculator or astrologer) as important functionaries in connection with the performance of these sacrifices.[3] In ancient India, *Varahmihira* was the first astrologer who divided the *'Jyotish-sastra'* into three branches namely *Tantra* (astronomy and Mathematics), *Hora* (Horoscope) and *Samhita* (applied astrology). His astrological work *Brihatsamhita* contains useful information such as the movement of heavenly bodies and their effect upon men, geography, architecture construction, excavation of tanks, laying out of a garden, special characteristic of different classes of women and animals, augury, marriage etc.[4] It appears that contemporary society was very much influenced with astrology. People used to consult astrologers in their day- to- day life. As one of the early Arab geographers, Abu Zaid[5] tells that some Indians, who were devoted to religion and these sciences, called as Brahmins, astronomers, philosophers, and diviners. 'They used to live in the courts of their kings and draw omens from the flight of crows etc.

The Sun, as a God, had a very important place among the Hindu deities since Vedic period. The different names of Sun God indicate the devotion to this deity by the people. During early medieval period Sun was worshipped in different ways. Various Sun icons have been found in different ways. An absolutely different method of representing the Sun icon is found in shape of nine planets i.e., '*Navgraha*' worshipped in the time of danger and carved in a row on the lintel of the main sanctum in Vaishnava or Shiva temple. These nine planets have been carved on the stone slab of Parasrameshwar temple of Bhuvneshwar and also found at Konarka in Orissa. Thus, it can be stated on the basis of archaeological remains that sun worship with nine planets was the most popular worship in the society during medieval period.[6] The sun eclipse is described in the *Purans* and *Smriti* literature as *Surya* has been eclipsed by *Rahu* (*Rahu Graste Divakar*). The time of eclipse has been regarded very sacred and people were advised to give *Dan* or alms on this auspicious occasion. The shadow of earth on Sun has been described as '*Rahu Grast Divakar*' though Aryabhatta, in 5th century A.D., had established the relation of planets and the cause of eclipses. It was nothing but the shadow of earth falling on the Sun and Moon. This scientific view had no value or importance for the people whose minds were absorbed in myths and superstitions.[7]

The Hindi Poet *Jayasi* has referred to a time-honoured Hindu custom of deriving omen from a number of things just as the time of a journey called *Yatra*. The medieval people took augur from sneezing. People believed in lucky and unlucky days. *Barani* says that the age of *Alauddin Khilzi* produced great astrologers and astronomers.[8] He further tells us that women of the *haram* of Alauddin Khilzi lavishly rewarded Hindu and Muslim astrologers for drawing horoscopes on the birth of princes. The elite class people of Delhi usually began some important work or undertook any projects only after consulting an astrologer.[9] Amir Khusrau's work "*Nu Sipiher*" shows his deep knowledge of astronomy. It indicates that astronomy and astrology played a vital role in the life of the medieval people.[10]

Thus, we find that the belief in the supernatural and the influence of the stars on the fate of man was universally recognised since ancient period. Moreover, during the medieval period, people in general were as superstitious and gullible as in the preceding eras. Both the Hindus and the Muslims shared this common faith in the supernatural.

In medieval period, astrology played an important part in the life of both Hindus and Muslims. People had an unshakable belief in astrology, evoked the help of saints, took omens from incidents and dreams, which, in their belief, revealed the mysteries of the world or cast shadows of coming events, Mauncci remarks,[10] that Astrology was paying profession. The *bazaar* was thronged with them. Both Mughal and Hindus were so credulous that they put faith in all that these men choose to tell them.

Astronomy is considered heterodoxy in Islam. But superstitious beliefs, which influenced the whole of the Muslim community, were practiced during medieval period. Astrology had influenced the Muslim mind since the time of Caliph Mansur. The influence was to such an extent that every good family had an astrologer of its own. However, the science of Astrology was not considered lawful in Islam.[12] Bernier remarks,[13] "The majority of Asiatics are so infatuated in favour of being guided by the signs of the heavens, that according to their phraseology, no circumstance can happen 'below', which is not written 'above'. In every enterprise they consult their astrologers. When two armies have completed every preparation for battle, no consideration can induce the generals to commence the engagement until the *Sahet* (propitious moment) be performed, that is until the propitious moment for attack is ascertained. In like manner no commanding officer is nominated, no marriage takes place, and no journey is undertaken, without consulting the Astrologer. Their advice is considered absolutely necessary even on the most triffling occasion, such as the proposed purchase of a slave, or the first wearing of new clothes. This silly superstition is so general in annoyance and attended with such important and disagreeable consequences that I am astonished it has continued so long, the astrologer is necessarily made acquainted with every transaction, public and private, with every project common and extra ordinary".

Bernier further writes[14] of the pernicious presence of astrologers in the bazaars of Delhi. 'Hither, likewise, the astrologer`s resort, both Mahometan and Gentile. These wise doctors remain seated in the sun on a dusty piece of carpet handling some old mathematical instruments, and having open before them a large book which represents the signs of the *Zodiac.* In this way, they attract the attention of the passengers and impose upon the people, by whom they are considered as so many infalliable oracles. They tell a poor man his fortune for a paussa (Paisa) and after examining the hand and face of the applicant, turning over the leaves of the large book and pretending to make certain calculations, these importers decide upon the *sahet* or propitious moment of commencing the business he may have in hand. Silly women, wrapping themselves in a white cloth from head to foot, flock to the astrologers, whisper to them all the transactions of their lives, and disclose every secret with no more reserve than is practiced by a scrupulous penitent in the presence of her confessor. The infatuated people really believe the stars have an influence which the astrologers can control'.

Bernier further states[15] that 'these were the poor bazaar-astrologers. Those who were eminent doctors became wealthy. The whole of Asia was degraded by the same superstition. Kings and nobles granted large salaries to these crafty diviners, and never engage in the most trifling transaction without consulting them; they read whatever is written in heaven, fix upon the *sahet* and solve every doubt by opening the '*koran*'.'

Thus, Bernier's account shows that the people had beliefs in superstitions. *Ain-i-Akbari* also records some beliefs of the people in black arts and sorcery.[16]

Manucci, the Venetian traveler also mentions[17] an episode of an astrologer, named Bhawani Das, who was personally known to him. He made befooled to Dara Shikoh by declaring that he would be a king.

Francisco Pelsaert also writes[18] high about some Brahmans, who enjoyed great reputation and respect among big men on account of their predictions about day-to-day life. He writes that without consulting these Brahmans, no one used to set out on an important journey, nor entered the city until the suitable day or hour had been predicted. He also describes street astrologers, who were believed by the poor people. Auspicious moments were taken into consideration to observe sixteen *sanskaras* from birth to death by the Hindus. Soon after the birth, a horoscope of the baby was drawn by the family priest. The school going ceremony was also observed at the exact hour fixed by the astrologer. Even the time and date of the marriage were fixed in consultation with an astrologer.[19]

A matrimonial alliance was celebrated with a *tilak* ceremony. An auspicious day was fixed for the marriage ceremony after consulting astrologers. Both Hindu and Mohammadans considered some months to be inauspicious.[20]

Astrology was a lucrative profession to the priestly classes like today. On the basis of astrology, people tried to explore the health, wealth, and prosperity in their life. In fact, astrology received the allegiance of all classes in the country. Hindus, Muslims, and half castes were not averse to consult the astrologer or *purohits*. The almanacs prepared by the priests were in use in families of all faiths. In northern India, astrology was practiced by Hindus and Muslims alike.[21] Dubois gives an elaborate outline of the principles on which astrologers calculated the influence of the celestial bodies, the phenomenon of eclipse etc. According to him, astrology was "a science which opens so vast a sphere to the imagination". Undoubtedly in India, priests had raised it to the status of almost an exact science.[22] He further states that Hindu astrologers believed themselves capable of telling the secrets as well as the future events of life. They even tried to find out not only the place but also the sex and the caste of the thief. They also told whether a person who had been long absent was dead or alive, sick, or healthy, at liberty or in prison and whether he would return or not.[23]

Besides astrological beliefs, some superstitions such as amulets and talismans were prevalent in society. Children were also armed with them from their very birth as these amulets were supposed to guard them from evil effects of various calamities, diseases, infirmities, and dangers. Colonel Tod says[24] that it was a popular practice with the Rajputs that on the birth of an infant the father tied round its arm a root of the species of the grass known as Amarbul. Different types of amulets and charms were worn on different parts of the body.[25] We also come across other types of superstitions deep rooted in society. People used to believe in certain omens as indication of good or evil, such as if a hare crossed the path, it was an ill omen. Similarly, owls, cats etc. were considered ill omens.[26]

In spite of the patronage to astrology given by the ruling class as well as common masses, during the period of Aurangzeb, the increasing volume and intensity of opposition to astrology generated a gradual withdrawal of eminent astronomer from the participation in astrological activities.[27] But at the same time, astrology had deep rooted influence in the society.

Education and Learning

In ancient period of Indian History, four types of "*Vidyas*" (education) are referred to by the thinkers like *Kautilya* and *Kamndaka*. These Vaidyas are (1) *Anvikshiki* (which contains Philosophy and Metaphysics), (2) *Trayi* (Rigveda, Samaveda and Yajurveda), (3) *Varta* – which consists of Education for livelihood, and (4) *Dandaniti* which is a science of good administration. But *Brihaspati*, a great thinker of ancient period, refers to only two main types of education i.e., *Varta* and *Dandaniti*. But he gives a long list of education in Varta for livelihood. The art of sooth saying, and astronomy is also covered in this long list. Kalidas, a Sanskrit poet also refers to 14 Vidyas. Astronomy and astrology are also two vidyas out of the 14. Thus, it is obvious that astronomy and astrology[28] were very important subjects of education since ancient times.

Upnayan Samskara' was followed by the '*Vadyarambha Samskara*'. It used to be performed when the sun came towards the northern hemisphere at an auspicious moment with the consultation of an astrologer. It began with the worship of *Brihaspati, Vinayaka, Gribadevta* and *Saraswati*.[29]

In medieval period also, the same *samskara* i.e., *Upnayna* and *Vidyarambh* sanskara were performed at about the age of five either by his father at home or by a teacher at school. The Mughals too would send their children after performing the maktab ceremony, which was usually performed at the age of four years four months and four days. Both Hindu and Muslims put their children to school at an auspicious hour after consulting the astrologer.[30]

During the medieval period, higher education was imparted in *madrasas*. The curriculum in the *madrasas*, generally speaking, included grammer, logic, literature, theology, metaphysics, jurisprudence, and medicine. Akbar, however, laid special emphasis upon the study of astronomy, mathematics, medicine, and philosophy. Abul Fazl refers to the curriculum for higher studies thus; every boy read books on morals, arithmetic, the notations peculiar to arithmetic, agriculture mensuration, geometry astronomy, physiognomy, household matters, the rule of government, medicine, logic, and history.[31] Badauni also makes it clear that in the age of Akbar, subjects like astronomy, medicine, mathematics, philosophy and poetry were considered beneficial and hence were widely pursued by the people.[32] Shah Waliullah, the famous Muhaddis of Delhi (1702-1760 A.D.), implemented his own courses of study. His work *'Tuzul-Latif* `consists of all the courses. One of these subjects was astronomy and Mathematics with several treatise.[33] Astronomy and astrology as well as some allied subjects were open to the students to study and specialize.[34]

It may be noted here that the study of the subjects referred to above also depended upon the whims of the ruler as we have seen that Humayun and Akbar laid special emphasis upon the study of mathematics, astrology, astronomy, philosophy, and medicine etc.[35.]

During early Mughal rule in India, Hindu education received practically no encouragement from early Mughal emperors due to engagement in wars for stability of the dominion. But Akbar felt that without support of Hindus, the stability and safety of the Mughal rule was not possible. And he decided to give due encouragement to the noble aspects of Hindu culture. A number of Hindu scholars received state patronage. Akbar gave reasonable state-assistance to the various classes of the learned men without any distinction of caste, creed, or race.[36] Almost similar policy towards Hindu education and learning was adopted by the successors of Akbar. The Hindus received their higher education in the *Chatuspathis*, popularly known as the *'Chauparis'* i.e., the four *Shastras* namely grammer, law, *puran* and *darshan.* Bernier gives a detailed account of the curriculum prescribed for higher education. It included the study of puran, *Vedas*, philosophy, medicine, astronomy and astrology, history, and geography.[37]

Astronomy and astrology were popular subjects among the people and the court, and their study was encouraged by all efforts. It formed part of the courses of study. Astronomy was a compulsory subject while astrology was an optional[38] one. Badaoni also remarks that some knowledge of astronomy was considered essential.[39] And Akbar issued a farman commending its study. Brahmans were famous for their skill in both these branches of knowledge, and they never failed even to a minute in predicting the time for the eclipse of sun or moon.[40]

The famous astrologers of the period were Jotikray, Maulana Chand, Kanjar Beg, Nuruddin Muhammad Tarkhan, Illiyas, Fat-ul-lah Sirazi, Imam Abul Muhmamad of Ghazni and Mulla Farid Munajjim.[41]

A few centers were particularly famous for the study of astronomy and astrology Thus, Banaras was famous for the study of astronomy and astrology.[42] Nadia in Bengal, a great centre of Hindu learning, had a chair of astronomy added in 1718 A.D. by Ramrudra Vidhanidhi.[43] Another big centre was Multan where students crowded from all part of India to study and specialize in difficult sciences like astronomy, astrology, mathematic, medicine etc. Brahmans scholars had mastery in these subjects. There is some evidence to indicate that some Muslim students attended the schools run by Hindu teachers for instruction in subjects like astronomy and astrology, medicine etc.[44] Quite a large number of libraries existed during the Mughal period. Humayun and Akbar seem to possess an enormous number of books on astronomy and astrology in their Libraries. Private libraries were also common in the period. Shaikh Faizi had a grand library consisting of 4,600 books on various subjects like medicine, astronomy, astrology, music, poetry, philosophy, science etc.[45] Abul Fazl, the brother of Shaikh Faizi, also seems to have books on astronomy and astrology. Maharaja Sawai Jai Singh of Jaipur (1699-1743) possessed an unrivalled library containing all the astronomical treaties such as Ptolemy's Almagest, the astronomical table of Ulugh Beg. La Hire's Tabulate Astronomical, Flamsteed's Historia etc.[46]

Myth, Belief and Astrological – *Vastu* Traditions in Mughal Architecture

The language of architecture of a given period is much more difficult to understand than that of any other arts, but once understood, it may be the most authentic source of history. The monuments and architecture of a country reflect its history, contemporary society, its faiths and beliefs, aesthetic outlook, and artistic approach of its people. Morgan writes, "Architecture is a printing press of all ages and gives the history of the state of society in which it was erected".[47] Architecture is the mother of the arts of sculpture, painting and allied decorative craft. It also reveals the continuous evolution.[48] In this way, the spirit of the Mughal age is also reflected in their monuments, which also reveal the insight tastes and temperaments of their builders. For example, a frequent use of the Hindu architectural features in the buildings erected by Akbar, denotes his liberal outlook and his generous patronage of indigenous artisans.

The Mughal art of building is often misunderstood as a result of the mixture of the elements of Saracenic architecture which is based on Islamic form. But it is proved through intensive study of the monuments that Mughal art of building was an assimilation of Indian art conceptions such as the Art of Gandhara.[49] Having inspired by Islamic art, the Mughal art evolved fundamentally on the basis of ancient Indian architectural norms. Thus, the Mughals employed the structural forms, e.g., the arch, the vault, the squinch and the dome alongwith the feature of typically India origin like pillar, bracket beam, chhajja, corbelled péndentive, orial window, *padamkosh* and *kalas.*[50] The constructional technique remained essentially Indian. The lines on the horizontal axis and the proportions of vertical sections were opted from the Indian ancient *Vastu*-texts. These texts also played a dominant part in planning.[51]

The word '*Vastu*' is derived from the Sanskrit Dhatu '*Vasa*' which means to live. So, "*Vastu Shastra* is the science which deals with the layout of the site and the building to be constructed".[52] Dr. S.R.N. Murthy elucidates that civil engineering and architecture are called *Vastu* in Sanskrit, since it is mentioned in the *Vedas* that the eight *Vastus*, viz. *agni, prithivi, antariksa, aditya, dyaus, chandrama,* and *naksastra* are held by the ground. Hence the earth is also called "*Vasudhara*". The lord of such a ground is addressed as "*Vastopati*."[53] In this way, *Vastu* also gives detailed knowledge about the construction of township palaces, complexes etc. The main objective of this '*Shastra* is to make humanity live in as perfect a harmony as possible with 'Mother Nature".[54]

According to Mansara, the term "*Vastu*" in its broadest sense implies[55] *dhara* (the Earth), harmya (building), Yana (conveyance) and Paryanka (bedstead). In this fourfold implication of Architecture, the building or *harmya* includes *prasada, mandapa, sabha, sala, prapa* and *ranga.* The conveyance or *Yana* includes *Adika, Syandana, Sibika* and *Ratha.* The bedstead or *Prayanka* includes *Panjara, Mancali, Manca, Kakastha, Phalakasana* and *Balparyanka.* It also denotes villages, towns, forts commercial cities, dwelling house, a group of houses and a site. According to mayamata, bhumi prasadas, Yana and Sayana constitute the *Vastu.*[56]

Vastu Shastra and Astrology

Vastu Shastra is one of the branches of Hindu Astrology. In the Vedic period, the *Rishis* had thought deeply on the *Karakatva* of the planets or their significance in formulating the principles of *Vastu.*[57] The principles of *Vastu* are supposed to be eternal in the changing world. The characteristics of the *Karakatva* (reasoning and relationship) of planets can not be changed. Through the implication of these principles of *Vastu*, i.e., the *Karakatva* of planets in building, dwelling places, the peace, and happiness can be achieved in our life.[58] According to Indian philosophy, the whole world is a manifestation of the *Panchmahabhutas*, or *Panch-tattavas*, viz., *Prithvi, Apa, Tejas, Vayu* and *Akasha*. The *Akashatattva* works in space, whereas the four basic *Tattvas* i.e., *Prithvi, Apa, Teja* and *Vayu* play a great role in the day-to-day human life. A house or a building consists of three components of the *Tattvas*, if there is any imbalance in following up the proper rules, the sufferings with anxieties will take place in the life.[59] The *Karakatva* of planets has responsibility of the situation. It is remarkable that the different directions have their planetary rulers, such as the East direction is ruled by the sun and West is ruled by Saturn. In the same manner, the North is ruled by Mercury, and the South is ruled by Mars. The North-East is ruled Jupiter, and the South-East is ruled by Venus. The North-West is ruled by the Moon and the South-West is ruled by Rahu.[60]

In this way, it is observed that some *Karakatvas* of the Planets played an important part of the *Vastu* principles: The Sun stands for fire, father, east direction, mental purity, copper, and mouth. The Moon stands for mind, water, heart, silver, mother, pond nourishment, pleasures of life etc. Like this, other planets also stand for specific areas[61] as it has been discussed earlier in Chapter II. So, the *Vastu* principles strictly follow the enmities and friendship of planets, certain *Karakatvas* of one planet may not be suitable for another planet. For example, fire will not go with air. Fire stands for Maras and Saturn stands for air. In the same way, South and North, East, and West, North-East and South-West and North-West and South-East are opposite directions that can not be harmonized mutually.[62] With this simple planetary understanding of the *Karakatvas*, it is very clear that *Vastu* principles are akin to astrology. Therefore, *Vastu* is within the purview of astrology. Whereas *Vastu-Purush* implies the complete theories of astronomy, astrology and *Vastu Shastra*. The celebrated astronomer, varahmihira's work *Braht-sambita* is one of the authoritative manuals on the *Vastu Shastra*. It may be called 'Applied Astronomy'.[63]

Impact of *Vastu Shastra* and Astrology on Mughal Architecture

In medieval India, Mughal emperors introduced a spirit of various cultural ideas instead of the theocratic conception of Islam. They were tolerant and refused to be influenced by the Ulema. Babur advised his son Humayun to pay due regard to the people with a religious bent of mind.[64] Superstition, myth and astrological beliefs were prevalent in medieval period. So, all these trends impressed them. As Elphinstone remarks, "The miracles of the *Yogis* were related by the orthodox writers with as perfect a conviction as could have been given to those in the Quran; witchcraft was universally believed; omens and dreams were paid the greatest attention".[65] As earlier discussed in Chapter III Humayun had deep interest and belief in astrology and arranged his court according to the four elements i.e., fire, air, water, and earth. He also used to wear the clothes each day according to the colour of the planet of that day.[66] His audience hall had seven chambers named after seven stars and each was used according to the influence of the presiding divinity, such as the Moon Chamber for poets, travellers, and ambassadors etc.[67] It was almost a conversion to the aesthetic and philosophical values and norms which the Hindu had been following from long times ago. It was the liberal trend of Akbar's age, which made the sincere efforts to bring about a cultural fusion by free attitude towards the popular beliefs.

Akbar employed indigenous artisans on the construction of his buildings at Agra and Fatehpur Sikri and gave them full freedom to display their art. So, the aesthetic impression as well as symbols and icons passed into Mughal architecture through the hands of these indigenous building. For example, the monuments at Agra, Fatahpur Sikri, and Delhi contain many symbolic art motifs like *chakra, padma, shrivatsa, purunakalah, swastikha* and *gavaksha*, which were used by Hindus as *Vastu* symbols. And each motif of Indian art had a meaning. These motifs were used by Mughals either symbolically or ornamentally.[68] It may be analysed as such as follows:

> *Purnakalash* also known as *Purankumbha, Purnaghata*, and *Mangalkalash* is one of the eight auspicious symbols of the classical Indian art. It is a symbol of plenty and creativity.[69] It is generally associated with "*Lakshmi*" or *Gajalakshmi* and with overflowing foliage composed of lotus buds, flowers and leaves.

The *Purnakalash* has been used as the base of nook-shafts at Jami Masjid of Fatapur Sikri.[70] It has been carved as an ornamental motif on the pillars of Panch Mahal. It is also used in various forms in Jodhabai Palace, Diwan-i-Khas and Jahangiri Mahal. *Purnakalash* motif is frequently used in the buildings of Shahjahan, such as: Khas Mahal at Agra fort, Shish Mahal, Shahjahani-Mahal, Machchhi-Bhawan as well as Jharokha pavilion. It may also be pointed out here that it is used on the domes as the most important part of the finial in Mughal Architecture from Akbar to Shahjahan. It is sometimes associated with *amalaka* i.e., on the *chhatries* of Akbar's buildings at Fatapur Sikri and Agra Fort. Sometimes the *Kalash* with *Padamkosh* can be seen in the buildings of Shahjahan.

The Padma (Lotus), used in Mughal Architecture frequently in various forms, is also an ancient Hindu symbol. It represents the principle of growth and denotes life floating on the surface of the creative waters and it is a prime symbol of creation.[71] The lotus symbols occupy an important position in Hindu cosmology. Water is the source and support of all things, and the lotus represents it. A.K. Comaraswamy opines that "growing in the mud and yet so clean, the lotus is a symbol of purity: a lotus-pool, with leaves and flowers in bud, widely opened and again dying down, is an image of the ebb and flow of human life (*Samsara*). Bodily centres of consciousness, such as the solar plexus, the heart, and the brain, are represented in lotus forms. While the whole universe is sometimes imagined as one great flower, whose petals are outlined by the starry worlds. In this sense probably, we should understand the flower held in the hand of deities".[72.]

The lotus has been used on a large scale in Mughal architecture, in a variety of forms. It has been carved in most of the buildings of Fatehpur Sikri. It can be seen at earliest in Jami Masjid on the Badshahi Darwaja. It is also carved at the Khwabgah, the royal palace, the Panch Mahal, the tomb of Salim Chisti and Akbar's tomb at Sikandarabad. The lotus was also used as Fringe of lotus-buds around the arches, ornamental and functional in the red sandstone buildings.[73] The *padmakosa* or sheath of lotus petals is the most important form of the use of lotus in Mughal architecture. It has been used almost universally over the domes and cupolas of the *chhatries*.[74] Various forms of Lotus are used very impressively in the white marble buildings of Shahjahan at the Nagina Masjid of Agra fort, the Moti Masjid of Red Fort, Delhi, and the Taj Mahal on the superstructure alongwith the *chhatries* and domes.[75]

Govaksa, i.e., eye of the cow assumed a symbolic significance during the Mauryan age. It was used in the semi-circular opening in the façade, so that the sun's rays passed into the interior through it. Thus, it was a sun-window and in the shape of an eye or curve, designated *gavaksa*.[76] This motif was used in the building of Akbar on a large scale, mainly on pillars. It appears in the Jami Masjid, so called Birbal's Palace, Khwabgah, the Sultana's house, the Panch Mahal and on the entrance of Salim Chisti's tomb at Fatehpur Sikri. It was not used at the tomb of Itmad-ud-Daulah. But later on, it appears in the buildings of Shahjahan.[77]

The *Kirtimukha* or the face of Glory, is the symbolic manifestation of the terrible aspect of Shiva according to Puranic mythology. The God Shiva had opened his third eye from which a physical shape of a lion headed demon appeared to kill the messenger 'Rahu' sent by Jalandhar the demon King, who challenged Shiva himself. Rahu was immortal due to drinking *Amrita*. But in a state of painful hunger the lion headed demon was commanded by Shiva to feed himself with his own hands, feet, arms, etc. When its face was left, the God Shiva (knowing that it was his own power) declared the face to be a face of Glory (Kirtimukh) and ordained him to be set forever at the door for worship by the people.[78] It is chiefly used in the brackets below the *chhajja* of Mariam's house.

Swastika was a solar symbol in Hindu mythology. Its symbolical meaning indicated the path of the 'Sun' across the heavens and the propitious direction for the priests on pious pilgrim to circumambulate.[79] It was used in the buildings of Akbar at Fatehpur Sikri. But it was not depicted in the tomb of Itmad-ud-Daulah or in the buildings of Shahjahan.

Chakra was a symbol of time. It denotes the cyclic movement in a rhythmic order. According to A. K. Coomarswami, the wheel (*chakra*) which later on becomes the mark of a *chakravartin*, the discus the Vishnu and the Buddhist Wheel of Law, originally represented the Sun.[80] It has a twofold aspect viz., the centre and the circumference. There is rest at the centre and movement in the circumference, unity in the centre and diversity in the circumference. The complete *chakra* presents a synthesis or harmony between the two.[81]

The *chakra* was used. though on a very small scale, in Mughal architecture. It is chiefly carved on pillars and arches. A few illustrative examples of the usage are Birbal's Palace at Fatehpur Sikri, the Panch Mahal, the Jahangiri Mahal, and on the tomb of

Akbar at Sikandra (Agra). But it disappeared in the later phases of Mughal art.

Srivatsa is also counted among the eight auspicious signs of classical Indian art.[82] According to T. A. Gopinath Rao, '*Srivatsa* is a mark, a sort of mole, which is conceived to adorn the chest of Visnu in association with the *Kaustubhamani*, which is a jewel.[83]

It is depicted on the lintels of the doorways of the Akbari-Mahal at Agra. Sometimes, it appears combined with the lotus. It can be seen on the upper pavilions of the Jahangiri-Mahal and on the so-called Jodhbai's palace. But it is completely absent in the buildings of Jahangir and Shahjahan.

The Chain and Bell Motif is a characteristic ornament of the Hindu Temple. And it is the sounding of a bell to invoke the deity incarnate. It is used in three monuments of Fatahpur Sikri.[84] It appears on a large scale on the shafts of the columns of the so-called Jodhabai's palace. It is also depicted on the first floor's pillar of Panch Mahal.

Satkona is the most important symbolic motif, frequently used in the buildings of ancient India. It was commonly used along with other symbols like the *triratna*, the lotus and the *swastika*. It was also used in temples particularly dedicated to worship of Shiva and Shakti. Sometimes it denotes the tantrism, the Yoga Sadhana, and the black magic.[85] It is depicted in the early Mughal buildings with a *bindu* in the centre, or a lotus inside it. It was used first in Mughal architecture in the Tomb of Humayun at Delhi built about 1565 A.D. during Akbar's reign. It appears next to the Delhi gate of Agra about 1569. In Jami Masjid it occupies a prominent position above the main *mehrab* over the sacred inscription.[86] A lotus is carved inside it.

The Satknoa was also used in other monuments of Fatehpur Sikri. It can be seen in Birbal's palace. Jodhabai's Palace, Jahangiri Mahal of Agra, the tomb of Akbar at Sikandara (Agra) and Salim Chisti's Tomb. The most surprising Satknoa is found carved on the west side of Salim Chisti's Tomb, in the form of six interlacing serpents which intricately combine around a central *bindu* like a *naga-pasa*.[87] Explaining the purpose of its depiction particularly in the monuments of Akbar, R. Nath writes,[88] the *Satkonas*, in different ways, show Akbar's belief in the occult sciences of the Hindus and the practices which lead to their accomplishment. He had contact with the jogis as Badaoni,[89] a contemporary writer, gives a detailed account of the emperor's association with the jogis and his belief in these practices. The emperor had faith in 'black magic' also. He seems to have favoured at least some sort of superstitious practices, though not followed himself as shown by an illustrated manuscript of talisman.[90] Some wall paintings at Khwabgarh and Marium's house showing winged fairy or mysterious angels, obviously served the purpose of *amils* (talismans) and satisfied the superstitious craze of the age – to which Akbar seems to have liberally favoured.[91]

Important evidence of Akbar's belief in such practices can be mentioned here. This is his own shield, which depicts the 12 signs of the zodiac (*Rasis*) with the name of each *rashi* inscribed in a circle over it in parsian letters. In the exact centre is the Sun with eyes and nose and long moustache and tilak. A *Satkona* is depicted on a corner. Few words like "*Buland Iqbal Shahenshah Akbar Sanh 10_2*" (the third digit of the date is missing) are inscribed in the centre of the *Satkona.*[92]

It is obviously shown by the personal shield[93] of Akbar that he was a firm believer of Astronomy. The Sun is the central theme of the shield. According to R. Nath, the shield is probably the most important item of the personal armour of an emperor, so it helped to protect him in a life and death struggle and the depiction of *Satkona* on the shield represents a strong belief in the "*Yantra*". The depiction of this *tantric* symbol indicates that it was regarded to be auspicious to ward off evil and protect him in all circumstances in battles.[94]

It seems that the *Satknoa* was depicted on the mosque, tomb, and residential buildings of Akbar, as its representation was considered auspicious to ward off evil. All these symbolic *yantra* and motifs show the association of Mughal Emperors with occultism. That is why they used these symbols so prominently and assertively mostly on the gateways. The tendency of commonly using the motifs in the buildings reflects the popular belief of the people and the spirit of the age.

It is very interesting to mention here an article "The Diwan-i-Khas of Fatehpur Sikri: A Symbol of Akbar's belief in Surya-Purusa" written by R. Nath.[95] He offers a fresh interpretation about the 'Diwan-i-Khas' a building in Fatehpur Sikri built by Akbar. He writes that it is totally misnomer to be identified as a Diwani-i-Khas, wherein Akbar used to sit in centre platform and the four bridges were occupied by his ministers. According to R. Nath,[96] such a small and dark place could not be used for any religious or political meetings. Indeed, its architectural beauty conveys that Akbar had something new in his mind. He says that the central column of Akbar's Diwan-i-Khas symbolized the axis of the cosmic order, i.e., ekstambha, represented in four quarters of space by bridges, which supported the *Surya-Purusa.* Akbar firmly believed in the efficacy of Sun-worship as the Sun is the origin of creation and the source of the phenomenal world. Abul Fazl[97] and Al-Badaoni[98] have also recorded his belief in the efficacy of sun worship. R. Nath opines that the existence of this building only symbolized Akbar's belief in the *ekstambha* doctrine of the '*Surya-Purusa*, i.e. the axis pillar of the cosmic order which is measured out by the Surya Purusa, this axis sustaining the three worlds in all the quarters of space, in accordance with the dictum, "*Aalamb stumbha Ekam Tribhuvan-Bhavanasya*".[99] A square canopy standing on a platform, known as the 'Astrologer's seat'[100] in the Diwan-i-Khas also supports of R. Nath's view.

Thus, we find so much evidence which prove the intense impact of astronomy and astrology on Mughal architecture. Different symbolical and animated motifs were depicted widely in their monuments. Such depictions were made possible by the indigenous artisans, who were liberally employed by Akbar. We also find that from Humayun to Shahjahan, all Mughal emperors firmly believed in astrology in their daily life. These motifs may simply be depicted keeping in view the decorative aspect of the monuments in later Mughal architecture. However, the monuments built up to the period of Shahjahan were influenced by occultism, prognaustical sciences and *VastuShastra.*

Impact of Astrology on Painting

Impact of astrology on painting, during Mughal period, may be seen since Akbar's reign. Babur and Humayun could spare little time in this field due to their indulgence in the battles. Though Humayun had temptations of wine, opium as well as ease, he spent a lot of energy for directing highly complicated astrological schemes. He prepared a huge tent, with compartment of each month, where his courtiers could gather according to astrological signs. He also possessed a large carpet with nine astrological circles, each named after a star, where courtiers stood according to rank.[101] However, two safavi artists were patronized by him.

The Mughal school, with distinct style, emerged by 1580, shows the imprint of the Safavid and Tumurid art traditions and some influence of the classical Indian schools. Painting of this period maybe described essentially as narrative art, which is also traceable in Persian and Indian art. The Mughal pictorial tradition comes out in a variety of ways in the art of book illustrations. The simplest way of the artist's expression is represented by the illustrations of the '*Tutinama*'.[102] Again the narration in Mughal school appears in the '*Hamaza Namah*' illustrations. In 1567, Akbar had established a atelier of Indian artist working under two Persian masters with the object of illustrating the *Hamza Namah* in 14 volumes, each containing a hundred paintings of large size on cloth.[103] The most mature form in the illustrations emerged in the *Tarikh-i-Khandan-i-Timuriya* (1584-7), the *Jami-ut-Tawarikh* (1597-8) and the *Akbarnama* (1602-5).[104] Besides these illustrations, the astrological influence may be seen also in the contemporary miniatures of the Deccan states. The "Nujum-al-Ulum (The Star of the Sciences) is a collection of remarkable miniatures.[105] Some parts of it are based on astrology. The work belongs to the years 1570-71 and probably was produced in the state of Bijapur. It is a compendium of Muslim and Hindu beliefs chiefly concerning astrology and magic, though many aspects of which have now become obscure. Its author is anonymous. It appears that this volume was owned by the Bijapuri ruler Ali Adil Shah (1557-79) who had mystic learnings and whose credulous personality seems to correspond with the combination of Hindu and Muslim beliefs in the *Nujum-al-Ulum*.[106] Ali Adil Shah had a Hindu in charge of his library and that the state of Bijapur was culturally receptive to a mixture of traditions and customs that accord with the diverse superstitions recorded in the *Nujum al-Ulum*.[107] It also contains much earlier unexplored information about social history. The illustrations reveal the astrological and magical theories that the authors present.[108] Some illustrations, which seem to be influenced by these theories, may be narrated as follows:

An illustration of Akbar's birth is corroborated by Gulbadan Begum (Humayun's sister) in '*Humayun Nama*'. The incidents following the birth of Akbar, depicted in the illustration, can be divided into three parts.[109] At the top, on the right, are Hamida Banu and the child, on the left the news is announced with sound. In the middle, the hour of birth is being communicated to the astrologers.

At the foot, the news is being given to Humayun by Tardi Beg and is welcomed by music and dancing.

We find that one part of the illustration shows the impact of astrology. The birth of Akbar's second son at Fatehpur Sikri was also a rejoicing movement. The related illustration of the event, comprises five units: the unit on the top right shows the queen with her new born baby attended by maids, while one of the units just below depicts a group of astrologers who are busy preparing the horoscope.[110] P. N. Chopra also mentions about a painting showing astrologers casting the horoscope of a prince on his birth.[111] The birthday of the ruling Mughal emperor was celebrated throughout the empire with great pomp and show. From the time of Humayun onwards, on this occasion, the emperor was weighed against certain precious metals and articles according to planetary position and these articles were given away in charity. A beautiful painting depicts "Akbar being weighed".[112] Another episode[113] weighing ceremony of Prince Khurrum later Shahjahan is described by Jahangir in his Memoirs, the event took place in 1607 A.D. Jahangir writes "On Friday ... I came to the quarter of Khurram which had been made in the Urta Garden, whereas it was the rule of my father to have himself weighed twice every year, once according to the solar and once according to the lunar year and to have the princes weighed according to the solar year and moreover in this year, which was the commencement of my son Khurram's sixteenth lunar year, the astrologer and astronomers represented[114] that a most important epoch according to his horoscope would occur. As the prince's health had not been good, I gave an order that they should weigh him according to the prescribed rule, against gold silver and other metals, which should be divided among *faquirs* and the needy". Hence, as so often in Mughal art, these miniatures depict the deep-rooted influence of astrology on Mughal emperors. The miniature depicts all commodities according to planets to distribute among the *faquirs.*

Another miniature was portrayed by Abul Hasan. This portrait was based upon the inquiries assisted by Jahangir. In the painting 'Shah Abbas embracing to Jahangir, both are standing on terrestrial globe with Sun and Moon's light behind Jahangir.[115]

Besides the astrological impact on Mughal painting, we find a comprehensive astrological and Hindu Tantric lore in the *Nujum al-Ulum*, as discussed earlier. In fact, India was renowned for its various complex types of astrological prediction from ancient times. A large part of the vast literature, produced in the Deccan, was procured by the Mughals after the campaign against Bijapur (1686) and Golconda (1687).[116] Thus, it is very much pertinent that a work such as *Nujum al-Ulum*, which contains various types of astrological superstitions, should have originated in this area only. Its author assumes the unity between cosmic factors which in turn affect earthly events. Many of the illustrations in the *Nujum al-Ulum* were originally visualized as having human relationships. For example, the planets are first shown as symbolic human being according to astrological system.

The *Nujum al-Ulum* commences with pictures of angles that are found according to Muslim belief at various heavenly levels. The pictures of constellations were also widely used but are especially decorative in the *Nujum al-Ulum*. The third section of the volume, which is quite long, illustrates a comprehensive system of astrology. In this section, the author sets out the associations between the planets, the signs of zodiac. This portion represents a significant part of the book; many of the individual miniatures, such as those portraying planets, are of exceptional fineness and the overall designs of the illustrating degrees of the zodiac, have a beautiful ornamental quality as well. The illustrations are here listed in their original sequence.[117]

The book '*Nujum al-Ulm* consists of five miniature groups. The first miniature group consists of angles of the various heavens. The miniature group no. two, three and fourth consists of the northern constellations, planets, *nakshatras*, sign of the Zodiac and their degree and the southern constellations respectively. But the fifth Group consists of '*Talisman*'. We find that miniature group number three gives a vivid picture of planets, *nakshatra* signs of the zodiac and their degrees.[118]

The section on astrology which follows the northern constellation, is based on ancient Indian system of calculating time according to the moon's changing position during the course of a lunar month of 27 days. The moon appears to reside in a succession of 27 "mansions" termed *nakshatra*, which are stars or star groupings and signs of the Zodiac were combined with '*Nakshatras*' for astrological prognosis.[119]

The astrological symbols illustrated in the *Nujum al-Ulum*, are divided into sections each including a planet followed by two signs of the zodiac, three *nakshatras*, thirty degrees of each zodiac signs. Twelve signs of the zodiac each with their thirty degrees are equal to the 360 degrees of a circle and correspond approximately to the days of a year. Rahu and Ketu also appear at the end of the section. Hindus have, in fact, worshipped the nine planets for about two millennia because of their supposed malevolent influence over daily life. The system, coordinating planets with the zodiac, appears in the order set out by Ptolemy: Leo (Sun), Virgo (Mercury), Libra (Venus), Scorpio (Mars), Sagittarius (Jupiter), Capricorn (Saturn), Aquarius (Saturn), Pisces (Jupiter), Aries (Mars), Taurus (Venus), Gemini (Mercury), Cancer (Moon).[120]

According to K. Khandaalavala and J. Mittal, Talisman was a fairly popular subject for illustration. And the first produced manuscript on the subject which was also contemporary of Nujum-al-Ulum belongs to Mughal paintings.[121] In miniature group five of *Talismans*, only one type of *talisman* associated with the planets is described.

To conclude we can say that there were myths, beliefs, superstitions, and astrological traditions prevailing in society so intensified that contemporary art, architecture and painting could not go untouched by the impact of these subjects or areas.

Endnotes

1. V. R. Pandit, "*Omens and Portents in Vedic Literature*", Proceedings of the All India Oriental Conference, Nagpur Session (1946), p. 76.
2. O. P. Jaggi, *History of Science and Technology*, *op. cit.*, pp. 98-100.
3. Ibid, pp. 99-100
4. Hardhar Pathak, *Cultural History of Gupta Period (1978)*, Delhi, Bhartiya Publishing House, pp. 227-28.
5. Elliot and Dowson, *The History of India, as told by its own Historians*, Kitab Mahal Pvt. Ltd: Allahabad (1978), Vol. I, p. 10.
6. Vasudeva Upadhayay, *The Socio-Religious Condition of North India*, Chowkhamba Sanskrit Series Office: Varanasi-I (India), pp. 255-269.
7. *Ibid.*
8. .P. Srivastava, *Social and Cultural Trends in Islamic India*, Vohra Publisher and Distributors: Allahabad, p. 45; Also see Iqtidar Husain Siddiqui, *Medieval India*, Manohar: New Delhi (2003), p. 20.
9. Iqtidar Husain Siddiqui, *op. cit.*, pp. 20-21.
10. R. Nath and Faiyaz Gwaliari, *India as seen by Amir Khusrou*, H.R.D: Jaipur (1981), pp. 28-29.
11. Manucci, Eng. Tr. W. Irvine Vol. II, p.213.

12. Yasin Mohammad, *Social History of Islamic India*, The Upper India Publishing House: Lucknow (1958), p. 93. Also see Hughes, *Dictionary of Islam*, p. 25.
13. M.A. Ansari, *European Travellers Under the Mughal*, Delhi, pp. 98, 121 and *op. cit.*, p. 94. Also see Bernier, p. 161. Monserrate p. 9; Terry, p.223; Careri, Part III, p. 251 and O. P. Jaggi, *op. cit.*, pp. 27-28.
14. Bernier's Francois, *Travels in the Mughal Empire* (1656-1668), Oxford, 1934. p. 161.
15. *Ibid.*
16. Ain-i-Akbari, Vol. I, p.340.
17. Manucci N. Storio do Mogor, *op. cit.*, Vol. I, p. 215.
18. Francisco Pelsaert, "Remonstrantie" (trans.) W. H. Moreland and P. Geyl, *Jahangir's India, Idagah-i-Adabiyat-I*, Delhi (19), p. 77.
19. A. L. Srivastava, *Akbar the Great*, Shive Lal Agrawala and Co.: Agra (1973), Vol. III, pp. 67, 201, 202 & 2045. Also see P.N. Chopra, *Life and Letters Under the Mughals*, Ashajanak Publications: New Delhi, pp. 132,180.
20. P.N. Chopra, *Life and Letters Under the Mughals*, op, cit., p. 180. Meer Hasan Ali, *Observations on the Mussulmans of India I*, pp. 353-55.
21. V. P.S. Raghuvanshi, *Indian Society of Eighteenth Century"*, Associated Publishing House, New Delhi, p. 155.
22. Dubois, p. 383, as quoted by V.P.S. Raghuvanshi, op, cit., p. 156.
23. Raghuvanshi, *Ibid.*, p. 157.
24. *Ibid.*, p. 163.
25. *Ibid.*
26. *Ibid.*, p. 167.
27. Howard R. Turner, *Science in Medieval Islam*, Oxford University Press: Delhi (1999), pp. 109-11.
28. Haldhar, Pathak, *Cultural History of Gupta Period*, *op. cit.*, pp. 167-69.
29. *Ibid.*
30. Abul Fazl, Beveridge (trans.), *Akbaranama*, *op. cit.*, Vol. I, p. 519, quoted by P.N. Chopra also.
31. Blochman (Trans.), *Ain-i-Akbari*, *op. cit.*, p. 289; also see B. K Sahay, *Education and Learning under the Great Mughals*, New Literature Publishing Co., Bombay (1972), pp. 13-14.
32. Badauni, p. 316; also see B. K. Sahay, *op. cit.*, pp. 14-15.
33. K. Sahay, *Education and Learning Under the Great Mughals*, *op. cit.*, pp. 14-15.
34. P. N. Chopra, *Life and Letters under the Mughals*, *op. cit.*, pp. 114-45.
35. Badauni, *op. cit.* quoted by B. K. Sahay and P. N. Chopra.
36. Blochman, *Ain-i-Akbari*, *op. cit.*, Vol. I, pp. 278-79.
37. Bernier's Travels, *op. cit.*, pp. 334-35.

38. Badauni, *op. cit.*, Vol. II, p.307 & 316; *Ain-i-Akbari*, *op. cit.*, Vol. I, pp. 288-89.
39. Badauni, *op. cit.*
40. Palseart, *op. cit.*, p. 77, also see P. N. Chopra, *op. cit.*, pp. 146-47.
41. P. N. Chopra, "Life and Letter Under the Mughal", *op. cit.*, p. 146.
42. *ibid.*, pp. 134-136.
43. *Ibid.*, p. 137; R. K. Mukerji, *Ancient Indian Education*, pp. 598-601, also see, B. K. Sahay, *op. cit.*, pp. 20-25.
44. *Ibid.*, p. 141.
45. *Ibid.*, p. 154.
46. *Ibid.*, p. 154; also see A. F. Soonewala, *Maharaja Sawai Jaisingh*, pp. 10-11.
47. As quoted by R. Nath, *The Evolution of Tomb in Mughal Architecture*, D.B. Taraporevala Sons: Bombay (1972), p. 4.
48. *Ibid.*, p. 4-5; Also see Clarks Fabri, *An Introduction to Indian Architecture*, Asia Publishing House, Bombay, New York (1963), pp. 36-40.
49. *Ibid.* also see Charles Paberi, *op. cit.*, pp. 40-46.
50. *Ibid.* Also see Surendra Nath Dasgupta, "Fudamentals of Indian Art", Bhartiya Vidya Bhawan: Bombay (1954), pp. 34-40.
51. *Ibid.*, Also see Surendra Nath Dasgupta, *Ibid.*, p. 11-20.
52. Gayatri Devi Vasudev (ed.), *Vastu Astrtology and Architecture*, Motilal Banarasidas: Delhi (1998), pp. 140-41.
53. S. R. N. Murthy, "Indian Architecture", in Gayatri Devi Vasundhra (ed.), *op. cit.*, p. 197.
54. Kowth Lalith Manohar, "The Efficacy of Vastu Shastra", in Gyatri Devi Vasundhra (ed.), *op. cit.*, p.114.
55. As quoted by D.N.Shukla, *Vastu Sastra*, Vastu Vangaya Prakashan: Lucknow (1960), il. I, pp. 38-40.
56. *Ibid.*, p. 39. Also see Dr. V. Ganapati Sathapati, *Sthapatya Veda*, Dakshina Publishing House: Chennai (2001), pp. 125-30.
57. V. Vanapati Sthapati, *Ibid.*, pp. 369-74.
58. T. S. Vasan, "Vastu in Astrology" in Gayatri Devi Vasudev (ed.), *Vastu, Astrology and Architecture*, *op. cit.*, pp. 115-16.
59. *Ibid.*
60. *Ibid.*, pp. 118-19.
61. *Ibid.*
62. *Ibid.*, pp. 119-20.
63. D. N. Shukla, *Vastu Shastra*, Vol. I, *op. cit.*, pp. 36-37.
64. M. L. Roychoudhary, *The Din-i-Ilahi*, Calcutta, 1941, p. 47, quoted by R. Nath, *History of Decorative Art in Mughal Architecture*, Motilal Banarasi Das: Delhi (1976), p. 4.

65. Elphinston, *History of India*, op.cit., p. 476.

66. Qanun-i-Huymayuni of Khwandamir (trans. Bani Prasad, Calcutta (1940), pp. 23-59; Iswari Prasad, *The Life and Times of Humayun*, Calcutta (1956), p. cit., pp. 52-57.

67. Raichaudhary, *op. cit.*, p. 51.

68. R. Nath, *History of Decorative Art in Mughal Architecture, op. cit.*, pp. 5-6.

69. V. S. Agarwal, *Indian Art*, Varanasi (1965), p. 51 as quoted by R. Nath in *Ibid.*, pp. 6-7. V. S. Agarwal has given a list of *Asthmangals* (eight auspicious symbols) of Indian art in his book – *Chakradwaja*, Varanasi (1964) as such: (1) *Swastika* (2) *Srivatsa* (3) *Mina Mithuna* (4) *Vaijayanti* (5) *Devgriha Vimana* (6) *Ratuapatra* (7) *Purnaghata* (8) *Mahasrak* (The great garland).

70. E. W. Smith, *The Mughal Architecture of Fatahpur Sikri*, A.S.I. New Imperial Series: Allahabad (894-98), Vol. XVIII (4 parts) part IV, Plate XXVIII and LXXXII as quoted by R. Nath, *op. cit.*, pp. 7-9.

71. V. S. Agarwal, *Studies in Indian Art*, *op. cit.*, p. 47.

72. A. K. Coomaraswmy, "Origin of the Lotus", *The Historical Quarterly*, Calcutta (1930), Vol. VI, p. 374.

73. R. Nath, *op. cit.*, pp. 14-15.

74. *Ibid.*, p. 15.

75. *Ibid.*, p. 18.

76. R. Nath, *op. cit.*, p. 21. Also see Stella Kramrisch, *The Hindu Temple*, Calcutta (1946), Vol. II, p. 355.

77. *Ibid.*, pp. 19-21.

78. Heinrich Zimmer, "Myth and symbols in Indian Art and Civilisation" (ed. Joseph Combell), New York (1962), p. 139, Kramrisch recounts a similar story and quotes Varahmihira's Brahat-Samhita', *op. cit.*, p. 325, as quoted by R. Nath, *op. cit.*, pp. 22-23.

79. E. B. Havell, The Ancient and Medieval Architecture of India, London (1915), p. 29, as quoted by R. Nath, *op. cit.*, p. 24.

80. A. K.Coomarswami, *History of Indian and Indonesian Art* (Dover ed.) (1965), p. 41. Also see R. Nath, pp. 27-28.

81. V. S. Aggrawal, *Chakra-dwaja*, Varanasi (1964), Preface, p. (i).

82. V.S. Aggrawal, *Indian Art*, *op. cit.*, p. 159.

83. T. A. Gopinath Rao, *Elements of Hindu Iconography*, Delhi (1968), Vol. I, Part I, p. 25, as quoted by R. Nath, *op. cit.*, p. 29, footnote.

84. R. Nath, *op. cit.*, p. 30.

85. R. Nath, *op. cit.*, pp. 31-40.

86. E. W. Smith, *The Mughal Architecture of Fatehpur Sikri*, A.S.I., New Imperial Series, Vol. XXIII (4 parts), Allahabad (1894-98), Part IV, p. 11, Plate LI, Also see R. Nath, *Ibid.*

87. E.W. Smith, *op. cit.*, Part III, Plate XXVIII and XXIII as quoted by R. Nath, *op. cit.*, p.32.
88. R. Nath, *Ibid.*, pp. 32-34.
89. Al-Badoni, Muntakhabul's Tawarikh, Vol. II, (tr. W. H. Lowe), Calcutta (1924), p. 265.
90. Karl Mhandalvala and Jagdish Mittal, *An early Akbari Illustated Manuscript of Tilasm and Zodiac*, Lalitkala, No. 14 (1969), p. 9.
91. R. Nath, op.cit., pp. 42-43.
92. *Ibid.*, pp. 43-44.
93. It is now preserved in the Prince of Wales Museum of Western India, Bombay, Item No. 16.100 as quoted by R. Nath, *Ibid.*, p. 43.
94. R. Nath, *Ibid.*, p. 44.
95. Published in the *Quarterly Review of Historical Studies*, Calcutta, Vol. XII, No. 4 (1972-73), also see, R. Nath, *Some Aspects of Mughal Architecture*, Abhinav Publication: New Delhi (1976), pp. 7-18.
96. Some Aspects of Mughal Architecture, *op. cit.*, pp. 16-18.
97. Abul Fazl, *Ain-i-Akbari*, op.cit., pp.10-15.
98. Al-Badaoni, *Muntakhabut's-Tawarikh*, *op. cit.*, *op. cit.*, pp. 268-69.
99. R. Nath, *Some Aspects of Mughal Architecture*, *op. cit.*, p. 18.
100. Percy Brown, "Monuments of Mughal Period" quoted by Monica Juneja (ed.), *Architecture in Medieval India*, Permanent Black I. P. Extention: New Delhi (2001), pp.190-92. Also see, Anand Coomaraswamy, *Introduction to Indian Art*, The Thesophical Publishing House: Adyar (1956), pp. 62-70.
101. Stuart Cary Welch, *Imperial Mughal Painting*, George Braziller Inc. One Park Avenue: New York (1978), pp.14-15.
102. Som Parkash Verma, *Art and Material Culture in the Paintings of Akbar's Court*, New Delhi (1978), p.18, Pl. XIV.
103. Karl Khandalavala, *The Development of Style in Indian Painting*, The Macmillan Co. of India Ltd: Delhi, Madras. Bombay, Calcutta (1974), pp. 70-71.
104. Irfan Habib, *Akbar and His India*, *op. cit.*, pp. 151-53.
105. Linda York Leach, *Mughal and Other Indian Paintings*, (from the Chester Beathy Library), Scorpion Cavendisl Ltd: London (1995), Vol. II, p. 819.
106. *Ibid.*, p. 820.
107. *Ibid.*
108. *Ibid.*, p. 823.
109. Gulbadan Begum, "Humayun Nama", Satkona A. S. Beveridge (trans.), *Idarah-i-Dabiyat-i-Delhi*, Delhi (1972), pp. 152, 158.
110. *Ibid.*, p. 154, also see Som Prakash Verma, *Art and Culture*, *op. cit.*, pp. 17-18, Pl. XII.

111. P. N. Chopra, *op. cit.*, footnote p. 199. Also see A catalogue of Indian Collections, Pt. VI.
112. A. K. Coomaraswamy, *Museum Fine Art*, Cambridge: Boston (1930), Pl. III-VI.
113. Sir W. A. Thomas, "A Catalogue of the Indian Ministers", ed. By J.V.S. Wilkinson, Vol. II, Pt. No. 33 as quoted by P. N. Chopra, *op. cit.*, footnote, p. 199.
114. Stuart Cary Welch, *op. cit.*, pp. 74-75, Plate No. 18. Also see Jahangir's Memoirs, *op. cit.*, Vol. I, p. 115.
115. Stuart Cary Welch, *Ibid.*, pp. 80-81, Plate No. 21.
116. Lind York Leach, *op. cit.*, pp. 823-24.
117. *Ibid.*, pp. 821-26.
118. *Ibid.*, pp. 827-50.
119. A. L. Basham, *op. cit.*, p. 490.
120. Linda York Leach, *op. cit.*, pp. 830-31 (footnotes).
121. K. Khandalavala and J. Mittal, *An Early Akbari Illustrated Manuscript of Tilasm and Zodiac*, Lalit Kala 14, (1969), pp. 9-20.

CHAPTER 6

Abul Fazl's Vision of Astronomy and Astrology

The knowledge of astrology and astronomy in India goes back to early vedic period as it has been discussed in various ancient texts such as Rigveda, Narad Puran, Vedanga Jotish, Yazurveda, Epics, Puranas, Brahmans, etc. Gargya, Sunashsepa, Parasara, Saktya, Gautama, Vamadeva, Aryabhatta, Srisena, Varahmihira, Brahma Gupta, Bhaskara I, Kalyanavarman, Bhattotpala, Bhaskara II, Lalla, Manjula, Shripati, Prithudaka etc. were famous astronomers in ancient India, while Varahmihira ws one of the famous astrologers too. Indian astronomers came into contact with Greek astronomy as a result five astronomical systems, called as 'Siddhantas' namely: Surya Pitamaha, Paulisa, Vasistha, and Romaka came into existence.

In the early medieval period, people were generally very superstitious. Rulers were very particular to know the auspicious and the inauspicious moments from the astrologers in the court of Al-Mansur (773 A.D.) some books on Indian astronomy were translated in Arabic. 'Brahmasphuta Siddhanta' of Brahma Gupta, 'Aryabhatiyam' or Aryabhatta and 'Khanda Khadyaka' were translated as Sindhind, Arjabahad and Arkand respectively. An assimilation of Indian and Arabic astronomical science can be seen in the court of later emperors or Arab. In this context the contribution of Al-Biruni is remarkable. His famous works are Kitab-ul-Hind-fi-Tahqiq, Mial Hind, Asarul Baqia and Qanun-i-Masudi. He probably enjoyed the reputation of a great Munajjim i.e. Astrologers and Astronomers. Pheru Thakkura (1291-1323 A.D.) was a good astrologer in the period of Ala-ud-din Khilzi. Zij astronomy appears in India for the first time, under the patronage of Sultan Ferozshah Tughlaq (1351-1388 A.D.). Hence, astrology has a long history in India. Astronomy is the study of individual celestial bodies as a whole, while astrology is the investigation of happenings of the celestial bodies and its impacts on individuals and on universe.

Abul Fazl was one of the remarkable personalities of medieval scholarship. He had an outstanding knowledge of astronomy and astrology during the Mughal period. Endowed with sharp and penetrating intellect, at the age of fifteen, he completed his education in the rational and traditional sciences. He was more than a mere conventional official historian[1]. His main writings i.e. Akbarnama and Ain-i-Akbari show his analytical study and expression of philosophy, religion as well as his scientific bent of mind. In the Ain-i-Akbari, there are sections on subjects like technology, metallurgy, veterinary science, medicine, physical and mathematical geography and on astronomical sciences[2]. In the Akbarnama he displays his learning by giving a string of astronomical and astrological terms[3].

In the present paper an endeavour has been made to highlight Abul Fazl's deep knowledge and understanding about the astronomical sciences and to explit cultural exchange between the Hindus and the Muslims. Attempt has also been made to reflect how contemporary society was influenced by astronomy, and astrology like modern times.

Akbarnama and Ain-i-Akbari were Abul Fazl's main historical works. Ain-i-Akbari is the supplementary work of Akbarnama. V.A. Smith[4] remarks, that "nothing at all resembling, it was ever compiled in Asia, and it would be difficult to find an authoritative compilation of this type even in Europe. In 1776, about 13 years before the French Revolution, when France was passing through acute financial crisis, Le.P. Tieffentaller published extracts from the rent rolls given in the Ain-i-Akbari in his "Description Geographique de l'Indostan". Abul Fazl perhaps was the first Indo-Persian historian to attract the attention of European scholars[5].

The Insa-i-Abul Fazl or the Maktubat-i-Allami, comprises letters and firmans written on behalf of Akbar by Abul Fazl to rulers and nobles[6]. The Munajat-i-Abul Fazl formally constituted his invocation to God. He also wrote Prefaces to the Tarikh-i-Alfi and the Persian translation of the Mahabharat[7]. Ayar Danish is another work to the credit of Abul Fazl,[8] these works contain just incidental remarks about astrology.

Harbans Mukhia, writes about the content of his chief writings that "apart from battles and similar events, Abul Fazl appends incidental notes on subjects such as the topography of an area or elephant or astrology. This kind of information is given only on occasions when Abul Fazl is describing an event of which it forms an element. If he were telling us, for instance, of the emperor's ride on a particularly difficult elephant, he would incidentally describe the kinds of elephants Akbar used to ride on. Similarly, if he mentioned the birth of a prince, he would also refer to the horoscopes under different systems prepared on the occasion"[9]. It indicates his knowledge about horoscope under different methods of astrology.

Abul Fazl gives an account of his deep knowledge about the basic principles of astronomy practiced by Hindu as well as Muslim astronomers. In the Ain-i-Akbari he mentions a list of 86 Muslim astronomers and astrologers, who had flourished the courts of emperors in Central Asia[10]. Displaying his analytical approach about the subject, he defines that 'Rasad' signifies 'watching' in the Arabic language. Therefore, the watchers are those who observe the movements of the stars and study their aspects. The result of their investigations regarding the spherical or terrestrial mysteries, which are tabulated, is called an "Astronomical table" or "Zij". This word is an Arabicized form of the Persian 'Zik" which means the threads that guide the embroiderers in weaving brocaded stuffs. In the same way an astronomical table is a guide to the astronomer in recognizing the condition of the heavens, and the liner extensions and columns, in length and breadth, resemble these threads[11]. He mentions important astronomers and their achievements from the historical perspective. He further defines that whatever astronomers set down, year by year from an astronomical table of the particular motions and individual positions of the planets, is called an Almanac, and in Hindi called` 'Patrah'. It embodies the progression of a planet from its first entrance into Aries to a determinate point in the Zodiac. He narrates the dedication of Indian sages towards astronomy as it is inspired by divine intelligences.

Abul Fazl seems to be well acquainted with Indian astronomy and astrology as he writes that the writings of Indian sages were termed as 'Siddhant'. He further mentions nine books, which are, still depends upon i.e., the Brahma Siddhant, the Suraj Siddhant, the Som Siddhant, the Brahaspat Siddhant, inspired respectively by Brahma, the Sun, Moon, and Jupiter. Their origin is traced back to time immemorial. The Garg Siddhant, the Narad Siddhant, the Pulast Siddhant and Vishista Siddhant are ascribed as earthly sources. He also displays the minute difference between Elkhani and Gurgani tables and discrepancies in the calculation of time. He gives an account of the history of Islamic astronomy. According to him, for the Muslims as well as Greeks, the astronomy only aims at "studying the apparent movement of the stars and giving a geometrical spherical astronomy and the theory of the instruments"[12]. Al-Baruni is Abul-Fazl's source of information about Indian works in astronomy.

In the beginning of Islam though the Arabs possessed some knowledge of practical astronomy, it was only in the 2nd century of Hijra (8th century A.D.) that the scientific study of astronomy was introduced, under the influence of two Indian books: the Brahma–Sphuta–Siddhanta of Brahmagupta (628 A.D.) and the treatise of Aryabhatt.[13]

Abul Fazl elucidates different popular eras of the Hindus. According to him every era was a new epoch in history. The Hindu astronomers regarded the months and years as of four kinds, according to the Zodiac sign. First is "Saurmas", which is the Sun's continuance in one sign of the Zodiac, and such a year consists of 365 days, 15 gharis, 30 pals and 22½ bipals. Second is "Chandramas" which is computed from the first day of the Moon's increase to the night of the new moon. This year is 354 days, 22 gharis and one pal. The difference between Saurmas and Chandramas is due to the calculation of the mean rate of motion of the Sun and Moon. The third kind of month is "Sawan Mas". Abul Fazl writes that Hindu astronomers fix its commencement at any day as they please. And it is completed in 30 days and, thus, the year consists of 360 days. The fourth one is "Nachhattar", which is calculated from the time-cycle of moon in "Nachehatras". This month consists of 27 days and the year of 324.[14.]

Abul Fazl further mentions six types of seasons, which are called Ritu, viz.

1. Basant, when sun remains in Pisces and Aries Zodiac sign.
2. Grisham, in which sun enters into Taurus and Gemini.
3. Barkha, when sun is in Cancer and Leo.
4. Sard, when sun remains in Virgo and Libra.
5. Hemant, sun enters into Scorpio and Sagittarius,
6. Lastly Shishra, when sun remains in Capricorns and Aquarius.

The year is again divided likewise into three 'Kals' beginning from Phagun. The Hindu astronomers called four hot months as Dhupkal, the four rainy months as Barkhakal and the four cold months as Shitkal. Abul Fazl further elaborates these 'Kals' according to Zodiac signs' divisions as follows; Pisces, Aries, Taurus, and Gemini are the summer; Cancer, Leo, Virgo and Libra, the rain and Scorpio, Sagittarius, Capricorns, and Aquarius are the winter. The solar year is divided into two parts. The first beginning with Aries to the extreme of Virgo is termed as "Uttargol", which is the sun's progress to the north of the Equator, and from the beginning of Libra to the extreme of Pisces, termed as "Dakkhangol", that is the sun's course to the south of the Equator. According to the declination of sun, the year is also divided into two parts: Uttarayan and Dachchhanayan. From the first of Capricorn to the end of Gemini as Uttarayan is the Sun's northern declination and from the first of Cancer to the end of Sagittarius as Dachchhanayan is the Sun's southern declination.

Abul Fazl further narrates that the whole day and night is divided into 60 equal parts as known as 'Ghaties', more commonly known as Ghari. Each Ghari is subdivided into the same number of parts, each of which they call Pal. In the same way, 'Pal' is sub-subdivided into Nari or Bipal also. And each Nari is equal to six respirations of a man of an equable temperament, not disturbed by running or any other emotions. The breath, which is respired and inhaled, termed as Swas and Parswas respectively. And both together are called as a Prane. Six Pranes make a Pal and 60 Pals a Ghari. An astronomical hour, which is the 24th part of a whole day and night[15] is equal to 2½ gharis. The whole day and night are equal to 2½ gharis. Each night and each day are again divided into 4 parts, each is called as 'Pahr'.[16] He seems to have known about the latitude and longitude of the cities also.[17]

The above description shows that Abul Fazl has acquired a deep knowledge of Hindu astronomy. No terminology or principle of the astronomical sciences seems to be unfamiliar to his knowledge.

Abul Fazl further narrates the popular eras of different countries of the contemporary age. He writes in detail about the Khatai Era of China, the Turkish Era, the Era of Adam, the Jewish Era, the Era of Bakht Nassar, the Era of Philipus (also known as the Era of Alexander of Macedonia), the Coptic Era, the Syro-Macedonian Era, the Augustan Era, the Christian Era, the Era of Amtonirus of Rome, Era of the Hijra, the era of Yazdajird, the Maliki Era, the Khani Era and the Illahi Era, which was started by Akbar. He discusses all aspects of the aforementioned Eras as in a same manner as the

Hindu Era.[18] He also gives a chart of the months and eras of various countries.[19]

H.S. Jarrett[20] has written a biographical note, which contains a long list of authors as Abul Fazl has given. It seems that the works of these authors might have been studied by Abul Fazl to acquire a deep knowledge of astronomical Sciences.

After going through the Akbarnama[21], it cannot be denied that Abul Fazl had a deep understanding of Astrology too. He was rather more aware of all numerical/ mathematical calculations of planets. Displaying his knowledge on Numerology and Gemology, Abul-Fazl referred to the works of his brother Faizi and Al-Biruni, who writes that the letters of the word AKBAR correspond to the numerical value. The letters of the name are a collection of the four fold degrees, i.e. the four elements and stages of Beauty, Majesty, Bounty and Perfection. These stages denote his excellent qualities i.e. bodily health, length of life, exaltation of sovereignty and lasting job. Thus, explaining the name AKBAR, he writes that Alif (A) is fire, K of (K) Water, Ba (B) Air and Ra(R) Earth.[22]

Abul Fazl mentions four horoscopes of Akbar, which are interpreted by different astrologers. The first and fourth, however, seem to be the same. Both were made by Muhamumadan, servants of Humayun-the first by Maulana Chand and the fourth by Maulana Ilyas of Ardabil. Maulana Chand had drawn up the horoscope according to the "New Table"[23] of Ulugh Beg Mirza who was Timar's grandson. Maulana Alya's horoscope was cast according to the Ilkhani or imperial table made by Nasiruddin Tusi. The second horoscope was made by Jotik Rai, who was Akbar's Hindu astrologer. It was drawn after many years of Akbar's birth. The third was made by Fathullah of Siraz after 1583 A.D.[24] Abul Fazl has marked a very thin line while describing the difference between the horoscopes made by Indian and Muslim astrologers.

Abul Fazl elucidates that both Maulana Chand and Maulana Ilyas put the birth of Akbar under Virgo. The Indian astrologers, however, put his birth in Leo because that sign is the house of the Sun. There was supposed to be a mysterious connection between the sun and Akbar. It means that Akbar has some qualities like sun. According to him, the difference between Indian astrologers and Maulana Chand amounts to 17o. But it seems that Fathullah-Shirazi did not adopt the Indian calculation. He based his calculation on the Greek and Persian Tables and found the cusp of the Ascendant to be 28o36' Leo. But on the whole, each horoscope is equally good in the matter of power, dignity, and sublimity.[25]

Abul Fazl gives an account of the explanation of the judgement or prediction contained in the horoscope of Akbar. The account, undoubtedly, placed Abul Fazl in high esteem among the contemporary astrologers of that time. He appears to be a well- read aspirant of the subject. The judgment of all 12 houses of the horoscope has been discussed elaborately. He mentions the degree of every planet and houses including its aspects, position of exaltation, and malefic also. The horoscope of the accession of Akbar is also mentioned by him. He writes that at Kalanaur, in a felicitous hour on Friday noon, the second day of Ravi-as-sani 963 of the lunar year, i.e., 14th February 1556, but by calculation i.e., 15th February, Akbar was sat on the throne. The calculation of planetary position was made by the astronomers as follows[26]: Though, Imam-Abu-l-Muhammad of Ghazni, who was one of the great masters of astronomy, had suggested that the Ascendant of Scorpio would be good, so that the tenth house might be Leo, the house of the Sun. But in the present horoscope the Sun itself comes in the tenth house. He, moreover, never forgot to describe the Zodiac sign and Ascendant of the horoscope of newly born child in the imperial court. He narrates horoscopes of Prince Salim, Murad, Danial, Khusro, Khurram etc. A brief account of their horoscopes referred to by Abul Fazl may be discussed here.

Abul Fazl[27] writes that in accordance with directions of Akbar, astronomers calculated the powers of the planets and prepared the horoscope of prince Salim. He further writes that horoscope was prepared according to the Greek and Indian methods, because these two methods are different in the matter of fundamental principles and method of forecasting. Abul Fazl himself has given an example of his deep interest and knowledge of astrology. He says that he (Abul Fazl) was ordered by Akbar to draw out a new horoscope in accordance with the Greek and Indian canon and to record its judgment for each year, so that it might be a code for horoscope makers of the age.[28] Maulana Chand's horoscope which he drew up according to the Greek canon appears most worthy.[29] But both (Greek and Indian) give Libra as the sign. At the ascension point of the 24th degree of Libra after seven hours had elapsed of the day of Rashn 18 Shahriywar, Divine month of 977 (30 August 1569).[30]

Abul Fazl also narrated the horoscope of Prince Shah Murad. On 7 June 1570, under the sign of Capricorn according to the Greek philosophers and Sagittarius, according to the Indian sages, a noble son 'Murad' was born in the fortunate quarters of Shaikh Salim in Fatehpur. The horoscopes[31] were made according to both canons, Greek as well as Indian.

A horoscope of Prince Sultan Danial is also mentioned in the Ain-i-Akbari of Abul Fazl. On 9th September 1572, under the sign of Aries according to the Greek philosophers and of Pisces according to the Indian sages, the Shahinshah (Akbar) was blessed with a son, in the blissful land of Ajmer. Its longitude of is 111.5 and latitude 26.[32] Abul Fazl further mentions that the horoscopes were inserted by him according to both methods of Greek and Indian tables but left the extraction of the judgments to the subtle eyes of astronomers.[33]

Abul Fazl was delighted to mention the horoscopes of the third generation of Akbar. He described the horoscope of Prince Khusrau. On the day of Din 24 Amardad (about middle of August 1587) in the bed chamber of Prince Salim (Jahjangir), Khusrau was born after the lapse of ten hours and thirty-six minutes. According to the Greek rules, the horoscope was the 9th degree of Capricorn and according to Indian astrologers; it was the 22nd degree of Sagitarius. Here, Abul Fazl was very hopeful regarding the planets of this newly born baby to be as an enlightened man with noble qualities. He also expressed his wish to give a full account of this horoscope.[34]

Abul Fazl has also given another description of the horoscope of Prince Khurram (Shahajahan). According to him, on the 26th Dai(month) of Devine Era, after four hours and 24 minutes, during the sign of Libra, the daughter of the Mota Raja gave birth to a son in the harem of Prince Salim in Lahore. His name was Sultan Khurram.[35]

One of the occurrences was the birth of Aram Banu Begam Abul Fazl narrates that on 12 Dai, 22 December 1524, divine month, and the 19th Degree of Sagittarius and according to the calculation of the Indians, one degree and 54 minutes, that night gleaming jewel of fortune appeared, and glorified the harem of the Shahinshah. He further says that astrologers announced the joyful news and the world's lord conferred on her that great name. It was to be hoped that the advent of this lady of the family of chastity would be the means of increased life and would be an adornment of the kingdom.[36]

He further mentions that on the eve of the 16th Ardibihisht (25 April 1586), the daughter of Raja Bhagwan Das, named Manbai, gave birth to a daughter in the house of Prince Sultan Salim, which was followed by various rejoicings. The horoscope according to the Greek method gave 18 degree of Sagittarius and according to Hindu calculation; it was 1 Degree 41 minutes.[37]

These descriptions of horoscopes show the deep interest of Abul Fazl in Astrology.

Description of the Appearance of the Comet in 1577 A.D.

Abul Fazl also narrates the occurrence of comets in his writings. He describes its effects on Hindustan as well as on the world. He might have been acquainted with the astronomical position in the atmosphere when the phenomenon occurred.

He referred to the occurrence of two comets. It is very interesting to note that, before describing the appearance of comet, he writes about the atmospherical process of vapor and smoke. According to him both are of two kinds. One becomes fixed in the ground and produces heat, hollow space in the earth and earthquakes. The other one spreads over the surface of the earth, and produces clouds, rain, storms, thunder, lightning etc. He has given astronomical reasons behind the phenomenon. He writes that whenever Mars is predominant in a country, the latter becomes aride and thick vapours and smokes rise up in it.[38]

He explains that when Mars specially is in the tenth house of the horoscope of the season and the house is with windy or fiery and malefic inclined with Moon and Mercury as a result of this phenomenon, the crops would, then, become bad and there would be the elements of a famine, sickness, and predominance of wrath.[39] He further explains the process of formation of meteor (Shihab) and comets (Zu-Zuaba). He narrates that when the viscous and hairy vapor first rises from the ground and joins the first stratum[40] of the atmosphere, viz. that, which is mixed with fire, it assumes beauty, just as the smoke of an extinguished lamp, becomes illuminated, when approached with a light. It is, then called a meteor (Shihab) also a shooting star. On account of the diverse nature of the atmosphere it assumes various forms. Thus, it becomes hairy, or it acquires a tail, or it holds a spear, or resembles a horned animal etc. According to differences in its qualities, it is either quickly consumed, or lasts a long time. In Indian books, the number of forms is mentioned more than one hundred. In Greek treatises, seven kinds are enumerated and they, all are regarded as of the natures of Saturn and Mars. The Zu-zuaba (the hairy one) and the Zu-zanab (the tailed) are regarded as the most malefic. He further narrates the opinion of Ptolemy that the Zu-zuaba and the sun are eleven Signs apart. Some of the Greeks are of the opinion that the Zu-zuaba shows themselves in the morning towards the east, and the Zu-zunabs appear at evening toward the west. It seems according to repeated observation.[41]

Abul Fazl also narrates the opinions of the Indian scholars as they have divided those (Comets) into two classes i.e., malefic, and benefic. But he mentions that all the scholars can agree about their influences and effects across the country whose zenith they pass or where they are visible to the inhabitants, or it depends on the nature of the sign in which they appear.

It appears that Abul Fazl has gone through the old books in detail regarding their influences. He, however, expressed his inability to describe it as a whole. He further mentions some of the occurrences in historical perspective. He says that the hairy comet appeared in the Hijra year 662, when sun was in the Sign of Leo.[42] It passed to the countries of Tibet, Turkestan, China, Kashgar, Farghana, Transoxiana and Khurasan and was visible for eighty- five days. There were disturbances in all these countries. He further narrates that in 803 Hijra (1400 A.D) a tailed comet appeared in the Zenith of Asia Minor. Maulana Abdullah Lisan Muhiu-d-din Maghrabi and a host of astronomers represented to Timur were of the view it that appeared according to wise sayings that an army from the east would conquer that country and capture its monarch.

Abul Fazl mentions another instance which occurred in Hijra 837 (1433 A.D.) when a tailed comet appeared in the first degrees of the sign of Libra near the Northern Crown. It became spear bearing and disappeared in eight months. As a consequence, a great epidemic occurred in Herat and its neighbourhood. Everyday more than a thousand persons died. He mentions that the important personalities like M. Ibrahim, the ruler of Fars, M. Baysanghar Arghun, the Shah of Badakhshan and S. Zainu-d-din Khafi died during this calamity.

He further writes about the aftermath of a comet's appearance. He says that according to the astrologers, if a comet appears in the angle of dominion, the sovereign of that country would die. And if it occurs in a falling angle, sickness and epidemic would increases, and there would be sudden destruction among the people.[43]

Lastly, Abul Fazl mentions a brief account of the great, wonderful phenomenon. He says that on the day of 25 Aban (5 November 1577) at the time, when sun was placed in Scorpio, the comet appeared in Sagittarians in the west, but inclined to the north. It had a long tail and was visible in some countries for five months. According to Abul Fazl, astrologers predicted that in some inhabited parts of India, grain would be dear and also mentioned the particular places of its occurrence. The places were Persia, Khurasan, Iraq etc.

Some astrologers made prediction of the death of Persian ruler and the disturbance in Iraq and Khurasan. Then, Abul Fazl accounts briefly about the malseffects of comet. He writes that the news about the death of Shah Tahmasp of Persia arrived to Akbar's court.[44] The occurrence was followed by many other disturbances and chaos in Persia. He mentions another appearance of Comet in the beginning of 1597, which was followed by dryness and scarcity in the empire.

In brief, we can say that during the days of Abul Fazl, people both Hindus and Muslims had an unshakable belief in astrology. The Mughals inherited their faith in astrology from their ancestors. Astrologers indeed played a very important role in the Mughal court.[45] Manucci, a traveler writes, "The king had his astrologers."[46] Astrology was a paying profession, soon after the birth, a horoscope of the baby, which took the exact time of the birth into consideration, was drawn up by the family priest.[47] Thus, it seems that as society was highly influenced by the astrology, so Abul Fazl also could not save himself from the impact of such phenomenon.

Abul Fazl was undoubtedly one of the great scholars of the time. Although it can be admitted that he was deeply indebted to Albiruni's Kitab-u'l-Hind, he still had a great understanding of the subject. His style of description or writing, however, is not free from defects. As K.A. Nizami writes[48] "his endless metaphors, allegories and allusions lose all meaning in translation and have not much sense in the original...His attempt seems to have been to overpower the reader with clever duplication of words rather than to convince him."

He further criticised, "It is strange that Abul Fazl, who was criticising religious superstition right and left and was condemning Ulema for their irrational approach, himself indulged in fabricating a paraphernalia of religious grandeur round the person of Akbar which man less lost in ambition would have felt ashamed of. He says that when Maryam Makani (Hamida Banu) was "pregnant with the holy elements of His majesty"...How ridiculous is the story that the astrologer asked Hamida Banu to delay the birth of the child as the time was inauspicious and the impulse passed off."[49] However, Abul Fazl had a deeply inquisitive mind. He was never satisfied by formal and traditional explanation of things, when passed through uneasy circumstances, he analysed it philosophically and astrologically.

List of Astronomers Reffered to by Abul Fazl*

S.No.	Name	Year	Place	Work
1	Ali Benou Amajour	885-933 A.D.	–	Canon: Al Bedia or "The Wonderful'
2	Abul Qasim Abdullah	–	Herat	Astronomical Table
3	Thabit-B-Qurrah B Harun	836-901 A.D. (AH 221-288)	Harran	Spherics of Theodosius
4	Husan b. Sinan	A.H. 290-360	Harran	Kitab-ul-Anroa, (Collection of Meteorological observations)
5	Thabit-b-Musa	–	Harran	
6	Muhanumad-b-Jabir-Al-Battani	877-8 A.D.	Harran then, Ruqqa (Inhabitan t)	Discoverer of motion of Apogee and Corrected the motion of Star determined by Ptolemy and length of year also.
7	Ahmad-b-Abdullah Jaba	–	–	Author of three canons: modeled on Sirlimd, Mumtahan, and shah, set of compited the tables by the Caliph's order.
8	Abu Rayhan Muhammad-b-Ahmad Albirum	973 -1048 AD	–	Kitab-ul-Hind
9	Khalid-b-Abdul-Malik	232 A.D.	Meru	Instituted The Shamma-Sigh observatory at Baghdad, Al Mamm's astaonomer

* 9Jarrat (Trans) *Ain-i-Akbari* of Abul Fazl Vol. III, pp. 5-12.

10	Yahya-b-Mansur	Died about 833 A.D.	Baghdad	Observer to Shammasiyah observatory at Baghdad and Mount Qasiun at Damascus. At – Mamun's famous astronomer.
11	Hamid Marwasudi	Died in 898 A.D.	Saghaw (Merv)	Maker of Astrolabes at Baghdad
12	Abul Wafa-Nurhari	939-998 A.D.	Buzjan (Nisabus)	Canon: Shamil, And Almagest
13	Kushyar-b-Kenanal Hanbali	–	Baghdad	Three canous: Jami, Sali, and Zij Kushyar
14	Ahmad-b-Died Ishaq Sarakshi 899 A.D.	899 A.D.	–	The Eisagaege of Porphirius
15	Gharari Probably, Al Fazari	–	-	Maker of Astrolabe, Author of A canon and several Astronomical wrok
16	Al. Haruni or Harum-b-al Munajjim	Died in 901 A.D.	Bagdad	–
17	Khwarazmi or Muhammad-b-musa	–	–	Author of canon
18	Samani or Abu Saad Abdul Karim Muhammad	A.H. 506-62	–	Author of 'Adab-fi -istimal il Hisab', and, a commentator on the canon of Potboy.
19	Ibn Sahra	749-846 A.D.	Bagdad	A, Reno rued Astrologer
20	Abul Fadhl Mashallah	Born in Al-Mansur's reign	Bagdad	Voluminous writings
21	Kabir of abu Mashar	Died in 885 A.D.	Balkh	A renowned Astrologer and Astronomer, Thirty Three works mentioned by First and his works also translated into Latin.
22	Abu-Tayyib Sind-b-Ali	–	–	Appointed as astronomer and superintendent of observatories

23	Abu-Ul-Aa'lain	925 A.D.	Bagdad	Astronomical Table
24	Abul Fath	–	–	Amended the table, termed 'Samarqandi'.
25	Masaudi	–	–	Canon writer of Masudicus
26	Muatabar of Sanjari	Services to Ali al Khazin of Marwazi	–	Writer of a canon
27	Ahmad Abdul Jalil Sanjari	–	–	Author of two treaties on stellar influences, and on astrologer.
28	Sultan Ali Khwarazmi	–	–	Author of a canon called "Shahi and a writer of a perstan abstract from the Rlkhani table called Umdal-ul-Klkhaniya'
29	Alai of Shiswani	–	–	Eminent astronomer and an author of several canons one is called Alai
30	J. Mshidi and	–	–	Astronomers, both together prepared a cannon
31	Ghiythu Ddin Jamshid	–	–	–
32	Nasiruddin Ibn Muhammed (Khwajah Nasiruddin)	A.H. 597-672	Tusi	Astronomer, Maker of Astronomical table, called as 'Elkham' Table.
33	Muhammed Turghai Ulugh Beg	1393 A.D to 1449 A.D.	Samarqand	Producible catalogue, corrector the plolemany's computation and compiled zij-i-Jadid-sultani.

Besides, this several names of astronomers are mentioned which follows: –

(1) Hipparchus, Ptolemy, Pythagoras, Zoroaster, Theon of Alexandria Sulayman-b-Muhammad, Abul Farad Hirazi, Abul Hasan Tusi, Yakub-b-Taus, Yusufi, Aasimi, Abul Sufi, Schalan Kashi, Ahwazi, Abul Jafar Bushauni Akkah rahibi, Wajiz-i-Muatabar,

Muhammad Hasib Tabari, Fakhir Ali Nasalr, Rahiri, Mustowfi, Abu Raza Yazdi, Kaydurali, Nasiri and Kamil of Abu Rashid.[1*]

List of Astronomical Works***

S.No.	Work	Writer/Maker	Instrument
1	The Jan	Kushyar-b-Kenan al	Canon
2	The Baligh or Sali	Hanbali	Canon
3	Teh Adhadi or Zij Kushyar	translated into Persian by md-b-Umar-b-Ali Tahib at Tabrizi	Canon
4	Safaih	–	Canon
5	Majmua	–	Canon
6	Adwar-i-Kirain	–	Canon
7	Wafi	A work of Ulugh Beg	–
8	Fi Maqawam al Juzhar	Shaikh Ibu-ul Oadir al Barallusi	Canon
9	Shahryan	Translated into Arabic by At Tamimi	Canon
10	Adani	–	Astronomical table
11	Taylasaui	–	Astronomical table
12	Asabai	–	Astronomical table
13	Kirmani	–	Astronomical table
14	Al Iklil	It is the Lunar station three the head of Scorpio	–
15	Khatai	–	Astronomical calendar in
16	Daylami	Kublai Khan of China, After conquering it, introduced astronomical learning three	North Chinas Astronomical table
17	Mufrad	Mel-b-Ayyub	Canon
18	Elkhani	Nasiruddin Tusi	Astronomical table
19	Gurgani	Vlugh Beg	Canon

*** Abul Fazl, Ain-i-Akbari, Vol. II, op.cit. pp. 5-12.

1* Jarrett (Trans) Writes that the detailed information of these astronomers is not traced out.

Endnotes

1. K A Nizami, *On History and Historians of Medivial India*, Delhi (Munshiram Manohar Lal Publishers Pvt. Ltd), 1983, pp.142-43.
2. Iqbal Ghani, 'Scientific Concept in Abul Fazal's Ain-i-Akbari', *Akbar and His India* (Irfan Habib Ed.) Delhi, 1997, Oxford University Press, p. 127-128; H.Blochmann (Tr.) *Ain-i-Akbari*, Vol. I, Delhi (New Taj Office), 1989, pp. 18-32., 126.
3. Abul Fazl, *Akbarnama*, H. Bevaridge (Tr.) Delhi, (M L.Chopra],1973,pp.34
4. V.A. Smith, *Akbar, The Great Mughal*, p. 4; quoted by A.K. Nizami, *op. cit.*, p. 141.
5. *Ibid*, p. 141.
6. Harbans Mukhia, *Historians and Historiography during the Reign of Akbar.* Delhi Vikas publishing House pvt Ltd (1976), p.60.
7. Ibid,p. 61
8. *Ani-i-Akbari*, vol I, *op.cit.*, Biography of Abul Fazl,p. LIV
9. Harbans Mukhia, *op. cit.* p. 66.
10. H.S.Jarrett, (Tr.) *Ani-i-Akbari of Abul Fazl*, vol. II Delhi, (New Taj Office), 1989, pp. 5-7.
11. *Ibid*, p. 4.
12. *Ibid*, p.14.
13. *Ibid*,pp.16,17.
14. *Ibid*, p. 18.
15. Jarrett writes it (day and night) in a term as *'Nycthemeron'*, Ibid, p. 18, 19.
16. *Ibid*, pp. 15-19.
17. *Ibid.*
18. *Ibid* p. 19 to 29
19. *Ibid*, p. 31
20. Jarrett, (Trans.) *Ain-i-Akbari of Abul Fazl*, Vol. III, *op.cit.*, pp. 33-37.
21. *Akbarnama of Abul Fazl.* H. Beveridge (Trans) Vol I, II, III.
22. *Ibid*, Vol. I, p. 14.
23. Ulugh Beg was born in 1393 A.D. and died in 1449 A.D. The ancient astronomy had produced only one catalogue of the fixed star, that of Hipparcus. Ulugh Beg after a long interval, produced for second time. His observatory at Samarqand in its days was regarded as one of the wonders of the world. He corrected Ptolemy's computations and compiled the "*Zij-i-Jadid-Sultani*" (Tr. by Hyde in 1665, by Sedillot in 1847.
24. *Akbarnama* Vol. I, *op cit, pp.* 125-126.; O.P.Jaggi, '*Science and Technology in Medieval India'*, Vol. VII,) Delhi, Atma Ram & Sons, (1977), p.55
25. *Akbarnama* Vol.I, op. cit., pp. 123, 126,127.

26. *Akbarnama,* Vol. II op cit, pp. 10,11
27. *Ibid,* Vol. II, p. 506
28. *Ibid*
29. *Ibid,* pp. 506 & 507.
30. *Ibid,* p.504
31. *Ibid* pp. 514, 515, Baveridge, (Tr.) mentions in footnotes that both horoscopes are givenwithout explanation. So these are not translated.
32. *Ibid,* p.542, Baveridge mentions in footnote that correct horoscope of Danial area given in B.M. MSS Add. 5610, pp. 540b and 541a and 5553, pp. 282, 83.
33. *Ibid,* p. 543.
34. *Akbarnama* Vol. III, Ibid, p. 799.
35. *Ibid,* p. 921, MS Add. 27, 247 write the name of Sultan Khurram. A space is left in the MS, for the horoscope, but it is blank, mentioned in footnotes by Baveridge.
36. *Akbarnama,* Vol. III , p.661
37. *Ibid,* pp. 746,47
38. *Ibid,* pp. 311, 12.
39. *Ibid,* p. 312.
40. It is stated in the *Ain-i-Akbari* (Jarrate, Vol. III, p. 38), that Fire is the first elemental sphere, and that it's convex adjoins the concave of the sphere of the moon.
41. Abul Fazl, *Akbarnama,* Vol. III, p.313.
42. *Ibid,* p. 314
43. *Ibid,* p. 315.
44. *Ibid,* 316.
45. M.A.Ansari, *Social Life of Mughal Emperors,* Delhi (Shanti Prakashan), 1974, p.179.
46. Manucci, Vol. I, p.213 (quoted by Ansari, *op. cit.* p.179.).
47. A.L. Srivastava, *Akbar, The Great* Vol. III, Shive Lal Agrawala and Company Agra, p.201.
48. K.A. Nizami, *op. cit.,* 155.
49. *Ibid,* p.151

Akbar's Horoscope
Sunday, 5 Rajab, 949 A.H.
= 15th October, 1542, Ci 2A.M

Figure No.1
Horoscope cast by Muslim
Astrologer Maulana Chand

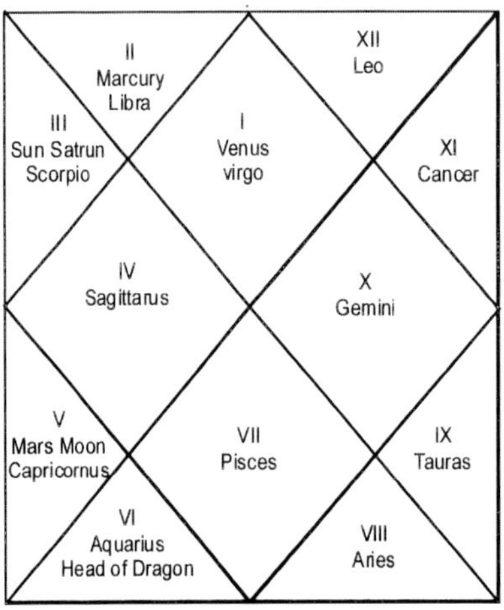

Figure No.2
Horoscope cast by Indian
Astrologer Jotik Rai

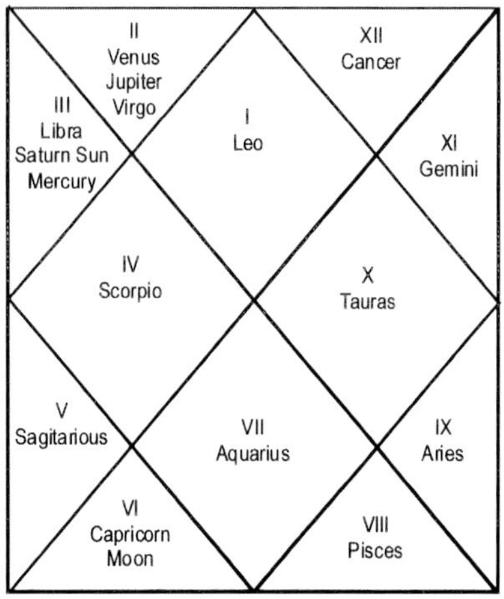

Figure No.3
Horoscope cast by Muslim
Astrologer Fathu-L-Lah of Shiraz

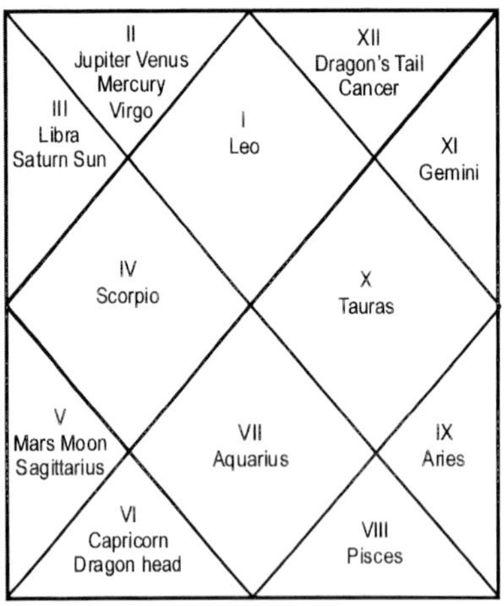

Figure No.4
Horoscope cast by Muslim
Astrologer Maulana Ilyas of Ardabil

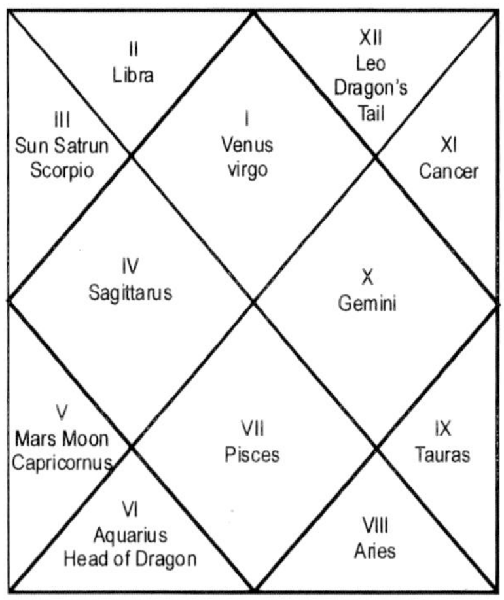

The Horoscope of The Accession Of Akbar

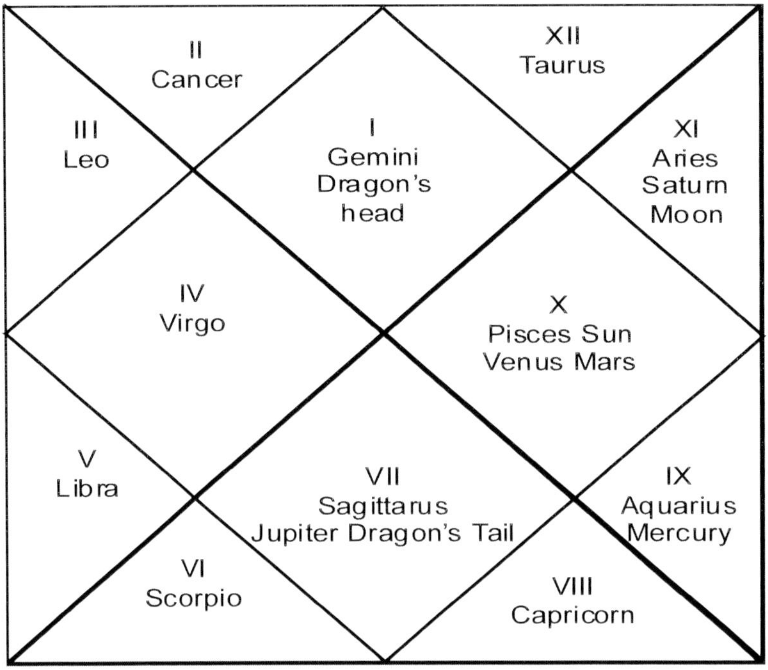
II
Cancer
XII
Taurus
III
Leo
I
Gemini
Dragon's
head
XI
Aries
Saturn
Moon
IV
Virgo
X
Pisces Sun
Venus Mars
V
Libra
VII
Sagittarus
Jupiter Dragon's Tail
IX
Aquarius
Mercury
VI
Scorpio
VIII
Capricorn

CHAPTER 7

Conclusion

Since the early civilisations of the World, man has been attracted by heavenly bodies, which have created myths and beliefs in his mind. In fact, myth is the result of a psychological operation. The psychological ideas behind these myths and beliefs somehow are always based on some logic and facts. In ancient India, the great Rishies, with the spiritual practice and meditation had acquired the knowledge of these heavenly bodies and their effects on living things. They have observed recurring order of the morning, noon and night, repetition of same season after a large number of days and nights. These observations provided them the knowledge about the increasing and decreasing phases of the Moon in a month. They also observed the heavenly path known as Zodiac, a belt in which the Sun, the Moon, and Planets travel. In this way, it was the first important landmark in their knowledge of astronomy. India in fact has a long astronomical tradition. As a result, it has become a basis rather scientific ground of Astrology.

Astrology has been discussed in various ancient texts such as Rigveda, Narad Puran, Vedanga Jyotish, Yazurveda, Epics, Puranas, Brahmans, etc. Gargya, Sunahsepa, Parasara Saktya, Gautama, Vamadeva, Aryabhatta, Srisena, Varahmihira, Brahma Gupta, Bhaskara I, Kalyanavarman, Bhattotpala, Bhaskara II, Lalla, Manjula, Shripati, Prithudaka etc. were famous astronomers in ancient India, while Varahmihira was one of the famous astrologers too.

Indian astronomers came into contact with the Greek astronomy. As a result, five astronomical systems, called as '*Siddhantas*' namely: *Surya Patimaha, Paulisa, Vasistha,* and *Romaka* came into existence. *Paulisa* and *Romaka* were foreign in origin as their name implied. Later on, Varahmihira wrote '*Panchsidhantika*' compiling all *Siddhantas* in a book form.

According to Narad Purana, astrology is divided into three parts – *Siddhantas, Samhitas* and *Hora. Siddhanta* is totally related to astronomy, while *Samhita* and *Hora are related* to astrology. Later on, the study of astrology was promoted as it helped in the calculation of time, in the preparation of horoscopes, and in the determination of auspicious hours for important decisions and occasions.

However, the practice of astrology was unequivocally condemned as an unorthodox science by early Buddhist, Jaina, Brahmanical writers. But these works show great popularity of astrologers among common folk. Persistency of beliefs, superstitions and omens were no exception in Indian society as Varahmihira mentions in his writings. However, astrology was a subject of learning. According to Varahmihira, "a real astrologer is one who knows mathematical astronomy as well as predictive part. He should be fully accomplished in natural astrology and be an efficient diviner". *Siddhantas, Tantras* and *Karmas* are three classifications of astronomical sciences, while astrology contains horoscopy, and predictions based on the planetary position in horoscope.

In the early medieval period, people were generally very superstitious. Rulers were very particular to know the auspicious and inauspicious moments from the astrologers. Both the Hindus and the Muslims had common faith in astrology. Kanka was the first Indian mathematician and astronomer, who introduced these sciences to the Arabs. In the court of Al-Mansur (773 A. D.) some books on Indian astronomy were translated in Arabic. '*Brahmasphuta Siddhanta*', by *Brahma Gupta*, '*Aryabhatiyam*' by Aryabhatta, and *Khanda Khadyaka* were translated as *Sindhind, Arjabahad* and *Arkand* respectively. Brahma-sputa *Siddhanta* was more popular among the people.

An assimilation of Indian and Arabic astronomical science can be seen in the courts of later emperors of Arab. In this context, the contribution of *Abu-Reham Al-Biruni* is remarkable. His famous works are *Kitab-ul-Hind-fi-Tahqiq Milal Hind*, *Asarul Baqia* and *Qanun-i-Masudi.* He probably enjoyed the reputation of a great Munajjim i.e., Astrologer and Astronomer.

The Sultans of Delhi, in the medieval period, were also influenced by astrology and astronomy. We find some evidence in contemporary sources like 'Nuh Siphr' of Amir Khusrau, showing the passion of scholars for the knowledge in this field. The court of Ala-ud-din Khilzi witnessed to have a good number of astrologers, whose services were enjoyed by the women of *Haram.*

Pheru Thakkura (1291-1323 A.D.) was a good astrologer in the period of Ala-ud-din Khilzi. His famous works are *Jyotisar, Vastu*

Shastra and *Ratna Pariksha*, which tell a lot about the knowledge of astrology and astronomy and its practical use by contemporary society.

Zij astronomy appears in India, for the first time, under the patronage of Sultan Ferozshah Tughlaq (1351 to 1388 A.D.). 'Zij', a Persian word, means a thread, especially warp and woof of a carpet. Due to the similarity between warp and woof of a carpet with astronomical tables, the books based on these tables are known as 'Zij astronomy'. Many astrolabes were constructed. Mahendra Suri composed a Sanskrit work on the astrolabe called "*Yantraraja*" on the basis of Arabic texts. Some books, on astronomy captured from the *Jwalamukhi* Temple by Firoz Tughlaq were translated into Persian. In early medieval period in India, people usually took augur and believed in superstitions. They used to consult astrologers and the book of *Hafiz* for omen before entering in an enterprise.

Hence, astrology has a long history in India. Astronomy is the study of the individual celestial bodies as a whole, while astrology is the investigation of happenings of the celestial bodies and its impacts on individuals and on universe. *Hora*, *Siddhanta*, *Samhita, Prashnashastra,* and *Shakuna Shastras* are five parts of Indian astrology. Zodiac, *Rasis*, planets, and constellations are astronomical facts, which form a basis of astrological calculations.

During medieval period Muslim astronomers of India remarkably contributed to the field of Zij astronomy, and constructed observatories and astrolabes. In fact, the Muslim community was equally influenced by the astrology. Mughal rulers were too influenced and also extended patronage to the astrologers.

Abul Fazl gives a list of 86 Mughal astronomers in his Ain-i-Akbari, who were great contributor in the field of astronomy before their advent in India. Their ancestor Ulugh Beg (15th Century) had built an observatory and left a book of tables. Among the famous astrologers of the Mughal period were Maulana Chand, Amir Fath-ullah-Shirazi, Jotika Rai, Kanjar Beg, Nurud-din Muhammad Tarkhan, Imam-Abdul-Muhammad of Gazani. Abul Fazl himself seems to be an astrologer as he had a deep knowledge about all astronomical facts as well as planetary position.

Babur, the founder of Mughal Empire in India, had a literary bent of mind. He wrote Tuzuk-i-Baburi. Though Babur is not considered to be a staunch believer of astrology, he was acquainted with Zodiac signs, planetary position etc. which he describes in his writings.

Humayun had a remarkable – inclination towards astronomical and astrological sciences, rather he was without rivals. He was a staunch believer of astrology as we find numerous instances in this regard in the writings of Abul Fazl. He used to wait for auspicious moments for any enterprise. He even chose an auspicious moment according to planetary position for the birth of his son Akbar. He had deputed Maulana Chand, an astrologer to calculate the planetary position at the time of birth of Akbar. His remarkable inventions and division of the dominion into three classes i.e., *Ahl-i-Murad, Ahl-i-daulat* and *Ahl-i-Saadat* were means of gaining everlasting auspiciousness in his court. He used to have a good association with famous astronomers like Maulana Chand, Maulana Illyas, Nuruddin-Muhammad Tarkhan, Kanjar Beg etc. He wanted to construct an observatory and had collected the necessary instruments for that purpose before his accidental demise. He also knew the casting of horoscopes, and the different calculation methods of planetary positions. He was acquainted with famous canons of Ullugh Beg and Ilkhani and Gurgani tables.

At the moment of untimely demise of Humayun, Akbar was away at Kalanaur. It was decided that Akbar's coronation ceremony be accomplished there under the auspicious planetary position. The date and time of accession was scrutinized by the astronomers and horoscope of accession was drawn. Akbar was also very influenced by this science. He had deputed famous astrologers to draw his birth chart and ordered to compare them. He invited Futh-ullah-Sirazi and asked him to re-examine his horoscope. He used to celebrate the anniversary of his accession, when the Sun enters in '*Aries*' sign of Zodiac i.e., an exalted position of the Sun. Moreover, he used to celebrate his birth anniversary according to solar and lunar months. We find that Akbar was so much influenced by astrology that he always took decisions or started any enterprise according to planetary position consulting an astrologer in his daily life. He even consulted an astrologer to fix an auspicious moment to enter into his capital or to go to battlefield. In 1577 A.D., when a long- tailed star, i.e., a comet appeared, Akbar ordered the astrologers to carry out the research on the matter. He himself used to pray and perform rituals at the time of eclipse to nullify its bad effect. He also promoted the education of astrology and astronomy in schools.

Jahangir, like his father, also had faith and interest in astronomical sciences as we find numerous instances in his memoirs "*Tuzuk-i-Jahangiri*". He loved to converse with Pandits and Hindu ascetics. He himself had some knowledge of zodiac signs; planetary positions as described in his memoirs. He believed in weighing ceremony on birth days of his sons and of himself. He always consulted his Hindu astrologer Jotika rai in daily life. Jotika rai had been felicitated many times by Jahangir. He used to consult him very frequently, about the horoscopes of his sons. He always chose auspicious moment for any new beginning. He had faith in Omens also. Some European travellers, like Terry, Pelsaert etc. also mention Jahangir's great belief in astrology.

The time of Shahjahan witnessed the development of astronomical sciences. Shahjahan had beliefs and took active interest in this science. He issued a royal command to Mulla Farid Ibrahim Dehlavi to prepare a new '*Zij*', based on the table of Ulugh Beg. He used to consult astrologers before any enterprise. Like Akbar, he used to perform weighing ceremony on birthday according to solar and lunar month. He was very mindful of his horoscope, and he even took his seat on the '*Peacock Throne*' at a propitious time fixed by the astrologers. *Zij-i-Rahimi Zij-Shahjahani* by Dehlavi were composed under his patronage. *Zij-i-Shahjahani* was also translated into Sanskrit by *Nityanand*, a Hindu court astronomer of Shahjahan. '*Sarvasidhantraja*' was also another work of *Nityanand*. '*Parasiprakasa*' composed by Malajit was a Persian-Sanskrit dictionary of astronomical and astrological terms in 1643 under the title 'Vedanagraya'.

Aurangzeb, though, was a fanatic Sunni Muslim, but never tried to condemn these sciences. He seems to have continued all rituals performed or practiced by his ancestors. Sometimes, he also consulted the astrologers as he himself admits in his letters that the pages of his horoscope composed by Fazil Khan, have been verified by actual experiences. Munucci, was an eyewitness of some rituals, which were observed by Aurangzeb to do away with any evil effect.

Sawai Jai Singh II of Jaipur, contemporary to later Mughal emperors, contributed a lot in the field of astronomy. He himself was a good scholar of astronomy. He wanted to correct the inaccuracy of the existing calendars. He built large observatories at Delhi, Jaipur, Banaras, Ujjain, and Mathura. His chief astronomer was Jagannath. He also invited many European astronomers to his court. Besides, some instruments and observatories, he also prepared a set of astronomical tables, known as "*Zij-i-Muhammad Shahi*" after the name of Mughal Emperor Muhammad Shah. Except it, eleven other Zijs were developed in Mughal period.

During medieval period Indian people in general believed in lucky and unlucky days. According to contemporary sources, people from all sections of society consulted astrologers before starting any work or undertaking any project. Contemporary foreign travellers like Bernier, Munucci, Pelsaert also speak highly of some astrologers, who had consequently secured a great reputation due to their prediction about day-to-day life. Besides astrological beliefs, some superstitions such as Amulets and Talismans were also prevalent in society. Emperor Akbar himself promoted the learning of astrology and astronomy. Banaras, Nadia, and Multan were the centers where education of astrology and astronomy was imparted.

It is very interesting to note that Astrology has influenced the Mughal architecture and painting also. Humayun's Audience Hall had different chambers after seven stars and each of these was used according to the influence of its presiding divinity, such as the Moon Chamber for poets, travellers, and ambassadors etc. Indigenous artisans had played an important role to pass the Indian symbols and icons into Mughal architecture. The monuments of Agra, Fatehpur Sikri and Delhi contain many symbolic arts, motifs like *Chakra, padma, shrivatsa, purnakalash, swastika, satkona* and *gavaksha* which were significantly used by Hindus as Vastu symbols, having significance. Mughals used them symbolically or ornamentally. The depiction of *Satkona* on the personal shield of Akbar represents his strong belief in the '*Yantra*'. This *Tantric* symbol had the implied belief that it would be auspicious to dwarf off evils and protect him from all dangers in battles. R. Nath has established a new concept about the 'Diwan-i-Khas' built by Akbar in Fatehpur Sikri. According to him, Diwan-i-Khas is a symbol of Akbar's belief in '*Surya Purusa*' or '*Ekstamba*' doctrine. A square canopy standing on a platform known as the 'Astrologer's seat', adjoining to '*Diwan-i-Khas*' also supports the above concept. However, the monuments built upto the period of Shahjahan were influenced by occultism, prognaustical sciences and Vastushastra.

We also find that Mughal paintings show the impact of astrology. There are numerous illustrations such as showing 'astrologers with drawing the horoscopes', 'Akbar being weighed' etc. Groups of

Talisman, the sign of Zodiac, comprehensive system of Astrology etc. are found in a work entitled '*Nujum-al-Ullum*' written during the Mughal period. So, beliefs, superstitions and astrological traditions were prevailing in medieval Indian society as well in the field of art architecture and painting also.

In the later medieval period, Abul Fazl mentioned the list of astronomers and astrologers in his writings. He himself had a deep knowledge and understanding about the astronomical sciences and astrological beliefs. All his works contained informative remarks about astrology and astronomy. When he mentioned the birth of anyone in Mughal court, he would also discuss the horoscope under different methods of astrology.

Abul Fazl gives an account of his deep knowledge about the basic principles of astronomy practiced by Hindu and Muslim astronomers. As he defines the astronomical terms such Rasad, Zij, Patrah, Zodiac signs, Ghati, Pal, Vipal, Nakchhatra, tables etc. He displays the minute difference between Elkhani and Gurgani tables. He further mentions six types of seasons (Ritus) in connection with the situation of the Sun in different Zodiac signs. He further elaborated 'Kals' namely Dhupkal, Barkhakal and Shitkal according to the divisions of zodiac signs. The terms like Dakhangol, Uthargol. Dachchhayan, and Uttarayan have been also elucidated according to the Zodiac sign and Sun's position. He narrates the whole day and night divided into 60 equal parts as known as Ghaties, which is further subdivided into Pal, Vipal or Nari, Swas, Parswas and Prane. He seems to have known about latitudes and longitudes of the cities also. No terminology or principle of astronomical science seems to be unfamiliar to his knowledge. He narrates the popular eras of different countries of the contemporary age like Khatai Era, Turkish Era, Jewish Era, Augustan Era, Christian Era, Hijra Era, Khani Era, Ilahi Era etc.

Abul Fazl had a deep understanding of astrology with all numerical/mathematical calculations of planets. He was aware of numerology and gemology also. He mentions four horoscopes of Akbar interpreted by Hindu and Muslim astrologers. The judgment of all 12 houses of the horoscope has been discussed elaborately. He also mentions the horoscope of the accession of Akbar. He narrates the horoscopes of prince Salim, Murad, Danial, Khusro, Khurram etc. He also narrates the occurrence of comets and their astrological malefic and benefic effects.

Briefly, we can say during the days of Abul Fazl people, both Hindus and Muslims had an unshakable belief in astrology. Abul Fazl could not save himself from the impact of such a phenomenon.

Hence, we find that the impact of astrology and astronomy was intense in 16th and 17th century in India. According to Will and Arial Durant, the stars were subjected to be science in most of the countries during this period. They mention in their work 'The Story of Civilisation' (Vol. VIII) about the progress in the field of Astronomy as it was a worldwide phenomenon. Several world reputed astronomers were Riccioli in Italy, Danzing Johaunes Hevelius, Jean Picard in France, Giovauni Domenies Cassini and so on. They further mention that though astrology and alchemy saw continued decline, but astrologers were numerous at the court of Louis XIV in France and at Vienna in Austria. Most of the British Kings still believed in ghosts, watched for omens, paid for horoscope, and calculated lucky and unlucky days. Hence the development and influence of astrology and astronomy were not only taking place in medieval India, but it was a worldwide phenomenon, like modern age.

Bibliography

Agarwal V. S. has given a list of *Asthmangals* (eight auspicious symbols) of Indian art in his book – *Chakradwaja*, Varanasi (1964) as such, (1) *Swastika* (2) *Srivatsa* (3) *Mina Mithuna* (4) *Vaijayanti* (5) *Devgriha Vimana* (6) *Ratuapatra* (7) *Purnaghata* (8) *Mahasrak* (The great garland).

Ahmad, Khwajah Nizamuddin, *The Tabaqat-i-Akbari*, tra. B.N. De. Bile Inds., Calcutta (1927-33), Vol. II.

Ahmad, Syed (ed.), *Tuzuk-i-Jahangiri*, Ghazipur and Aligarh (1863-64), Eng. Tr. Beni Prasad and Beveridge, Delhi.

Al-Badaoni, Muntakhabru't-Tawarikh, W.H. Lowe (tra.), *Idarah-i-Adabiyat-i-Delhi*, Delhi (1899, 1973), Vol. II.

Al-Badoni, Muntakhabul's Tawarikh, Vol. II, (tr. W. H. Lowe), Calcutta (1924).

Al-Badoni, Muntakhabul's Tawarikh, Vol. II, (tr. W. H. Lowe), Calcutta (1924).

Ali, Meer Hasan, *Observations on the Mussulmans of India I.*

Ansari, M.A., *European Travellers Under the Mughal*, Delhi.

Ansari, M.A., *Social Life of the Mughal Emperors*, Shanti Prakashan, New Delhi (1974).

Ansari, Muhammad Azhar, *Social Life of the Mughal Emperors*, Shanti Prakashan, Allahabad and New Delhi (1974).

Ansari, S.M.R., "Ghulam Hussain Jaunpuri and his Zij-i-Bahadurkhani", *Studies in History of Medicines and Science* (New Delhi), Vol. XVI, nos. 1-2, New Series (1995-96).

Ansari, S.M.R., "Islamic Astronomy in India during 16th-18th centuries and its interaction with traditional Indian Astronomy, written in 500 years of Tantrasangraha".

Ansari, S.M.R., "On the Transmission of Arabic-Islamic Astronomy to Medieval India (1995)", *Archieves International d'Historire des Sciences*, Vol. 45.

Bag, A. K., "Aryabhatata-I's Achievement in Ancient Indian Mathematic and Astronomy", *Journal of the Asiatic Society*, Kolkata (2005), Vol. XLVII.

Bandyopadhyay, Amalendu, "Astronomy During the period from 5th to 12th Century A.D.", *Journal of Asiatic Society*, Kolkata, Vol. XLVII (2005).

Banerjee, G. N., *Hellenism in Ancient India*, Chapter XIII, Munshiram Manoharlal, New Delhi (1998).

Barani, Hasan, *Albiruni, His Life and Works* (Urdu), Muslim University Press, Aligarh (1927).

Basham, A. L. *A Cultural History of India*, Clarendon Press, Oxford (1975).

Basu, B., "Vedic Astronomy, Its Relevance Today", *Journal of Asiatic Society*, Kolkata (2005), Vol. XLVII.

Begum, Gulbadan, "Humayun Nama", Satkona A. S. Beveridge (trans.), *Idarah-i-Dabiyat-i-Delhi*, Delhi (1972).

Beveridge, Rogers (Trans), *Humayun Nama –Gulbadan*, Muhammad Ahmad Idarah-i-Adabiyat-Dellh (1972).

Beveridge, Rogers (Trans.), *Jahangir's Memoirs*, Munshiram Manoharlal, New Delhi (1978), Preface.

Bhagi, M.L., *Ancient India, Culture and Thought*, The Indian Publication, Ambala Cantt (2001).

Bhambi, Pandit Ajay, *Be Your own Astrologer*, Wisdom Tree Darya Ganj, New Delhi (2004).

Bhasham, A. L. (ed.), *A Cultural History of India*, Clarendon Press, Oxford (1975).

Bhatnagar, V.S., *Life and Times of Sawai Jai Singh*, Impex India, Delhi (1974).

Bhattacharji, Sukumari, *Myths, Vedic Buddhist and Brahmanical*, Progressive Publishers, Kolkata (July 2002) Preface.

Bhattacharya, Ramkrishan, "Science and Superstition in Indian Astronomy", *Journal of Asiatic Society*, Kolkata (2005), Vol. XLVII.

Bilimoria, Jamshid H. (Trans.), *Ruka'at-i-Alamgiri* (Letters of Aurangzeb), by *Idarah-I-Adabi-yat-1*, Delhi, Qasim Street, Delhi (1972).

Brown, Percy, "Monuments of Mughal Period" quoted by Monica Juneja (ed.), *Architecture in Medieval India*, Permanent Black I. P. Extention, New Delhi (2001).

Catalogue of the Persian Manuscripts in the British Museum, 2, 459, 60, quoted by Nadvi, *Islamic Culture*, 280.

Chaudhuri, Sandipan, "Scientific Rationale of Astrology", *Journal of Asiatic Society*, Kolkata, 2005.

Chopra, P.N., *Life and Letters Under the Mughals*, Ashajanak Publications, New Delhi.

Coomaraswamy, A. K., *Museum Fine Art*, Cambridge, Boston (1930), Pl. III-VI.

Coomaraswamy, Anand, *Introduction to Indian Art*, The Theosophical Publishing House, Adyar (1956).

Coomaraswmy, A. K., "Origin of the Lotus", *The Historical Quarterly*, Calcutta (1930), Vol. VI.

Coomarswami, A. K., *History of Indian and Indonesian Art* (Dover ed.) (1965).

Coomarswami, V. S., *Chakra-dwaja*, Varanasi (1964), Preface, p. (i).

Dasgupta, Surendra Nath, "Fudamentals of Indian Art", Bhartiya Vidya Bhawan, Bombay (1954).

Edward, S.M., *Babur Diarist and Despot*, Haritage Publication, New Delhi (1977).

Elliot and Dowson, *History of India, as told by its own Historians*, London (1977), Vol. V, Aligarh Reprint (1952).

Elliot and Dowson, *The History of India as told by its Own Historian*, Vol. VII.

Elliot and Dowson, *The History of India, as told by its own Historians*, Kitab Mahal Pvt. Ltd, Allahabad (1978), Vol. I.

Elliot and J. Dowson, *History of India as told by its own Historians*, Kitab Mahal Private Ltd, Allahabad (1964), Vol. VII.

Erskine, William, *History of India under two first Sovereigns, Babur and Humanyn*, Idarahe-e-Adabiyat-i-Delhi, Delhi (1973), Vol. II.

Fabri, Clarks, *An Introduction to Indian Architecture*, Asia Publishing House, Bombay, New York (1963).

Fazl, Abul, *Ain-a-Akbari*, H. Blockman (tra.), New Taj Office, Delhi (1989).

Fazl, Abul, *Ain-i-Akbari*, Eng, tr. Jarrett, New Taj Office, New Delhi (1989), Vol. III.

Fazl, Abul, *Akbarnama*, Beveridge (Tra.), Asiatic Society of Bengal and Manmohan Satish Kumar Rare Books, Delhi (1972), Vol. I.

Francois, Bernier's *Travels in the Mughal Empire* (1656-1668), Oxford, 1934.

Garral, G.T. (ed.), *The Legacy of India*, Black and White Sandip Prakashan, New Delhi (2005).

Ghasemlou, Farid and Negar Naderi, "Persian Astronomical Tables Composed in India" (Article) written in *500 years of Tantrasangraha* by M.S. Sriram, Ramsubramanium and Srinivas, Inter University Centre, Indian Institute of Advance Study, Shimla (2002).

Gyaneshwar, Umesh Puri, *Prachin Bhartiya Phalit Shastra*, Randhir Prakashan, Haridwar (1996).

Habib, Irfan, (ed.), *Akbar and his India – Science and Superstition under Akbar and Jahangir, The Observation of Astronomical Phenomena* by Shireen Moosvi, Delhi Oxford University Press, Calcutta (1997).

Hassan, Mohibbul, *Babur*, Manohar Publication, New Delhi (1985).

Havell, E. B. The Ancient and Medieval Architecture of India, London (1915), as quoted by R. Nath.

Hughes, *Dictionary of Islam.*

Islamic Culture, Hyderabad, Vol. XIX, January 1945, reprint, New York (1971).

Jaggi, O. P., *Science and Technology in Medieval India*, Vol. VII, Atma Ram & Sons, Delhi (1977).

Jaggi, O. P., *Scientists of Ancient India and Their Achievement*, Atma Ram & Sons, Delhi (1966).

Jaggi, O.P., *History of Science and Technology in India*, Vol. II, Chapter 9, Atma Ram and Sons, Delhi (1984).

Jahangir, *Tujuk-i-Jahangiri*, Alexander Rogers (Trans.), Munshiram Manoharlal, Delhi (1978), Vol. I.

Jain, Nem Kumar, *Science and Scientists in India*, Indian Book Gallery, 2691, Gali Baradari Ballimaraw, Delhi (1982).

Jauhri, R. C., Firoz Tughlaq, ABS Publication, Jalandhar (1990).

Kapoor, Gauri Shankar, *Learn Astrology*, Rajan Publication, New Delhi (2004).

Kaye, G. R., *A Guide to the Old Observatories at Delhi, Jaipur, Ujjain, Benaras*, The Academic Press, Gurgaon, Haryana (1985) (Reprint Published).

Khan, Khafi, 'Muntakhabu-l-Lubab', quoted by Elliot and Dowson, Vol. III.

Khan, Mùtemad, *Iqbalnama-i-Jahangiri*, Elliot Down (tra.) Vol. 3, Nawal Kishore, Lucknow (1870).

Khandalavala, K. and J. Mittal, *An Early Akbari Illustrated Manuscript of Tilasm and Zodiac*, Lalit Kala 14, (1969).

Khandalavala, Karl, *The Development of Style in Indian Painting*, The Macmillan Co. of India Ltd, Delhi, Madras. Bombay, Calcutta (1974).

Khusrau, Amir, *Qiran ul-Sa'dain*, ed. Ismail Meeruti, Aligarh (1918).

Kochhar, Rajesh and Jayant Narlikar, *Astronomy in India, A Perspective*, Indian National Science Academy, New Delhi (1994).

Kochhar, Rajesh, "Pre Telescopic Astronomy in India" in D. P. Chattopadhaya (ed.), *History of Science, Philosophy and Culture in Indian Civilisation*, Vol. III, Part I, Oxford University Press, Delhi (1999).

Kramrisch, Stella, *The Hindu Temple*, Calcutta (1946), Vol. II.

Lamb, Harold, *Babur the Tiger, first of the great Mughals*, Great Britain (1962).

Lanepoole, Staley, *Babur*, Clarendon Press, Oxford.

Leach, Linda York, *Mughal and Other Indian Paintings*, (from the Chester Beathy Library), Scorpion Cavendisl Ltd, London (1995), Vol. II.

Mhandalvala, Karl and Jagdish Mittal, *An early Akbari Illustated Manuscript of Tilasm and Zodiac*, Lalitkala, No. 14 (1969).

Mohammad, Yasin, *Social History of Islamic India*, The Upper India Publishing House, Lucknow (1958).

Moosvi, Shireen, "Science and Superstition under Akbar and Jahangir", in *Akbar and his India,* Irfan Habib (ed.), Oxford University Press, Delhi (1997).

Mundi, Peter, *Travels of Peter Mundi in* Asia, ed. R.C. Temple, London, 1914.

Nadvi, Syad Suleman, "Some Indian Astrolabe Makers", *Indian History Congress IX* (1935).

Nath Brajendra, (Trans.), *Tabaquat-i-Akbari –Nizamuddin Ahmad.*

Nath, R., and Faiyaz Gwaliari, *India, as seen by Amir Khusrau*, Historical Research Documentation Programme, Jaipur (1981).

Nath, R., *Some Aspects of Mughal Architecture*, Abhinav Publication, New Delhi (1976).

Nath, R., *The Evolution of Tomb in Mughal Architecture*, D.B. Taraporevala Sons, Bombay (1972).

Niccolao, Manucci, '*Storia do Mogor*', tra. W. Irvine, London, 1906, Vol. II.

Nizami, K.A. work, *On History and Historians of Medieval India.*

Pandit, V. R., "Omens and Portents in Vedic Literature", *Proceedings of the All India Oriental Conference*, Nagpur Session (1946).

Pathak, Haldhar, *Cultural History of the Gupta period*, Bhartiya Publishing House Delhi, Varanasi (1978)

Pelsaert, Francisco, "Remonstrantie" (trans.) W. H. Moreland and P. Geyl, *Jahangir's India, Idagah-i-Adabiyat-I*, Delhi (19).

Pheru, Thakkur, *Ratna Parikshadi Sapt Grauthsangrah*, ed. by Agarchand and Bhanwar Lal Nahta, Rajasthan Prachya Vidya Prishthan, Jodhpur (1961).

Pingree, David, "Islamic Astronomy in Sanskrit", 1978, *Journal of History and Arabic Science*, Vol. 2, (1978).

Prasad, Bani, (trans.) Qanun-i-Huymayuni of Khwandamir, Calcutta (1940).

Prasad, Ishwari, *The Life and Times of Humayun*, Orient Longman, Bombay, Calcutta, Madras (1955).

Prashad, Munshi Devi, *Shahjahanama*, tra. by Raghubir Singh and Manohar Singh, Rawat Publication Scheme, Jaipur (1990).

Qanun-i-Huymayuni of Khwandamir (trans.) Bani Prasad, Calcutta (1940).

Quarterly Review of Historical Studies, Calcutta, Vol. XII, No. 4 (1972-73).

Quarterly Review of Historical Studies, Calcutta, Vol. XII, No. 4 (1972-73).

Raghuraman, V., *Vedic Nadi Astrology*, Sterling Publisher (P) Ltd., New Delhi (1996).

Raghuvanshi, V.P.S., *Indian Society of Eighteenth Century*", Associated Publishing House, New Delhi.

Rahman, A. (ed.), *History of Indian Science, Technology and Culture*, Oxford University Press, New Delhi (2004), Vol. III, Part I.

Rahman, A., *Maharaja Sawai Jai Singh II and Indian Renaissance*, Navrang, New Delhi (1987).

Raman, B. V., *How to Judge A Horoscope*, Motilal Banarasidas Publishers Private Ltd., Delhi, (2002), Vol. I.

Raman, B. V., *Planetary References on Human Affairs*, UBS Publishers & Distributors, New Delhi (1992).

Rao, T. A. Gopinath, *Elements of Hindu Iconography*, Delhi (1968), Vol. I, Part I, as quoted by R. Nath.

Roychoudhary, M. L. *The Din-i-Ilahi*, Calcutta, 1941, quoted by R. Nath, *History of Decorative Art in Mughal Architecture*, Motilal Banarasi Das, Delhi (1976).

Sachau, Edward, *Alberuni's India*, Rupa Co., New Delhi (2002), Preface I.

Sahay, B. K, *Education and Learning under the Great Mughals*, New Literature Publishing Co., Bombay (1972).

Saksena, Banarsi Prasad, *History of Shahjahan of Delhi*, Central Book Depot, Allahabad (1958).

Sarasvati, Swami Satya Prakash, *Founders of Sciences in Ancient India*, Part I, (Pb. Vijay Kumar, Govindram Hasanand, Nai Sarak, Delhi (1990).

Sarkar, J.N. 'Aurangzeb' Publication Scheme, Jaipur (1985), ed. by Raghubir Singh.

Sarma, K. V., *History of Science and Technology in India*, edited by G. Kuppuram K. Kumudamami, Sandeep Prakashan, Delhi (1990), Vol. II.

Sarma, Ramswarup (ed.), *Brahmasphuta Siddhanta*, Indian Institute of Astronomical and Scientific Research, New Delhi (1966), Vol. IV.

Sarma, S.R., "The Lahore Family of Astrolabists and their average", *Indian History Congress (55th Session)*, Aligarh (1994).

Sastri, P.S. (Tra.), *Jaimini Sutram*, Rajan Publication, New Delhi (1992.

Sathapati, V. Ganapati, *Sthapatya Veda*, Dakshina Publishing House, Chennai (2001).

Satyarthi, Swami Krishna and R. C. Verma, *Bhartiya Jyotish Avam Lal Kitab*, Hare Krishna Trust, Chandigarh (1996).

Sen, S. N. and K. S. Shukla, *History of Astronomy in India*, Indian National Science Academy, New Delhi (1985).

Shastri, Ajay Mitra *Varahmihira and his Times*, Kusumanjali Prakashan, Jodhpur (1990).

Shastri, Ajay Mitra, *Arthashastra*, IX-4; V.3.

Shastri, Ajay Mittra, *Ancient Indian Heritage Varahimhir India*, Vol. II, Aryan Book International, New Delhi (1996).

Shastri, Nemichand, *Bhartiya Jyotish*, Bhartiya Gyan Peeth Prakashan, New Delhi 1983).

Shukla, D.N., *Vastu Sastra*, Vastu Vangaya Prakashan, Lucknow (1960).

Siddiqui, Iqtidar Husain, *Medieval India*, Manohar, New Delhi (2003).

Thomas, Sir W. A., "A Catalogue of the Indian Ministers", ed. By J.V.S. Wilkinson, Vol. II, Pt. No. 33 as quoted by P. N. Chopra.

Smith, E. W., *The Mughal Architecture of Fatahpur Sikri*, A.S.I. New Imperial Series, Allahabad (894-98), Vol. XVIII (4 parts) part IV, Plate XXVIII and LXXXII as quoted by R. Nath.

Sobirov, G., *Samarkand Scientific School of Ulugh Beg, Dushanbe*, 1975 (in Russian) quoted by G. R. Kaye.

Somayaji, A. A. (trans.), *Sidhanta Shiromani of Bhaskaracharya*, Kondriya Sanskrit Vidyapeeth, Tirupati (1980).

Soonawala, M. F., *Maharaja Sawai Jai Singh II of Jaipur and His Observatories*, Jaipur Astronomical Society, Jaipur (1952).

Srivastava, A. L., *Akbar the Great*, Shive Lal Agrawala and Co., Agra (1973), Vol. III.

Srivastava, M.P., *Social and Cultural Trends in Islamic India*, Vohra Publishers and Distributors, Allahabad (1972).

Thaekston, M. (ed. and trans.), *Baburnama*, Free Gallery of Art, Washington D.C., USA (1996, 2002).

Thomas, Sir W. A., "A Catalogue of the Indian Ministers", ed. By J.V.S. Wilkinson, Vol. II, Pt. No. 33 as quoted by P. N. Chopra.

Tod, James, *Annals and "Antiquities of Rajasthan*", Routledge and Kegan Paul, London (1829), Vol. II.

Turner, A. J., *The Time Museum, Catalogue of Collections Part I, Astrolabes, Astrolabes-related Instruments Rock for 1985*.

Turner, Howard R., *Science in Medieval Islam*, Oxford University Press, Delhi (1999).

Upadhayay, Vasudeva, *The Socio-Religious Condition of North India*, Chowkhamba Sanskrit Series Office, Varanasi-I (India).

Vasan, T. S., "Vastu in Astrology" in Gayatri Devi Vasudev (ed.), *Vastu, Astrology and Architecture.*

Vasudev, Gayatri Devi (ed.), *Vastu Astrtology and Architecture*, Motilal Banarasidas, Delhi (1998).

Verma, Som Parkash, *Art and Material Culture in the Paintings of Akbar's Court*, New Delhi (1978), Pl. XIV.

Welch, Stuart Cary, *Imperial Mughal Painting,* George Braziller Inc. One Park Avenue, New York (1978).

Zimmer, Heinrich, "Myth and symbols in Indian Art and Civilisation" (ed. Joseph Combell), New York (1962). Kramrisch recounts a similar story and quotes Varahmihira's Brahat-Samhita', as quoted by R. Nath.

Ziyaulddin, Barani, *Tarikh-i-Firoz Shahi*, Calcutta (1862).

Illustrations

16

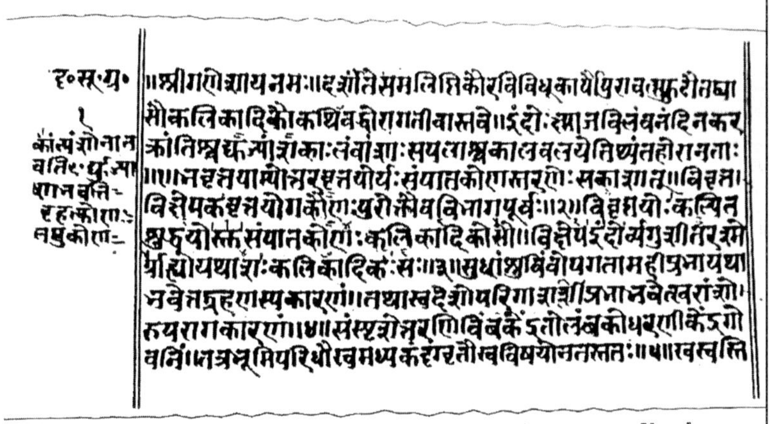

A page from *Drkpaksasaranyam-suryagrahanam* of royal astronomer Kevalrama preserved at Rajasthan Oriental Research Institute, Jodhpur.

An astronomer and his tools from an album of paintings in Jahangir's libarary. *Iindian Miniatures of the Mughal School, Prague,1960,plate18*

The sign Libra, Majma 'al-Ghara'ib, c.1650-60

An illustration showing 'Venus', a planet, in personification

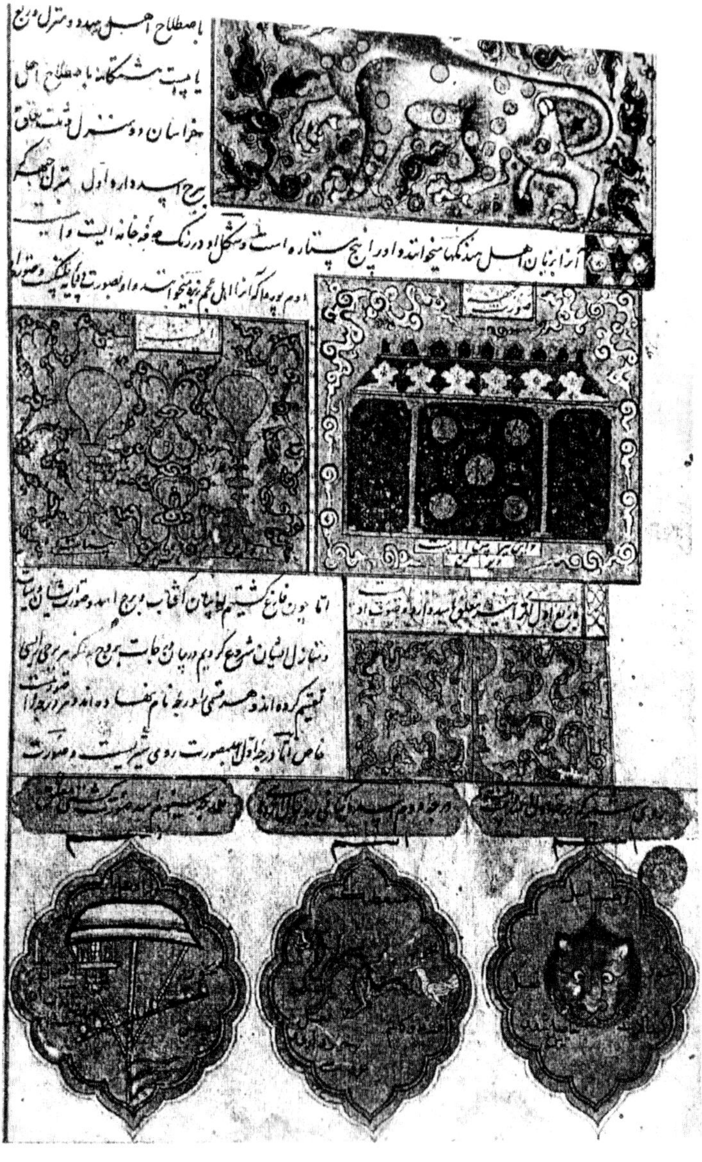

An illustration is showing –Leo, a zodiac sign, accompanying Nakshutra and Degrees

Jupiter as a heavenly king, Nujum-al-'Ulum, Bijapur

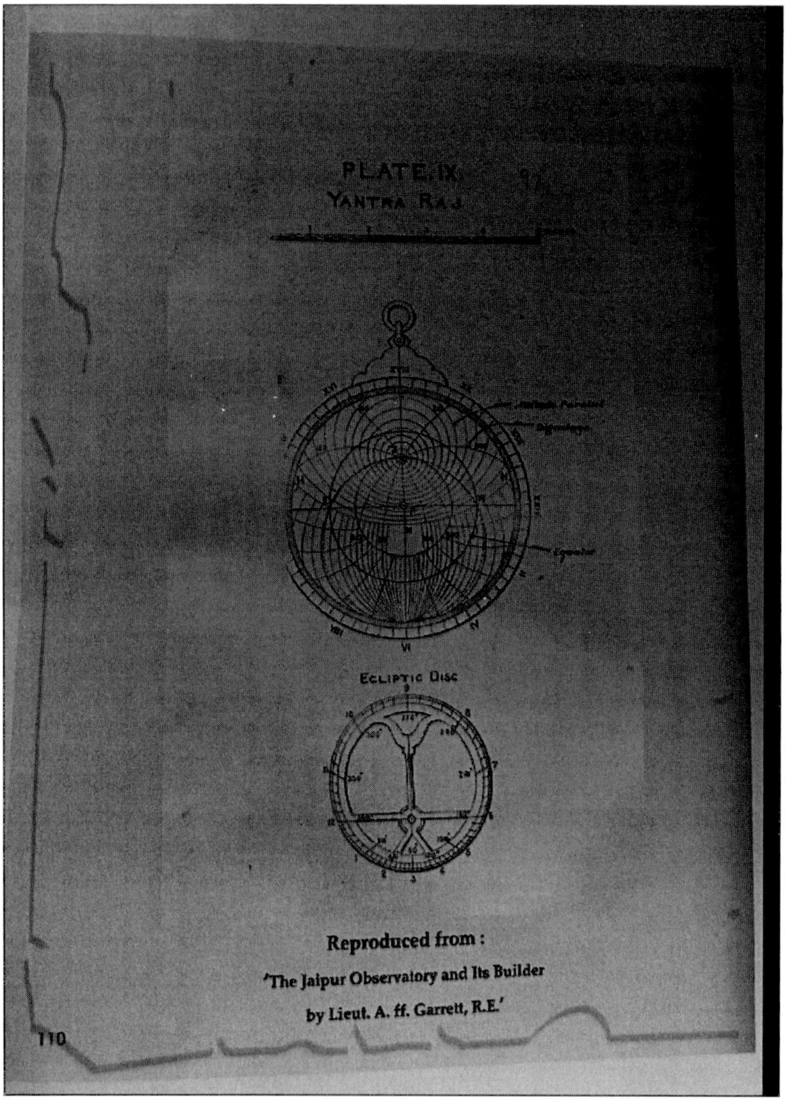
PLATE IX
YANTRA RAJ
ECLIPTIC DISC
Reproduced from :
'The Jaipur Observatory and Its Builder
by Lieut. A. ff. Garrett, R.E.'
110

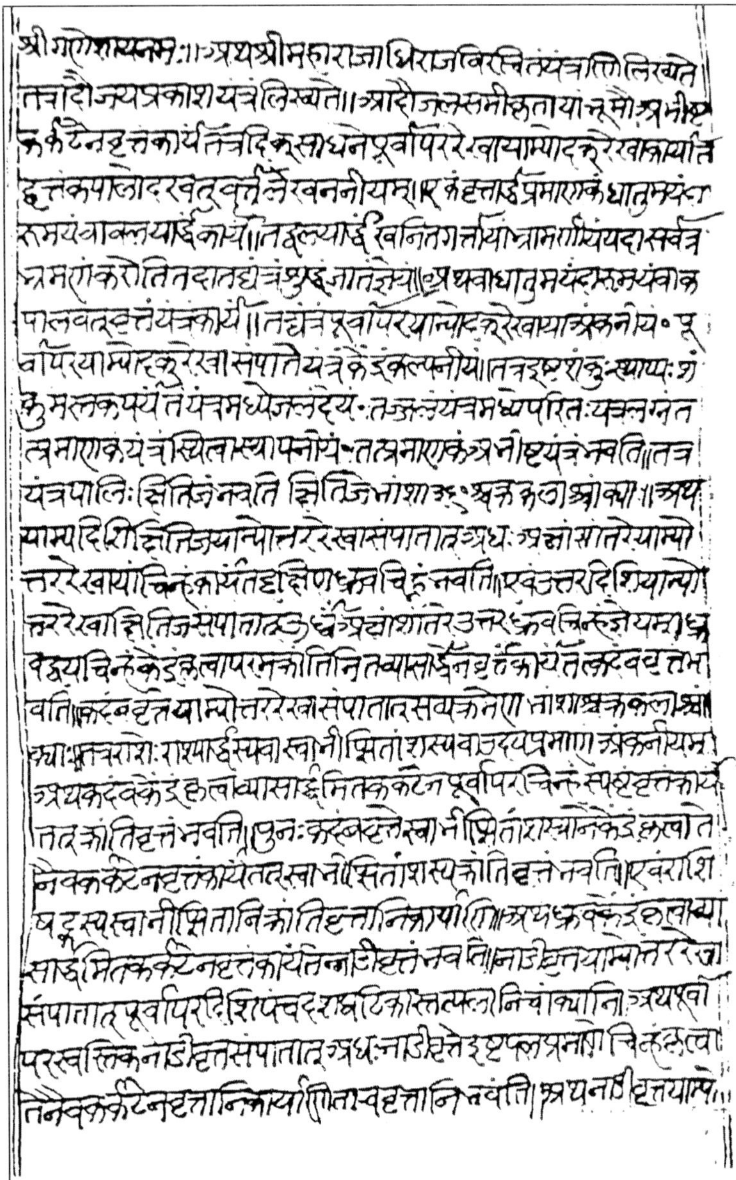

A page from *Yantraprakara* prepared by Jagannâtha Samrat,
Jai Singh's religious guru

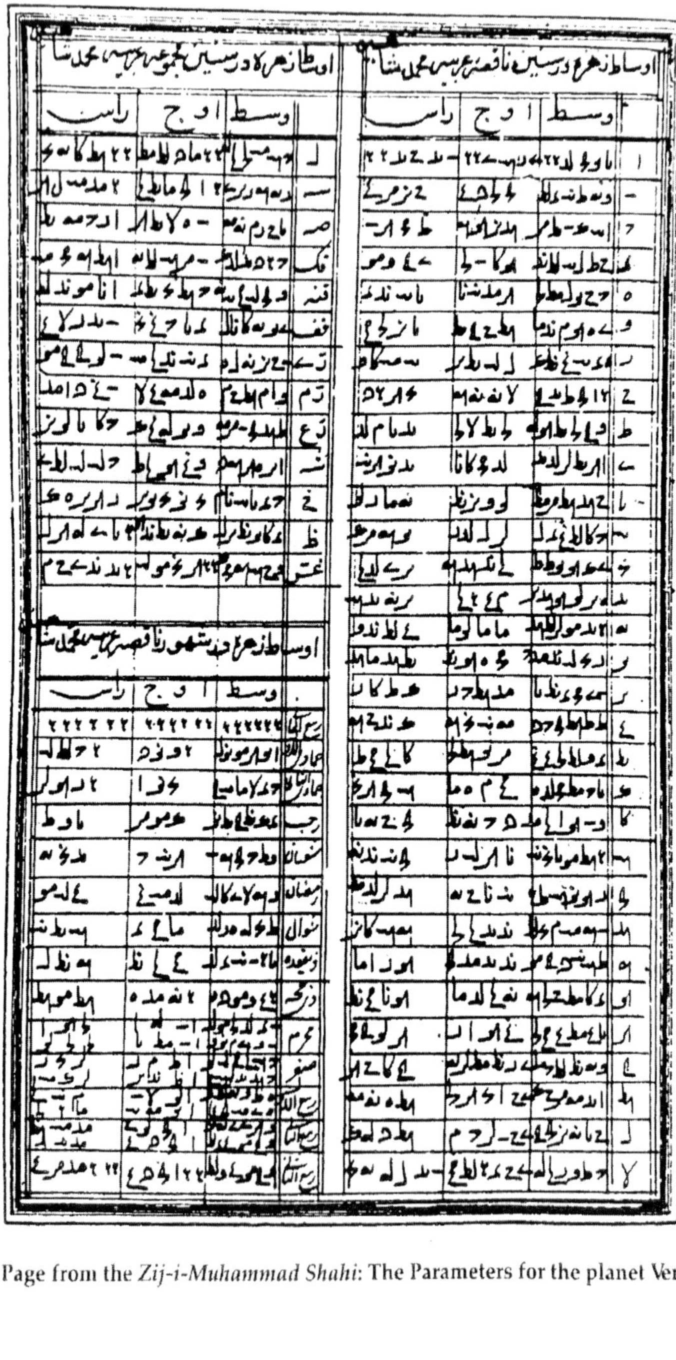

A Page from the *Zij-i-Muhammad Shahi*: The Parameters for the planet Venus

Index

A

Abu-Rihan Al-Biruni, 35
Ahmad, Nizam-ud-din, 101
Alyas, Maulana, 7, 70, 82, 83, 91
Angavijjapainnayam, 31
Angavinischaya, 33
Anterior conjunction, 90
Anvikshiki, 139
Applied Astronomy, 143
Arabic astronomical science, 159, 179
Arabic bibliographical tradition, 125
Aryabhata, 7, 21, 24, 25, 26, 28, 41
Aryan religions, 15
Astrological advice, 111
Astrological beliefs, 30, 31, 134, 138, 144, 183, 184
Astrological Magazine, 64
Astrological sciences, 116, 181
Astrological system, 152
Astronomical activities, 26
Astronomical calculations., 8, 28
Astronomical events, 116
Astronomical information, 17, 61, 129
Astronomical knowledge, 16, 17, 22, 72, 118
Astronomical position, 167
Astronomical systems, 22, 159, 178
Astronomical table, 161, 172, 173, 174
Asturlab, 122

B

Badshahnama, 114
Bhaskara I, 7, 22, 28, 41, 61, 159, 178
Bhaskara II, 7, 28, 29, 30, 42, 159, 178
Bhattotpala, 26, 29, 159, 178
Brahmasphuta Siddhanta, 29, 45, 159, 179, 190
Brihatsamhita, 134
Buddhism, 23

C

Capricorn, 51, 56, 62, 72, 84, 89, 94, 153, 163, 166
Celestial globe, 121, 123, 124
Chach-Nama, 37
Circumstantial felicity, 85
Constellations, 55
Contemporary Badauni, 101
Contemporary writer, 74, 147

D

Dachchhanayan, 163
Dasagitika-Sutra, 24
Day-to-day life, 137, 183
Double-natured Mercury, 85

E

Early medieval period, 29, 135, 159, 179, 180
Eclipses, 18, 103, 109
European astronomy, 119
Extinguished lamp, 167

F

Fakhr-i-Mudabbir, 38

G

Ganitanuyoga, 24
Geographical longitudes, 128
Geometrical spherical astronomy, 162
Greek astrologers, 77
Greek astronomy, 21, 22, 25, 27, 159, 178
Greek canon, 89, 165
Greek philosophers, 166

H

Hindu cosmology, 145
Hindu Tantric lore, 151
Humayun, Badakhshan, 78

I

Ibrahim, Asamuddin, 91
Imperial army, 77
Indian astrologers, 87
Indian astronomical, 22, 25, 33, 70, 107
Indian astronomy, 21, 22, 25, 117, 159, 161, 179
Indian Standard Time (IST), 61
Indo-Persian historian, 160
Instrumental technology, 121
Islamic astronomy, 40, 161

K

Kalyanavarman, 28, 29, 159, 178
Karakatvas, 143
Khan, Mùtemad, 109, 130
Kishnpacc, 96

L

Luni-solar calenders, 17

M

Malwa troops, 99
Mathematical geography, 160
Mathematical sciences, 121
Matrimonial alliance, 138
Medieval Indian society, 49, 184
Meteorites, 103, 108
Meteorological fact, 66
Mughal architecture, 144, 145, 146, 147, 149, 183
Mughal period, 8, 69, 101, 121, 127, 141, 149, 160, 180, 183, 184
Mughal pictorial tradition, 150
Muhammad, Qasim, 123, 124
Muslim astrologers, 39, 115, 135, 164, 184
Muslim community, 40, 136, 180

N

Naksatra-dusakas, 31
Nau-roj, 96
Northern Crown, 168

P

Padmakosa, 145

Paitamaha Siddhanta, 23, 27
Panchmahabhutas, 143
Panch-Siddhanta, 25, 26
Parasara Saktya, 20, 178
Philosophical values, 144
Physical sciences, 102
Planets, 19, 52, 53, 62, 143, 178
Popular etymology, 15
Primordial myth-making activities, 15
Prognaustical sciences, 149, 183
Psychological ideas, 7, 15, 178

R

Rigvedic hymns, 18
Romaka Siddhanta, 23, 25, 26
Ruhulla, Maulana Masihuddin, 73

S

Samvatsara, 30, 31
Sanskritize instrumentation astronomy, 40
Satapath Brahmana, 19
Scorpian-kinsmen, 85
Shah, Muhammad, 36, 118, 120, 128, 183
Siddhanta, 28
Siddhantas, 22, 23, 25, 26, 33, 40, 41, 159, 178, 179
Smriti literature, 135
Solar Month, 57
Stereographic projections, 122
Sutra period, 17
Syro-Macedonian Era, 163

T

Taittiriya Brahmana, 19
Tarkhan, Nuruddin Muhammad, 140
Topography, 160

V

Varahmihira, 7, 20, 22, 25, 26, 159, 178, 179, 191, 192
Vastu Shastra, 39, 142, 143, 144, 155, 180
Vedanga Jyotisha, 16, 19, 21
Vedic Aryans, 17, 134
Vedic astronomy, 19
Vedic civilisation, 30, 134
Vedic literature, 17, 21
Vedic period, 7, 17, 19, 26, 49, 134, 135, 142
Vrihad-Yatra, 27
Vrihat-Samhita, 27

W

Weighing ceremony, 97, 108, 115, 151, 182
William Erskine, 104
World-adorning banners, 96

Y

Yantraraja, 40, 42, 180

Z

Zij Astronomy, 39, 125
Zodiac, 8, 16, 38, 50, 51, 58, 161, 162, 163, 165, 178,
Zodiac signs, 33, 52, 71, 152, 182, 184